GENERAL JOSEPH WARREN REVERE

THE GOTHIC SAGA
OF PAUL REVERE'S GRANDSON

WILLIAM R. CHEMERKA

BearManor
Media

Albany, Georgia

Published in the USA by:
BearManor Media
P.O. Box 1129
Duncan, OK 73534-1129
www.BearManorMedia.com

ISBN 1-59393-241-3

Design and layout by Allan T. Duffin

Printed in the United States of America

Dedicated to
Harry G. Carpenter,
Founder and first President
of the North Jersey Civil War Round Table

TABLE OF CONTENTS

ACKNOWLEDGMENTS

Many people have provided assistance of one kind or another in the making of this book.

First and foremost, I thank all those individuals who are associated with The Willows, the home of Joseph Warren Revere, at Fosterfields Living Historical Farm in Morristown, New Jersey. The farm complex is part of the Morris County Park Commission, an authority dedicated "to develop and preserve a dynamic and unique system of diverse natural, cultural and historic resources, and to provide innovative education and recreation opportunities of regional value, while exercising environmental and fiscal responsibility."

The staff members and volunteers at Fosterfields have been particularly gracious. Special thanks to Lynn Laffey, Assistant

Director of Historic Sites/Division of Culture and Environmental Resources, who granted me access to the Revere Family Papers and the Revere Research Files. Lynn, who also serves as Curator of Collections and Exhibits, provided me with important comments and suggestions regarding the manuscript. Thanks also Joan Schaible, Senior Historical Program Specialist/Volunteer Coordinator, who supplied me with copies of important Revere documents during events held at The Willows in the 1990s and made me more aware of Revere's complex and interesting life. And thanks to Mark Texel, former Director of Historic Sites. He now serves as Director of State Park Service, New Jersey Division of Parks and Forestry.

Among others associated with Fosterfields who should be recognized include Nancy E. Strathearn, Roberta Bramhall, Nick and Mary DeRose, Bruce Hunter, Eleanor Kennedy, Heather Dempsey, Rebecca Kirkman, Sharon Carroll, Terry Kenneweg, Peter Doroshenko, Kathie Cirelli, Tom Coulter, Becky Hoskins, Peggy Kelly, Sue Youngman, Marilyn Franey-Austin, Jennifer Friedland, Delores Durso, Eleanor Kappock, Sherry Morse, Susan Martin, Cathie Sandbach, Laura Balogh, Shirley Vanderhoof, Merrie Tuttle, Rita Guibert, Mary Chatfield, Linda Barsch, Maryanne Rettino, Mary Darter, Joe Youngman, P. Gordon, C. Glacken, Gioia Weber, Keith Bott, Marie Ruzicka, Martha Bostick, Linda French, Peter and Madeleine Brennan, Jean Hanley, Rob Kibbe, Dorothy Swid, Christine Glazer, Chris Rain, and photographer Ralph Iacobelli.

I must acknowledge the late Caroline Foster, the daughter of Charles Grant Foster, who bought The Willows and the surrounding eighty-eight acres of land from Revere's widow, Rosanna, in 1881. Like her father, Caroline Foster maintained the wonderful house in its mid-nineteenth century appearance, although a number of upgrades–from central heating and electricity to room renovations–were performed over the years. The remarkable Ms. Foster willed the land and buildings to the Morris County Park Commission in 1979, the year she died–at age 102. The Revere Family Papers were donated to the Morris County Park Commission as part of Caroline Foster's estate after her death.

Thanks also to Dr. Cynthia Levine, Stephanie Levine, Jon Levine, and Sarah Levine for their support during living history programs at The Willows.

A salute of gratitude goes to all the historical interpreters–past and present–of the recreated Seventh New Jersey. Thanks to Lou Kaufer and the members of the Seventh New Jersey, Company A, and Fred Mossbrucker and the members of the Seventh New Jersey, Company D, who bring Joseph Warren Revere's regiment to life at various living history events and Civil War reenactments.

Thanks also to Mike Boldt, Earl Sutton, illustrator Wade Dillon, Robert Jones of the recreated Thirty-third New Jersey Volunteer Infantry, Jude Pfister of Morristown National Historical Park, and Francine Becker, Aide-de-Camp of the Washington Association of New Jersey.

I appreciate the help and encouragement of Donald Pfanz, a staff historian at Fredericksburg and Spotsylvania National Military Park. Pfanz, who authored *Abraham Lincoln at City Point* and *Richard S. Ewell: A Soldier's Life*, reviewed select portions of the manuscript.

Steward T. Henderson, President/Corporal of the recreated Twenty-third United States Colored Troops, was kind enough to provide assistance at the historic Chancellorsville Battlefield Visitors Center. Thanks also to the United Kingdom's Joe Irving, who served as an intern at Chancellorsville in 2012.

Thanks to Jim Burgess, Museum Specialist, Manassas National Battlefield Park, for his guidance regarding select sections of the manuscript.

Colonel Kevin Farrell, Academy Professor, Military Division Chief of the Department of History at the United States Military Academy, was also kind enough to examine portions of this work.

I appreciate Dr. David G. Martin of Longstreet House publications, who supplied me with a courtesy copy of *Louis Raymond Francine Brevet Brigadier-General U. S. Volunteers*, which was originally published in 1910. Thanks also to Joseph G. Bilby, author of *Remember You Are Jerseyman!, A Military History of New Jersey's Troops in the Civil War*.

A proper acknowledgment must go to Harry G. Carpenter, Founder and First President of the North Jersey Civil War Round Table (NJCWRT), to whom this book is dedicated, and to Norman Tomlinson, a co-founder of the NJCWRT. Thanks also to Rich Rosenthal, current President of the NJCWRT, Jim Lamason, and Jonathan Lurie, Professor of History emeritus at Rutgers University, for their help.

I appreciate the assistance provided by Sue Verzella, the business manager of the Victorian Society in America; James Amemasor, Library Reference Associate at the New Jersey Historical Society; Patricia Keats, Director of Library and Archives at the Society of California Pioneers in San Francisco; Andrea Cronin, Library Assistant at the Massachusetts Historical Society; and Gabriel Swift, Reference Librarian for Special Collections, Rare Books and Special Collections at Princeton University's Firestone Library.

Thanks also to Kate and Jim Malcolm of the Madison (NJ) Historical Society. Jim edited *The Civil War Journal of Private Heyward Emmell, Ambulance and Infantry Corps: A Very Disagreeable War*.

I am grateful for efforts provided by the staff of the Morristown and Morris Township Public Library's North Jersey History and Genealogy Center. And thanks to Sara Weissman, head of the reference department at the Morris County (NJ) Library, and the staffs of the Barnegat and Toms River branches of the Ocean County (NJ) Library.

I value the help provided by Diana Loughman, Cemetery Director of the Holy Rood Cemetery in Morris Township, New Jersey, where Joseph Warren Revere and members of his family are buried. Thanks also to George and Mary Ann Johnston.

Thanks to Joanne Cosh, Northern District Director, New Jersey Daughters of the American Revolution and Katherine D. Bowers, State Historian, New Jersey Daughters of the American Revolution.

Legal questions concerning the estate of Joseph Warren Revere and his family were answered by Charles S. Bargiel. Thanks again, Chuck.

Thanks also to editor Tom Soter [www.tomsoter.com], who also provided generous assistance with *Fess Parker: TV's Frontier Hero*.

Special thanks to the talented and highly respected George Skoch, who created the Chancellorsville battlefield map, and John W. Kuhl for the use of Civil War images from his impressive collection.

I am grateful to the late Sharon Reider, who devoted many hours to the Morris County Trust for Historic Preservation. Sharon also portrayed Rosanna Duncan Lamb Revere at The Willows for a number of years. After Sharon's passing, my wife, Deborah, portrayed Revere's wife at The Willows. Of course, thanks again, Deb!

Thanks to Ben Ohmart, Sandra Grabman, Brian Pearce, Allan Duffin, Jessica Fries, and the rest of the staff at BearManor Media for their continued support and guidance.

PROLOGUE

MAY 12, 1863

HEADQUARTERS ARMY OF THE POTOMAC
CAMP NEAR FALMOUTH, VIRGINIA

B rigadier General Joseph Warren Revere stood at attention. He looked straight ahead and said nothing.

Revere appeared impressive. His short, dark hair was carefully parted on the left side; his uniquely styled beard flared into three separate points—the center section reaching a horizontal plane on his wool uniform, where he proudly displayed three medals that had been issued to him prior to the Civil War: the first from the United States, the second from Spain, and the third from Mexico. And he had been honored by other nations as well. He was an author and an artist, a husband and a father, the commander of his home county's militia, and a well-respected man in his community.

Revere had served many years as an officer in the U.S. Navy and was later appointed colonel in the Seventh New Jersey Volunteer Infantry months after the Civil War began. He was appointed a brigadier general in 1862 and was wounded at the Second Battle of Bull Run. Above all, he had been acknowledged by Major General Joseph Hooker, the commander of the Army of the Potomac, who had called him "the best disciplinarian in the service."

In five days, Revere would turn fifty-one years old. But thoughts of a birthday celebration with his family at his home in Morristown, New Jersey, or a return to his field command had been replaced by the moment at hand: the verdict in his court-martial. Revere had said that his military reputation was founded upon twenty-five years of service of the United States. And he was proud of that. But more than his military reputation was at stake.

Revere faced two charges: "Misbehavior before the enemy" and "Neglect of duty, to the prejudice of good order and military discipline" during the dramatic Battle of Chancellorsville in Virginia. Revere understood that the carefully worded charges translated simply to acts of *cowardice*. If he were to be found guilty of either charge or both, he could be dismissed from service or imprisoned—a disgraceful end to his military career. And the historical Revere name would be tarnished forever.

Perhaps, as he stood before the court, his amazing, adventurous life flashed before him.

CHAPTER ONE

BEGINNINGS

"I always look back to this period of my life with pleasure."

The United States was on the eve of war with Great Britain when Joseph Warren Revere was born in Boston on May 17, 1812. His father, Dr. John Revere, was a son of Revolutionary War figure Paul Revere and his wife, Rachel.[1] Joseph Warren Revere, like one of his uncles, was named after Paul Revere's good friend Joseph Warren, a Revolutionary War hero who died at the Battle of Bunker Hill in 1775.

Dr. John Revere graduated from Harvard College in 1807 and traveled to Scotland, where he studied medicine at the University of Edinburgh. Following his return to the United States, he and his wife, Lydia LeBaron Goodwin, briefly resided in Maine.

The couple's first child, Helen Louisa, was born on February 22, 1809, in Portland. Dr. John Revere suffered from bronchitis and some of his colleagues suggested he move to a warmer part of the country. After Joseph Warren Revere's birth, the family moved to Richmond, Virginia, and later to Baltimore, Maryland.

The Reveres moved back to Boston, where John Frederick was born on September 7, 1815; however, he died less than two years later on May 2, 1817. Two days before Joseph Warren Revere's sixth birthday, his famous 83-year-old grandfather died in his Boston home. Lydia Revere gave birth to another son, Frederick Ballestier, on October 27, 1823, while residing in Baltimore. Eight years later in Philadelphia, Dr. John Revere "was appointed professor of medicine in the Jefferson College of that city."[2]

Revere Family Crest. Illustration by Wade Dillon.

Over a period of fourteen years, the Reveres lived in Massachusetts, Maine, Virginia, Maryland, Pennsylvania, and New York. Each residence shared a common element: a port city.

The larger towns' harbors were filled with commercial sailing ships, naval vessels, fishing boats, and assorted sloops, schooners, and skiffs. And the portside taverns, inns, shops, and warehouses were filled with diverse souls who punctuated their daily activities with lively conversations of the sea–topics ranging from legendary storms and the whaling industry to memorable journeys and the War of 1812's international naval battles. The atmosphere of the places was vibrant and exciting. Even from outside, one could smell the tobacco smoke and hear the sounds of boisterous rum-fueled laughter and the clash of clanking tankards and tin cups. Along the docks, veteran seamen shared their stories and tall tales to anyone who was willing to listen–and young Joseph Warren Revere was eager to hear them. He seemed to be particularly fond of the adventurous tales that described long-distance journeys to places that he had never heard of.

In time, Revere went to sea.

"Following the bent of an early predeliction for foreign travel, I entered the United States navy at the age of fourteen years, as a midshipman; and, after a short term spent at the Naval School at the New-York Navy Yard, I sailed on my first cruise to the Pacific Ocean on board the *Guerrière,* bearing the pennant of Com. Charles B. Thompson, the summer of year 1828," explained Revere, who was nearly sixteen years old when he was appointed to the rank of midshipman, the lowest ranking naval officer, on April 1, 1828.[3] The USS *Guerriere* shared the name of HMS *Guerrière,* the 49-gun British frigate that had been destroyed by the USS *Constitution* during the War of 1812.[4] The USS *Guerriere* was an impressive ship. Manned by a crew of approximately 400, the frigate was armed with over fifty guns–thirty-three 24-pounders and twenty 42-pounder carronades. In 1830, Revere received an additional $68.40 for "traveling expenses" incurred on his voyages.[5]

"For three years I served in the Pacific squadron, and was duly initiated into the tough discipline then in vogue in our navy, the rigorous practice of which had been in vogue during the war of 1812," noted Revere.[6] The most infamous example of "tough discipline" at the time was the use of flogging, the beating or whipping of a sailor. However, Revere never condemned the harsh discipline policies, which were widely criticized.[7] In fact, he appreciated the impact that such regulations had on crew effectiveness. Decades later, he would employ similar policies as an officer in the U.S. Army.

In November and December of 1832, Revere attended a naval school in Norfolk, Virginia. The "so-called naval schools at the navy yards [lasted] from six weeks to three months" and were places where "young officers were sent prior to examination for promotion."[8] He was assigned to the celebrated USS *Constitution*, which was commanded by Captain Jesse Duncan Elliott. Launched in 1797, the 44-gun *Constitution* defeated four British ships during the War of 1812 and had earned the nickname "Old Ironsides." Following an end to the conflict, the USS *Constitution* and other American ships operated in the Mediterranean. "I served for several years on this station in different ships, and, during the time, visited almost every port in that classic sea, besides making a trip to the Baltic," wrote Revere.[9] "I always look back to this period of my life with pleasure; for I had many fine opportunities of seeing places and persons of historic interest."

Service in the U. S. Navy included "sea service" and "other duty," which included extended periods of time on land, and Revere took advantage of the time he spent away from his assigned ship. Among the notable personalities that Revere met on his "other duty" travels were Czar Nicolas of Russia ("the handsomest man I ever saw in any country, and the most perfect embodiment of the regal power and dignity that the imagination can picture"); Letizia Romolino, Napoleon's mother ("the lines of her mouth and chin gave an expression of firmness, courage, and determination to a fine physiognomy"); King Otto of Greece ("the young king has just ascended to the throne"); Mahud II, Sultan of the Ottoman Empire ("in full health and strength and had a considerable share of good looks"); international sojourner Lady Hester Lucy Stanhope, niece of William Pitt the Younger ("her mind was somewhat unsettled in consequence of the death of her affianced husband, Sir John Moore"); and Ibrahim Pasha of Egypt ("he was of a restless and uneasy temper"), among others.

After a brief service aboard the schooner USS *Grampus*, Revere "spent about ten weeks at the naval school in New York" in 1833.[10] He sailed in the West Indies aboard the USS *St. Louis* from September 1833 to February 1834 and took his exam for the rank of lieutenant and "passed midshipman" in Baltimore on June 14, 1834.[11] Revere was eligible for the promotion as soon as an opening for a lieutenant became available, but he would have to wait nearly seven years. In March 1835, he was ordered back to the USS *Constitution*.[12] Under the leadership of Captain Elliott, the ship departed from Sandy Hook, New Jersey, on March 7, but ran into a gale and returned to its place of departure two days later. Once the weather improved, the USS *Constitution* set sail for Europe.[13]

Revere arrived in Lisbon, Portugal, in early September 1836 and later traveled to Spain, where, at Yuste in the Extramadura area, he viewed the Convent of San Geronimo, the celebrated retreat of King Charles V, who had reigned from 1519 to 1556. "I ascended to the roof of the cathedral, and stood entranced by the magnificent and smiling panorama of which is the centre; and again climbed to it on the morning of my departure to carry away with me the freshest possible memory of a spot so lovely," remarked Revere.[14] His affection for San Geronimo would remain with him for the rest of his life.

Revere's sojourns through Spain were filled with intrigue and adventure. He successfully intervened in a man's scheduled military execution; paid homage to the home of the legendary warrior El Cid; viewed bull fights; and was confronted by guerilla leader Martin Zurbano.

He contracted a guide, Manuel Blasco y Gusman, a one-eyed rogue and storyteller who later got into an altercation with a non-commissioned officer in the Spanish artillery over the affections of a woman. Blasco, as Revere called him, was charged with "aggravated assault," a charge punishable by death. "In Spain, summary executions so often follow an arrest in times like the present, that I was seriously alarmed," said Revere. Fortunately, Revere intervened on Blasco's behalf and the "weighty matter" was "brought to a satisfactory conclusion."[15]

Revere was fascinated with architecture and he particularly enjoyed his travels in Burgos. "The venerable old town has a noble seat, rising gradually on the banks of the Alanza, with its dominating castle, and the graceful spires of its unrivalled cathedral," explained Revere. "This wonderful temple is well known to all admirers of medieval architecture as among the finest specimens of florid Gothic in the world."[16] Revere was impressed and captivated by the Gothic style with its vertical lines, pointed arches, vaulted interiors, and its history.

Revere's meeting with Martin Zubrano came during the First Carlist War, a Spanish civil war that lasted from 1833 to 1839.[17] Zubrano and his followers took up arms against the counter-revolutionary traditionalists who sought to establish and maintain the royal house of the Bourbons on the Spanish throne. Revere had accompanied Lieutenant Colonel Rafael Soler and a "Carlist force of about nine hundred" to Logroño, a town situated by the Ebro River in northern Spain, where the troops engaged in a skirmish and captured a number of residents who were thought to be revolutionaries. But the fight escalated and soon the Carlists "were getting the worst of it" and pulled back from the town.

Zurbano returned with reinforcements and retook Logroño. The guerrillas captured a number of prisoners, including Lieutenant Colonel Soler and his wife, Doña Florencia Soler. Revere, as a foreign officer, was briefly detained. But while he waited in an apartment under the protection of two guards, Revere heard the musketry of the execution squads. The Solers had been shot and Revere was appalled at Zurbano's "horrible crimes." After Zurbano and his men departed the town, Revere assisted "at the burial, in consecrated ground, of the ill-fated Solers." Revere later reflected on the episode: "And thus it is in all civil wars, which are notoriously more rancorous and vindictive than hostilities between rival nations."[18]

Revere traveled next to France on "other duty," where he spent some time in Paris. During his stay in the French capital, he met the famous poet and songwriter Pierre-Jean de Béranger. "Béranger was at that time really a power in France," said Revere. "His *chansons* had an immense circulation, and doubtless had a mighty influence in bringing about the revolution of 1830." The internal struggle resulted in the abdication of King Charles X.[19]

Revere returned to Spain and traveled to Gibralter, where he rejoined his ship. He admired Spain's "loveliness and romantic character," but viewed its government with disdain. "In no other country has the monarchical principles of government obtained so much discredit," noted Revere. "For four centuries the Spanish crown has never been worn by an enlightened sovereign devoted to the interests of his people."[20]

While aboard the USS *Constitution*, Revere and his fellow officers discussed the need of a national naval academy, an idea which had been proposed earlier by President John Quincy Adams and others. The group drafted eight resolutions, which included the "establishment of a naval school" that would replace the existing system of ship schoolmasters, who provided instruction aboard ships, and the assorted schools located in New York, Boston, Philadelphia, and Norfolk. The enumerated recommendations were sent to the Secretary of the Navy, who was requested by Revere and the officers to submit them to the "chairman of the Committee on Naval Affairs" in the U.S. Senate. On April 23, 1836, the Senate acknowledged the officers' document.[21] In 1845, with the support of George Bancroft, Secretary of the Navy, a national naval school was established at Fort Severn in Annapolis, Maryland. Five years later, the school became the United States Naval Academy at Annapolis.[22]

After serving on the USS *Constitution*, Revere was assigned to the USS *Flirt*, which operated along the Florida coast during the Seminole uprisings. "Though the Seminole War was in progress, no encounters with the enemy occurred to mitigate the tedium of my situation; for excepting a few prisoners I saw at Tampa, including the celebrated Osceola, I never beheld an Indian," said Revere, who also met an ally, the war-painted David Moniac, "a young Creek chief who had been educated at the Military Academy at West Point."[23]

Revere was ordered "to take command of a large felucca-rigged boat, pulling forty oars, and armed with a long twelve-pounder… to capture a noted pirate named Benavides."[24] After two weeks of searching for the infamous buccaneer, Revere and his crew explored an estuary on the Cuban coast and finally located the unguarded pirate's cave, which contained a number of rusty weapons and a "keg of dollars." However, Benavides and his men failed to return. Revere confiscated the spoils and divided the treasure with his men after they left the area.

Despite the brief excitement associated with his hunt for pirates, Revere's early tour of duty was particularly unpleasant. His time in Florida was also marked by illness ("the loss of one of our men from fever induced by mosquito-bites") and a devastating hurricane which caused many deaths, leveled houses, damaged ships, and destroyed "millions of dollars worth of crops." Revere and his fellow sailors were glad to depart the peninsula.

Revere next crossed the Atlantic for Africa, where he settled in to a "most monotonous" experience searching for slave ships.[25] "At sea we alternately were drenched with heavy equatorial rains and scorched by the fierce tropical sun," noted Revere. "And the boat service in the rivers was simply detestable."

The USS *Flirt* caught a Portuguese slave ship disguised as an American schooner. Supported by sixteen sailors, Revere was given command of the ship and instructed to take it into port. As the USS *Flirt* sailed away in another direction, Revere encountered the most repulsive aspect of the "peculiar institution" for the first time. He had seen slaves working the shipyards of Baltimore, but he had never witnessed the horrors of the slave trade's so-called "Middle Passage."

"The main hold contained all the adults of the male sex, shackled by the leg to long bars running fore and aft in rows; and the women were in steerage abaft them, unshackled, but separated from the males by strong bulk-head,"[26] explained Revere, who soon became aware that the slaves saw no difference between their former captives and the Americans.

9

The lack of a wind for several days and a shortage of fresh water made matters worse. After three days, the water supply was exhausted. A brief rain provided "about ten gallons" of drinking water, but by the next day, it was consumed. "At the end of the twenty-four hours, we had no water left, and the slaves grew clamorous and reasonably too; for thirst is the most terrible punishment one can suffer in the heated atmosphere, amid the reflections of the glassy sea," said Revere. "There was no alternative, however, but to continue to keep them below; for our lives depended on retaining them in subjection."[27]

Besides running out of water, Revere and his men ran out of the ship's crew provisions. They resorted to a concoction of "slave rice cooked with salt water." Revere managed to find a small amount of rum and Muscovado sugar, which he rationed among his men. On the fifth day, they managed to spear a dolphin and later discovered a cask of drinking water, which was distributed to the slaves.

The next day, without the benefit of a breeze, the vessel drifted slowly to a shore line. Revere was tired and by early afternoon took a nap on deck. Suddenly, he was awakened by a "tumult in the hold." A few slaves had managed to slip out of their irons and began breaking down the bulkhead. "The fight had lasted about half an hour, and several slaves had been killed, whose bodies were brought on deck, and launched overboard," wrote Revere, who placed armed guards below deck to prevent further rebellion.[28]

The following day, a wind developed and Revere was able to sail the ship into a nearby port, where he deposited his human cargo. He was saddened to discover that the Africans would not be sent free; instead, they would be sold again to the highest bidder. Revere believed that the only practical way to stop the slave trade in Africa was for the nations of the world to colonize the continent.

By halting the trade in human cargo, Revere thought that slavery itself would one day end. But in the United States, only a bloody civil war would decide that question.

Revere and his crew departed for Cape Mesurado in Liberia, a nation that had been created in 1822 by the American Colonization Society as a place where slaves could return to Africa as free people. Formed during the presidency of James Monroe, Liberia's capital was named Monrovia in honor of the American leader and became the new nation's commercial center.

After making arrangements for the return journey to the United States, Revere and his crew boarded "a large heavily-laden cutter" that capsized in the heavy surf. As Revere reached for a floating oar, he noticed the dorsal fin of a shark. And then another. Soon the waters around him were filled with sharks, which began attacking the crew. One shark turned and swam towards him. "But I struck out boldly, and made all the noise I could without exhausting myself, until boats from the landing-place at Monrovia came to our assistance," said Revere.[29] Although in the water for approximately forty-five minutes before being rescued, Revere stated that "only fourteen persons…were saved from drowning and the sharks."

NOTES

1. The legendary Paul Revere (1735-1818) and his first wife, Sarah Orne (1736-1773), were parents to seven girls and one boy. Shortly after Sarah's death, Revere married Rachel Walker (1745-1813) in 1773 and the couple produced three girls and five boys. Revere's sixteenth child, John Revere (born in 1787), the last offspring of the famous "midnight rider," was the father of Joseph Warren Revere. See "The Revere Family" in *The New England Historical and Genealogical*

Register (October 1991), 291-316; "Paul Revere's Ancestry," New Jersey History vertical file, Morris County (NJ) Public Library.

2. Dr. Valentine Mott, *Biographical Memoir of the Late John Revere, M. D., Professor of the Theory and Practice of Medicine in the University of New York* (New York: Joseph H. Jennings, 1847), 22-23.

3. Joseph W. Revere, *Keel and Saddle: A Retrospect of Forty Years of Military and Naval Service* (Boston: James R. Osgood and Company, 1873), 1. On April 1, 1828, Revere would have been fifteen years and eleven months old. He is mistaken calling himself "fourteen" at the time of his midshipman appointment. Revere's home is listed as New York according to a roster of the ship's officers in the February 6, 1829 edition of Washington's *Daily National Intelligencer*. See also Francis B. Heitman, *Historical Register and Dictionary of the United States Army, from its Organization, September 29, 1789, to March 2, 1903* (Washington: Published under Act of Congress, 1903).

4. Revere or his publisher incorrectly used the name of the British *Guerrière* ship, with its accent mark over the letter "e," instead of the *Guerriere*. The USS *Guerriere* was built in Philadelphia and launched in June 1814. The frigate was initially commanded by Commodore John Rogers, who had bravely engaged the British sloop *Little Belt* in 1811 and the British frigate *Belvidera* in 1812. The USS *Guerriere* was subsequently commanded by the celebrated Captain Stephen Decatur during successful operations against the Barbary States. Later, under command of Captain Thomas Macdonough, the USS *Guerriere* sailed to Russia and ports in the Mediterranean before returning to the United States in 1819, where she served as a school ship in the Norfolk, Virginia, navy yard for nearly the next eight years. The ship was newly equipped in 1828 prior to Revere's association with the vessel. HMS *Guerrière* was captured and burned by the crew of USS *Constitution* on August 19, 1812.

5. Navy Department to the House of Representatives, Twenty-first Congress: Statement of the pay, emoluments, and allowances of

every officer and agent in the naval service, including the Marine Corps, May 29, 1830, 707. Revere was paid fifteen cents per mile.

6. Revere, *Keel and Saddle*, 2.

7. Flogging was widely criticized following the War of 1812. Writers, reform organizations, and public officials brought the practice to the attention of the general public. William McNally's 1830 publication, *Evil Island Abuses in the Naval and Merchant Service*, and petitions supported by the American Seamen's Friend Society were important. Herman Melville's 1850 novel, *White Jacket; or, The World in a Man of War*, also detailed the brutality that was common sailing on the USS *United States*. Senator John P. Hale of New Hampshire, who had read Melville's book and was influenced by it, introduced a bill to abolish flogging; the practice was eliminated in 1850. Hale, an abolitionist and the Free Soil Party's candidate for President in 1852, also succeeded in getting Congress to eliminate the navy's daily liquor ration in 1862.

8. Captain John B. Heffernan to Jos. A. Sullivan, October 7, 1947, Revere Research Files, Collection of the Morris County Park Commission. At the time of the letter, Heffernan was the director of the Naval Records and Library.

9. Revere, *Keel and Saddle*, 17.

10. Heffernan to Sullivan, October 7, 1947.

11. Letter from DeAnne Blanton, Military Reference Branch, Textual Reference Division, National Archives, Washington D.C. to Evelyn B. Roy, Morristown, NJ, 07960, April 20, 1993, Revere Research Files. Heitman's *Historical Register and Dictionary* incorrectly identifies Revere as having secured the rank on June 4, 1834. See also *Philadelphia National Gazette*, July 19, 1834, 2.

12. *Nantucket Inquirer*, March 21, 1835, 3.

13. Boston *Saturday Morning Transcript*, March 14, 1835, 111.

14. Revere, *Keel and Saddle*, 63.

15. Ibid., 75-77. Revere acknowledged that Blasco was an entertaining companion; as a matter of fact, Revere devoted sixteen pages (chapters XII and XIII) to a translation of Blasco's tragic romantic tale of Baltazar de Zuñiga, Count of Miranda.

16. Ibid., 96.

17. The Carlist Wars continued late in the nineteenth century. After leading yet another revolt in 1844, Martin Zurbano was arrested and subsequently executed on January 21, 1845. He has been called a "martyr to Spanish liberty."

18. Revere, *Keel and Saddle*, 103.

19. Charles X, a French Bourbon monarch who ruled from 1824 to 1830, was replaced by his cousin Louis-Philippe.

20. Revere, *Keel and Saddle*, 121.

21. American State Papers 026, Naval Affairs, Vol. 4, Publication No. 628: "Proceedings of certain officers of the Navy and Marine Corps, recommending the establishment of a Naval Academy." Officers of the USS *Vandalia* also signed the document.

22. The need to properly train young officers before they went to sea was hastened by the so-called "Somers Affair" in 1842. On its first major cruise, USS *Somers*, under the command of Captain Alexander Slidell Mackenzie, served as a naval school for apprentice seamen. During a passage through the West Indies, an alleged mutiny was uncovered and three young men, including Philip Spencer, 19, the son of Secretary of War John Canfield Spencer, were sentenced to hang without the benefit of a court-martial. Some believed that if the men had been properly trained at a land based naval school before they went to sea, they would have been more prepared and would never have initiated a mutiny. As such, the "Somers Affair" contributed to the establishment of the United States Naval Academy. The incident also may have influenced Herman Melville's novella *Billy Budd*; in fact, the author may have secured information about the event from his cousin, Guert Gansevoort, who served as an officer on the ship.

USS *Somers* sank in a storm during the blockade of Vera Cruz during the Mexican War on December 8, 1846.

23. Revere, *Keel and Saddle*, 2-3. Moniac, who Revere called a friend, was a Native American of mixed ancestry (his father, Sam, served as a scout during the Creek Indian War, 1813-1814; his mother, Elizabeth Weatherford, was the sister of William Weatherford, the famous Creek chief) who graduated from West Point in 1822, thirty-nine in a class of forty cadets. Although he resigned his commission, he later fought as a major commanding a mounted Creek Regiment in the Second Seminole War (1835-1842). He was killed during the Battle of Wahoo Swamp (in what is now Sumter County, Florida) on November 21, 1836. In *Keel and Saddle*, Revere refers to Moniac's death at the "battle of Okeechobee." Revere also incorrectly places this episode before his tour of duty on USS *Constitution*.

24. Ibid., 3.

25. Although slavery existed in the United States, the importation of slaves was forbidden by the United States Constitution (Article 1, Section 9).

26. Revere, *Keel and Saddle*, 12.

27. Ibid., 14.

28. Ibid., 15.

29. Ibid., 16.

CHAPTER TWO

CIRCUMNAVIGATING THE GLOBE

"I felt the good ship tremble through all her timbers."

Joseph Warren Revere turned twenty-four years old in 1836. He had spent his most recent years at sea, in international ports, and on foreign lands. Domestic events in the United States–Martin Van Buren winning the Presidential election, Texas achieving independence from Mexico, and Arkansas becoming the twenty-fifth state–seemed distant and somewhat removed from his daily existence on the high seas. Revere looked to the world beyond his home and more international adventures awaited him. Once again, he sailed aboard the USS *Constitution*.

"About a year after my Spanish tour–which interval had been spent in cruising in the Mediterranean–the ship arrived in the harbor of Algiers," remarked Revere, who called the French-controlled city "an inextricable labyrinth, full of oddity and mystery."[1] While in the city, Revere met an officer of the French Foreign Legion, who invited him on a supply mission. "It was composed of two companies of infantry...and a squadron of...native cavalry; the whole under command of Capt. Senneval," noted Revere.[2] After departing at dawn, the group advanced towards its bivouac point near the town of Blidah, but soon encountered a force of "stealthy, wandering Kabyles." A battle developed quickly and the sounds of musketry filled the air.

"Men were falling; and a soldier in front of me was killed by a bullet, slightly spattering me with blood and brain," said Revere.[3] Greatly outnumbered, the situation looked bleak for the legionnaires. The Kabyles charged the French lines and soon the adversaries were engaged in fierce hand-to-hand combat. However, Revere made no mention of his participation in the fight. The day was saved when a unit of French cavalry arrived and routed the Kabyles. Surprisingly, among those in the cavalry ranks was Revere's Spanish companion, Manuel Blasco y Gusman. Revere enjoyed his reunion with Blasco, who remained "as garrulous and declamatory as ever."

Revere returned to Algiers, boarded his ship, and sailed home. He was confident that he fulfilled the expectations of the USS *Constitution*'s commander, who also served as the commander of U.S. Naval Forces in the Mediterranean. Captain Elliott acknowledged Revere's "excellent deportment" and described him as "an officer and gentleman."

Proud of his performance aboard the USS *Constitution* and confident of his future in the navy, Revere decided to have his portrait painted. In 1837, he commissioned Jared Bradley Flagg, a young New Haven, Connecticut-based artist, to paint the canvas. During a stay in Boston, he made an acquaintance with Rosanna Duncan Lamb, the daughter of Benjamin Waldo Lamb and Deziah Lamb. Members of the Lamb family were prominent Bostonians who were successful shipping merchants. Rosanna's grandfather, Thomas, served as a lieutenant in the Continental Army during the American Revolution. Revere initiated a courtship with Rosanna, but it was quickly interrupted with a naval assignment.

"After returning from the Mediterranean, I was almost immediately ordered to join the squadron of Com. George C. Read, and with it made a cruise of circumnavigation," noted Revere, who sailed out of Boston aboard the USS *John Adams* on September 13, 1837.[4] The ship was not the first American naval vessel to sail around the globe–the USS *Vincennes* accomplished that between September 3, 1826, and June 8, 1830–but its voyage marked another effort by the United States to increase its presence as a world power on the international high seas. The Connecticut-born Read, who had served on the USS *Constitution* and later became its commander, was well respected by Revere and the other officers.

Revere stopped at the Madeira archipelago and the "cape" before sailing through the Mozambique Channel and arriving in Zanzibar.[5] "Our cruise extended to the Red Sea, Muscat, the ports of the Persian Gulf, and Surat; and we finally anchored in the harbor of Bombay, where the squadron rendezvoused."[6] At the time, the highest-ranking British officer was Lieutenant General John Keane, commander-in-chief of the Bombay Presidency, a province of British India. Revere was reported to have been involved in a rescue mission with the British man-of-war HMS *Ganges*, which was saved from a potential shipwreck. As a result of his efforts, Revere was presented with a sword of honor by the governor-general of India.[7] At about this same time, he received a temporary promotion when he was elevated to "Acting master," a rank at which Revere was in charge of basic seamanship and navigation.[8]

While in Bombay, Revere and the other naval officers were invited to witness a huge military procession involving tens of thousands of soldiers–including British regulars and Sepoy irregulars–and camp-followers. Although impressed by the "cosmopolitan throng of men and women, in all the varied costumes of the East," Revere was irritated by the crowd which viewed the martial spectacle. "This motley crowd were all talking and hallooing amid the rout and dust, in strange contrast to the silence of the disciplined masses that preceded them."[9]

Revere and the rest of Commodore Read's squadron continued to Goa and Colombo in Ceylon.[10] While in Colombo, Read was informed about "several acts of piracy," including the murder of the captain of the *Eclipse*, an American vessel that had originally sailed out of Salem, Massachusetts. For the next three months, Read's ships searched the coast of Sumatra for the bandits. The town of Muckie was destroyed after Read learned that some of its residents assisted the pirates who had plundered the *Eclipse*. The expedition against the pirates was going to continue, but an outbreak of cholera and dysentery curbed further actions. "The squadron was compelled to quit the coast; and March 1839, saw us anchor at Singapore," noted Revere. "From Singapore we went to China, and remained there for some months [and were] attending to American interests."[11] At that time, the United States was strengthening its trade ties with China, which was developing a large worldwide tea market.

The departure from China was uneventful until the American squadron encountered "a terrible typhoon" in the China Sea. Revere provided no additional details years later in his autobiographical *Keel and Saddle* about the devastating tropical cyclones which had affected ships for thousands of years. The squadron continued to Hawaii and other Pacific islands. Revere was fascinated by his next stop: Pitcairn Island, the place made famous by some of the mutineers who rebelled against Lieutenant William Bligh aboard the HMS *Bounty* on April 28, 1789.[12] Revere noted that there "were originally five couples of English and Tahitians; and from these had descended the population of the island–three hundred and more–at the time of our visit. The widow of Fletcher Christian, the ringleader of the mutiny [on] 'The Bounty,' was still living."[13] Revere remarked that "in 1840 there were but ten survivors of the first generation." He believed that the reason for what he called the "premature decay" of the islanders was a "state of monotonous peace and contentment" that lacked "the passions of hope and fear, the desire of achievement, and the triumph of success."[14]

Revere completed his circumnavigation journey when the USS *John Adams* returned to Boston in June 1840 and had earned his first medal, which was simply marked "Sumatra, 1837." However, he remained home for only a few months. He renewed his courtship, but soon returned to the sea aboard the USS *St. Louis,* which was bound to join the Pacific fleet off the coast of California.

Revere and his shipmates were sailing with calm winds "among the Windward Islands, westward from St. Thomas" when they experienced a unique and terrifying sea. "On the lee-beam the ocean seemed much agitated; and soon a huge 'comber' appeared, extending to the horizon on either end, over thirty feet in height above the sea-level," said Revere.[15] Quickly battened down by the ship's carpenters, the *St. Louis* "headed for the great wave, which rushed onwards with a terrible roar and irresistible momentum." The wave crashed into the ship and, according to Revere, "the ship, her crew, and every thing about the deck, were completely submerged." Revere thought that the *St. Louis* was going to remain under the surface before sinking to the ocean floor. "At my post on the poop [deck], I felt the good ship tremble through all her timbers under the weight of water on her deck, and clung to the mizzen-rigging, in which I had lashed myself," he recalled.[16] But the ship surfaced with "water pouring from her port holes like torrents." Three additional waves of decreasing size followed, but the *St. Louis* easily rode through them. Revere believed that if the large wave had struck the ship at night or on her side, the *St. Louis* and her crew would have been lost.

The strength and resiliency of ships were constantly being studied by naval engineers and designers. The deterioration of ship hulls was a particular concern–and Revere's father wanted to do something about it. For years, Dr. John Revere had been searching for an inexpensive alternative to copper sheathing and he was successful in 1829. "It is stated that Dr. John Revere is the inventor of the method of sheathing ships with iron, protected by zinc; in such a manner as to avoid rust."[17] But an Englishman quickly filed for a patent. In a newspaper article, the *Savannah Georgian* complained: "A patent has been taken out in England for a discovery, made by an American."[18] However, a patent was "granted in England to Dr. Revere."[19] In 1831, the United States granted a patent to Revere for a "Compound for sheathing ships."[20]

Years later, President John Tyler acknowledged Dr. Revere's effort in an address to Congress: "The object of his invention is to employ sheet iron instead of copper for sheathing ships, protecting it from corrosion by the agency of zinc."[21] Interestingly enough, the United States Navy had been securing copper from the Revere Copper Company, the firm created by Paul Revere and his son, Joseph Warren Revere, in Canton, Massachusetts, in 1801.[22] Most notably, the hull of the USS *Constitution* had been sheathed with Revere copper. Despite the patent for galvanized sheathing, the United States continued to purchase copper from the Revere Copper Company for its wooden ships; in fact, the nation continued its purchases throughout Joseph Warren Revere's naval career.[23]

On February 25, 1841, Revere was promoted to lieutenant, a rank which paid $50 a month and four rations a day.[24] Proud of his promotion and with a stronger sense of financial security, he married Rosanna Duncan Lamb on October 4, 1842, in Boston.[25] The *Boston Daily Atlas* printed their marriage notice two days later.[26]

But his time with his new bride was limited. Revere was assigned to the USS *Bainbridge*, which sailed out of Boston for Puerto Rico on January 31, 1843.[27] The *Bainbridge*, under the command of Zachariah F. Johnston, returned to the United States and departed in June for Vera Cruz. It returned to Norfolk, Virginia, on September 25, 1843, before departing once again for international waters.[28] However, Revere did not sail with the ship; he was granted three months' leave.[29] At the end of the year, a report issued by the Secretary of the Navy noted that Revere had served eight years and eight months at sea and two years and three months of "other duty."[30]

Revere remained home with his wife during the early months of 1844. The couple's first child, John, was born on November 26, 1844.

NOTES

1. Joseph W. Revere, *Keel and Saddle*, 122.

2. Ibid., 125.

3. Ibid., 128.

4. Ibid., 132. This date is also confirmed in a copy of a U.S. Navy document listing Revere and four other men in the Revere Research Files. Revere had served earlier on the *John Adams*. According to the May 11, 1837 edition of the *New-York Spectator*, Revere was aboard the ship when it arrived in New York from a trans-Atlantic journey.

5. In *Keel and Saddle*, Revere mentioned the "cape." In all probability, he was referring to Cape Town. At the time of Revere's journey, the African port settlement had been controlled by Great Britain; the Netherlands had yielded it to Great Britain in the Anglo-Dutch Treaty of 1814.

6. Revere, *Keel and Saddle*, 134.

7. *Biographical and Genealogical History of Morris County New Jersey*, Vol. I. (New York: The Lewis Publishing Company, 1899), 96.

8. *New-York Spectator*, November 30, 1837, 3. This temporary rank may have been inspired by the governor-general's sword presentation.

9. Revere, *Keel and Saddle*, 136.

10. Ceylon became Sri Lanka in 1972.

11. Revere, *Keel and Saddle*, 137.

12. The island was named after Robert Pitcairn, a teenaged midshipman who first sighted it on July 3, 1767, while serving on HMS *Swallow*.

13. Revere, *Keel and Saddle*, 138.

14. Ibid., 139. Revere mentioned Lord Byron's 1823 poem, *The Island*, as a published example of the "Mutiny on the Bounty," but there had been some earlier works written about the event. Mary Russell Ritford wrote the 1811 poem *Christina, the Maid of the South Sea*, which heralded the discovery of the last of the *Bounty's* mutineers, John Adams (a.k.a. Alexander Smith), by American captain Mayhew

Folger and the crew of the *Topaz* in 1808. Another creative work was the British ballet, *Pitcairn's Island*, which opened in 1816, following a British Navy visit to the island two years earlier. The most thorough work written about the event during Revere's naval years was Sir John Barrow's *The Eventful History of the Mutiny and Piratical Seizure of the H.M.S. Bounty: Its Cause and Consequences* in 1831. The Pitcairn Islands–Pitcairn, Oeno (and nearby Sandy Island), Ducie, and Henderson–became British colonies in 1838. Additional literary accounts by the likes of Mark Twain, R. M. Ballantyne, and others followed. The story of the famous naval mutiny reached larger audiences through such twentieth century films as *In the Wake of the Bounty* (1933), *Mutiny on the Bounty* (1935), and *The Bounty* (1984).

15. Revere, *Keel and Saddle*, 140.

16. Ibid.

17. Charleston, South Carolina *City Gazette and Commercial Daily Advertiser*, May 19, 1829, 2.

18. *Savannah Georgian*, May 18, 1829, 2. England's Henry Crawford received a patent for galvanizing in 1837.

19. *New-Bedford Mercury*, July 9, 1830, 3.

20. Patents Granted in 1831. Letter from the Secretary of State to House of Representatives, Twenty-second Congress, First Session, January 5, 1832, 51.

21. Message from the President of the United States to the two Houses of Congress at the commencement of the third session of the Twenty-seventh Congress, December 7, 1842, 716. Dr. John Revere began his experiments with galvanization on June 14, 1827. He delivered an address on the subject, which had been printed in the *American Journal of Science*, to the Historical Society of New York on March 17, 1829, at which time Joseph Warren Revere was sailing the Pacific aboard USS *Guerriere*. The Revere Research Files contains a "patent file" that includes a number of documents that mention patents for galvanized plates and wire; however, there is no detailed information

about the specific items or assigned federal patent numbers because the original patent documentation may have been lost in the U.S. Patent office fire of December 15, 1836.

22. Report of the Secretary of the Navy with a statement made by the commissioners of the Navy Board during the year 1827: Exhibit of Navy Contracts for the year 1827, 6. Paul Revere retired from the company in 1811 and his son, Joseph Warren Revere, assumed the role of president of the firm.

23. A year after Revere resigned from the navy in 1850, the United States purchased 49,140 pounds of copper from the Revere Copper Company. See Message from the President of the United States to the two houses of Congress at the commencement of the first session of the Thirty-second Congress. Part II. December 2, 1851, "List of contracts," 108.

24. A. P. Upshur, Secretary of the Navy, to John White, Speaker of the House of Representatives, Twenty-seventh Congress, Second Session, March 31, 1842, 2. The same year as his promotion, the USS *Guerriere,* the ship Revere first sailed on, was dismantled at the Norfolk, Virginia naval yard. The ship had been decommissioned in 1831.

25. Letter from Blanton to Roy, April 20, 1993, Revere Research Files. See also Francis B. Heitman, *Historical Register and Dictionary of the United States Army, from its Organization, September 29, 1789, to March 2, 1903* (Washington: Published under Act of Congress, 1903).

26. *Boston Daily Atlas,* October 6, 1842, 2. According to the newspaper, the ceremony was performed by Reverend Young and Rosanna was identified as "the daughter of the late Benj. W. Lamb, Esq."

27. *New-York Spectator,* February 1, 1843, 1; *Boston Evening Transcript,* January 27, 1843, 2.

28. Ibid., September 30, 1843, 2.

29. Charleston *Southern Patriot*, October 5, 1843, 2. Revere left Norfolk and traveled either to Boston or New York.

30. Report of the Secretary of the Navy, communicating a statement showing the length of sea and other services of the commissioner officers and passed midshipman in the Navy of the United States, December 11, 1844, 11.

CHAPTER THREE

THE MEXICAN WAR

"I had the honor to hoist the flag at Sonoma."

The Battle of the Alamo on March 6, 1836–the most memorable event of the Texas Revolution–began a series of events that would eventually involve Joseph Warren Revere.

The famous 13-day siege of the Alamo, in which an outnumbered garrison of Anglo and Tejano defenders–including David Crockett, James Bowie, and William B. Travis–fought to the death against an overwhelming Mexican force, was avenged by General Sam Houston and his ragtag army at the Battle of San Jacinto on April 21, 1836. Weeks later, the Mexican commander, General Antonio López de Santa Anna, who also served as his nation's president, signed the Treaty of Velasco, which seemingly granted Texas its independence. But Santa Anna only pledged to "persuade the Mexican government to receive a Texan commission so that the independence of Texas was recognized."[1]

Upon his return to Mexico, Santa Anna repudiated the treaty, arguing that as Houston's prisoner "he had ceased to be president of the republic" and had no authority to make an agreement with the embryonic Texas Republic.[2] For the next ten years, the Republic of Mexico considered Texas nothing more than an illegal state.

While Revere circumnavigated the globe, the subject of Texas' annexation was discussed in the halls of Congress and the offices of European ministers. In the summer of 1837, an annexation proposal was submitted to President Martin Van Buren, but it was rejected because it had the possibility of sparking a war between the United States and Mexico. The annexation debate also included the issue of slavery. Although American abolitionists opposed the admission of Texas as another potential slave state, those who favored expansion–like James K. Polk, the Tennessee Democrat who won the 1844 presidential election–eventually won the day. Texas was annexed on December 29, 1845.

Some European nations–notably Great Britain–were concerned about the growth and influence of the United States west of the Mississippi River. Great Britain was not only interested in maintaining its control of Canada and part of the Oregon Territory, but it sought to curb American ambitions in the West. Revere evaluated Great Britain's role in the region. "The threatening aspect of our relations with Mexico, and of the expectation which then prevailed that England might interfere in case our forces on the Pacific should land to take any portion of the Mexican territory," noted Revere.[3] A powerful imperialistic doctrine soon materialized which would engulf the United States and Mexico in war.

Manifest Destiny, the belief that the fate of the United States was to expand from sea to shining sea, was the sentiment of the nation during the 1840s. And, to be sure, the U.S. Navy's circumnavigation of the globe underscored American intentions that the United States was setting its sights in other parts of the world. A strong naval fleet would need more than just friendly international ports; it would need its own ports. The Polk administration coveted the natural harbors that punctuated Mexico's California coast and, in 1845, sent diplomat John Slidell with an offer to purchase California. But Mexico refused to receive Slidell.

Polk was still determined. The president decided to secure California–and much of the southwest–by provoking war with Mexico. He ordered General Zachary Taylor to march an army to the Rio Grande River, which marked the border between the United States and Mexico. However, Mexico had stated that Texas' southern border was the Nueces River, which was situated farther north. The land in between the two rivers became disputed territory that was claimed by both nations. Taylor entered the territory and established a camp on the north side of the Rio Grande, opposite the Mexican city of Matamoros. Mexico prepared to defend its sovereignty.

On April 25, 1846, Mexican troops fired upon Taylor's men. Polk subsequently declared that "Mexico has passed the boundary of the United States, has invaded our territory and shed American blood on American soil." A few weeks later, the United States won decisive victories at Palo Alto (May 8) and Resaca de la Palma (May 9) in southern Texas. Despite arguments against Polk's actions by the opposing Whig Party, Congress promptly declared war on May 13, 1846; however, it would take weeks before news of the conflict reached California.[4] But events were underway that eventually secured California for the United States–and Revere would play a historic role.

The previous summer, Revere had sailed the Pacific aboard the USS *Cyane*, a sloop-of-war.[5] The ship's voyage was relatively uneventful except for a fire that broke out when the *Cyane's* hospital steward brought a turpentine mixture too close to a candle. With "thick smoke pouring up the main hatchway," the entire crew jumped into action. Before it could ignite a larger vessel of flammable spirits, the fire was extinguished. Revere carefully explained that only through "coolness, discipline, and courage" was a disaster averted so far from shore.[6]

Revere transferred to the USS *Portsmouth* on February 14, 1846. The ship, commanded by Captain John Berrien Montgomery, was part of the Pacific fleet, a mix of ships of the line, frigates, and sloops.[7] Within weeks of his arrival, Revere became quickly aware that Montgomery was a strict disciplinarian. Several courts-martial occurred on board, and one verdict, on March 2, 1846, was particularly memorable for its brutality. A seaman named James Osborne received seventy-five lashes with a cat of nine tails (a multi-tailed leather whip) on his back. That same day, another sailor from another ship was given one hundred lashes–his punishment divided among three ships, including the *Portsmouth*.[8]

During patrols of the California coast, Captain Montgomery frequently sent his officers ashore in Monterey, California, where they were expected to scout the area and befriend American settlers. On one visit, Revere and fellow officer Lieutenant Henry Bulls Watson were among several people who attended a party. "Previous to supper, we had some music on the guitar & some waltzing by Mrs. H. and Lt. Revere," noted Watson.[9] Several weeks later, Revere and Watson went ashore again. After picking some flowers, they went to the home of Thomas O. Larkin, the American consul at Monterey, and his wife, Rachel. "When we returned we called and paid our respects to Mrs. Larkins (sic)," remarked Watson. "Revere remained on shore and I came on board at sun set."[10] On June 5, Revere and the ship's purser went ashore for several days. When he returned six days later, Lieutenant Watson noted that Revere was "very much pleased with the hospitality of the people." In his journals, Watson noted nothing improper with Revere's relationship with the married woman. He appeared– at least to Watson–to be conducting himself as an officer and a gentleman.

Arriving in Yerba Buena–now San Francisco–Revere and a shipmate secured horses and rode to the missions of Dolores, Santa Clara, and San Jose, where they helped establish positive relations between the U.S. Navy and the local communities. They also visited nearby ranches and a quicksilver (mercury) mine. "Quicksilver is destined to become a most important article of California commerce, and one of its great sources of wealth," stated Revere. "Gold, platina, silver, lead, copper, iron and coal, are all known to exist in California; and to her mineral wealth there will be no end."[11]

Revere was eager for the United States to "secure a footing in California, and seek to divert her golden streams into distant countries."[12] He believed that California could greatly expand its economic opportunities if a transatlantic railroad was built connecting "some point on the Mississippi" River. Furthermore, Revere championed the telegraph as "a means of communication, not only with the thousands of countrymen in Oregon and California, but also with our vast and growing commerce in the Pacific and in Asia."[13]

QUICKSILVER MINE - NEAR SANTA CLARA.

Quicksilver Mine–Near Santa Clara.
Illustration by Joseph Warren Revere.

Control of Oregon was also a goal of the United States. Four nations–Spain, Russia, Great Britain, and the United States–had made claims on the Oregon territory, a region that now included all of Oregon, Washington, Idaho, and parts of Montana and Wyoming. But Spain lacked the power to maintain its claim and Russia abandoned its stake in 1824. However, Russia's Russian-American Company still operated several commercial sites and settlements in northern California during the 1840s.[14]

The Polk administration was concerned with Great Britain, which controlled all of neighboring Canada, but winning a war against Mexico was the president's first objective. Polk became active on all fronts. The president supported the mission of John C. Frémont, an intrepid adventurer who left St. Louis with a band of over sixty men and arrived at John Sutter's Fort in Sacramento on December 10, 1845. Once in California, Frémont recruited more volunteers and formed the California Battalion, an eight-company unit of several hundred rugged frontier fighters.

Frémont sought California's independence from Mexican rule and confronted General Mariano Vallejo, the highest ranking Mexican official in the region, at the officer's Sonoma home. "The insurgents intended never to lay down their arms until they had established the independence of their adopted country, to which they had been invited with promises of lands and a republican government, but instead of which they had been prohibited to occupy lands, and had been oppressed by a military despotism," said Revere.[15] Vallejo acquiesced to the group's demands and was later imprisoned. U.S. troops occupied one of Vallejo's buildings and used it for a barracks. Revere traveled to Vallejo's property and was impressed. "The barracks were in a good habitable condition for accommodating three hundred men while occupied by me," noted Revere.[16]

"The 14th of June, 1846, must be regarded as a memorable day in the history of California; for then, her 'manifest destiny' became apparent, impelling her to 'gravitate' towards the Union," wrote Revere.[17] "On that day, at early dawn, a party of Americans detached from a body collected together in or near Sutter's Fort, at New Helvitia on the Sacramento, rode into Sonoma, and suddenly presented themselves in arms to the astonished eyes of the Californians, as a Revolutionary party."[18] And the group raised its rudimentary banner of independence. "A flag was also hoisted bearing a Grizzly Bear rampant, with one stripe below, and the words 'Republic California' above the bear, and a single star in the Union," remarked Revere, who later went to Frémont's camp to maintain a communication channel between the intrepid explorer and Captain Montgomery.[19]

During the same week the Bear Flag was being raised, the United States and Great Britain signed the Oregon Treaty, which settled the two nations' conflicting claims and established a boundary at the forty-ninth parallel.

Upon his return to the *Portsmouth* on July 4, Watson described Revere as "much fatigued." Several days later, a U.S. naval squadron arrived at Monterey. "On the 7th of July, 1846, Com. [John D.] Sloat issued his proclamation taking formal possession of the Californias in the name of the United States, landing his forces at the same time, and hoisting the American flag," wrote Revere.[20] The American flag was also raised at other locations.

On July 9, 1846, Revere made his mark in California's history when he lowered the Bear Flag and replaced it with the stars and stripes. "In command of a party from the ship, I had the honor to hoist the flag at Sonoma; and, in less than a week, all Upper California was in our possession," stated Revere.[21] Supposedly, Revere experienced some difficulty in lowering the Bear Flag. Captain Montgomery's teenage son, who served as a clerk aboard the *Portsmouth* and witnessed the ceremony, called the bear on the flag "Cuffy." When the banner got snagged a few times coming down the pole, young Montgomery noted in a letter to his mother sixteen days later: "Cuffy came down growling." Once the American flag was hoisted, a celebration erupted. "Bells were rung, guns were fired, whisky barrel tapped, and hilarity became the order of the day," remarked one soldier. Later, another American flag replaced the original and Revere kept his historic banner.

Two days later, Revere informed Captain Montgomery about the raising of the American flag. "I am happy to report that great satisfaction appeared to prevail in the community of Sonoma, of all classes, and among both foreigners and natives, at the country having been taken possession of by the United States," wrote Revere.[22]

Sloat, who was ill, yielded command to Commodore Robert F. Stockton. The new senior officer promptly initiated a land campaign against the forces of General José Antonio Castro, the commandante-general and acting governor of upper California. Outnumbered, Castro hastily retreated without engaging Stockton.

Larger military operations were underway by the summer of 1846. Zachary Taylor followed his initial victories in Texas by crossing the Rio Grande and occupying Matamoros, Mexico. Brigadier General Stephen W. Kearny commanded the Army of the West and led it from Fort Leavenworth, Kansas, to the New Mexico territory where he captured Santa Fe on August 18. Kearny's force entered California, but was confronted by a local military force. "He was attacked by a party of Californians under Andres Pico at San Bernardino: several of the officers and soldiers of his escort were killed and wounded, and his baggage and a field-piece fell into the enemy's hands," said Revere. "Kit Carson, who was with the general, brought the news of his arrival to San Diego; and he was safely brought into our garrison by a party sent for the purpose."[23]

Despite Revere's support of the war and the California uprising, he was concerned about the racism that pervaded the ranks of the insurgents. "The majority of the men...were ignorant of the Spanish language [and] deeply imbued with prejudice against the Mexican race," wrote Revere.[24]

Revere and his fellow crew members departed and set sail for Mare Island–actually a small peninsula–about two dozen miles north of San Francisco, where they "breakfasted." Revere was fascinated by a wild mare that was feeding alongside a band of elk. Some of the sailors wanted to shoot some of the elk, but as they approached, the animals darted safely away. "But better than the slaughter of these innocents was the exciting and novel spectacle they presented," noted Revere.[25]

Revere finally reached Sutter's Fort–a compound "enclosed by adobe walls, fifteen feet high and two feet thick"–where he met John Sutter, the Swiss-born adventurer and entrepreneur. "I doubt if a more remarkable instance of individual energy, perseverance and heroism, has ever been displayed under similar circumstances," stated Revere. "This unceremonious way of settling down in a strange country, and founding a sort of independent empire on one's 'own book,' is one of those feats which will excite the astonishment of posterity."[26]

Due to the lack of army officers, Stockton had to utilize his naval officers whenever it was necessary to initiate land operations and Revere was pleased by the commodore's order to "exchange the quarter-deck for the saddle." Revere enjoyed his occasional adventures on land. "Although I had often before done duty on shore with my 'charge of foot,' this was the very first time I had ever served in the cavalry–and albeit not exactly a 'horse marine,' I found this kind far more to my taste than remaining on board ship, in a war with an enemy incapable of opposing us in our proper element," explained Revere.[27] He also enjoyed the camaraderie of the other officers–especially Lieutenant Jacob Zeilin of the United States Marine Corps, who would later sail with Commodore Matthew C. Perry's expedition to Japan in 1854.

Revere was given command of Sonoma, where most of his garrison was composed of farmers and laborers, armed with their own rifles and "dressed in buckskin shirts and leggings, fringed and ornamented."[28] In October 1846, he secured "twenty-five horses, one saddle, and a small lot of percussion caps" for his unit and Frémont's from Moses Carson, the brother of Kit Carson.[29]

Revere led his men against roving bands of mounted loyalists and captured a number of them and their weapons during one raid. But after that, Revere saw no additional fighting. While he awaited orders, he went on an elk hunt, explored the area, and fell in love with the countryside. "The finest portion even of this universally magnificent country," he noted.[30] Revere reserved most of his accolades for Napa Valley. "The soil is of almost incredible fertility, the yield of wheat being as high as a hundred-fold, while corn and vegetables of all kinds, including the finest potatoes I ever saw."[31]

Southwest of Napa Valley was an attractive forested basin: the San Geronimo Valley. Within the confines of the valley was Rancho San Geronimo, acreage which Mexican governor Manuel Micheltorena had granted to Rafael Cacho, a friend of General Vallejo, on February 12, 1844.[32] However, by the beginning of hostilities in 1846, Cacho was eager to sell the property.

Although on active service, Revere saw an opportunity that he could one day take advantage of as a civilian. "In October, 1846, while in command of the military post of Sonoma, I purchased the estate of San Geronimo, consisting of two square leagues (*dos sitios de ganada mayor*), about five miles from the old mission of San Rafael, in what is now called Marin County," he remarked.[33] It must have pleased Revere when he learned that the name of the ranch was the same as his beloved Spanish San Geronimo convent. Besides Revere, other naval officers also purchased land in the area around San Francisco Bay.

Despite his new status as a California landowner, Revere was still a naval officer and subject to the authority of Captain Montgomery. On the evening of December 3, 1846, Revere came aboard "quite excited by drink." Lieutenant Watson said that he "was met on the quarter deck, and ushered into the cabin, where he was suspended by the Captain" for several days.[34]

On December 6, 1846, American forces were victorious at the Battle of San Pasqual, where naval officer Edward F. Beale stealthily passed through the Mexican ranks and secured reinforcements. On December 21, Revere and other officers signed a congratulatory letter to Beale for "his bravery in the field of action."[35] By the end of the month, Commodore Robert F. Stockton and General Stephen W. Kearny took control of Los Angeles. Revere joined a force commanded by Stockton and Kearny at La Mesa on January 9, 1847, where they engaged a larger mounted group of native Californians under General José María Flores. The day-long battle ended when Flores' men abandoned the battlefield–and essentially all of California.

The major fighting was over. The Treaty of Cahuenga formalized the end of hostilities on January 13, 1847, but additional battles were fought off the coast. A number of Mexican privateers were captured by American ships and U.S. naval landing parties skirmished with local militia bands before raising the stars and stripes in a few additional coastal communities.

In 1847, the USS *Portsmouth* participated in a blockade against Guaymas, an important commercial port which was located nearly 250 miles south of the future U.S.-Mexico border. The Mexican schooner *Eliza*, which had been taken as a prize, was brought within the blockade line on February 25. Acting Master N. B. Harrison took charge of the ship and its small crew, but after two weeks on board, he requested to be relieved. On March 9, Revere replaced him. That afternoon, an unidentified ship several miles away fired a shot and Revere immediately set sail and gave chase. When the *Eliza* approached "within two to three miles of her, [Revere] fired a gun, as a signal for her to heave too, which she did not regard." Revere fired another shot and the ship raised English colors, but quickly lowered them. "The hoisting of the English colors was no doubt a ruse," noted Lieutenant Watson.[36] Revere fired again and the blockade runner retired.

Two days later, Revere initiated a daring ruse of his own when he spotted the *Madalina*. The ship, sailing close to shore to avoid contact with the American blockade, was destined for Mazatlan with a cargo of 42,000 pounds of flour, two barrels of olives, 180 pounds of bread, and other items. As the *Eliza* came within view of the *Madalina*, Revere hoisted the Mexican colors and ordered his crew below; he allowed the few captured sailors to remain on deck. Revere "dressed himself in a Glazed hat and serappa [sic], and stood out to meet the vessel." The *Madalina*, believing the *Eliza* was still under Mexican command, raised its national flag and approached the ship. "And when within a few yards of him, Revere hauled down his Mexican colors and hoisted American," noted Lieutenant Watson. "He then sent some men on board of her who took charge of her."[37] The captain and crew were later offered in exchange for some captured American prisoners who were being held in Guaymas. In two days, Revere had chased a blockade runner back to shore and captured another. It was a fine display of initiative, creativity, resourcefulness, and bravery.

On April 8, 1847, the USS *Portsmouth* seized the *Admittance*, an American merchant ship which had allegedly traded with Californians loyal to Mexico. *Portsmouth* commander Captain Montgomery appointed Revere as the *Admittance's* prize master, the highest ranking officer aboard the captured ship. Clearly, Montgomery was impressed by Revere's exploits during the previous month and no longer placed any significance on his drunken behavior in December.

Revere and six seamen were responsible for the ship. On April 21, Revere was ordered to secure wood and water in preparation for a sail back to Monterey on April 23. Then, on June 2, 1847, Montgomery informed Revere that he was being replaced. "Mid[shipman] [N. B.] Harrison is ordered to relieve you," wrote Montgomery. "You will turn over the Ship and every thing pertaining to, or on board of her–[including the] original papers taken with the Ship which were sealed-enclosed and handed to you at the anchorage of San José."[38] During his tenure on the *Admittance*, Revere's father died in New York on April 30, 1847.[39]

On June 16 and 17, Revere was "sick, but not seriously so."[40] After recovering from his brief illness, he continued his duties aboard the *Portsmouth* and was invited by Captain Montgomery to go ashore at Sonoma in mid-August. While serving as the officer of the deck during the predawn hours of August 20, "the ship was very near being run on shore." Revere stated that he "steered the courses which he was directed to go to by the Capt." Captain Montgomery replied that he did not issue such orders and promptly suspended Revere.[41]

Guaymas was soon to fall. "In October, 1847, we bombarded this place with the frigate Congress and the sloop-of-war Portsmouth, and took military possession of it," noted Revere, who, like other officers, received an Aztec Club medal for his service in the war.[42] But Revere was also presented the flag of the California Battalion's Company B "as a token of their regard."[43]

As the fighting wound down in California, major land operations continued in Mexico. Months later, General Winfield Scott led a large American force against Mexico City, the celebrated "halls of Montezuma," where he was confronted by General Santa Anna.[44] Fighting raged at Cerro Gordo on April 18, 1847. Revere and his shipmates aboard the USS *Portsmouth* didn't learn of Winfield Scott's victory over Santa Anna until June 20.[45] The successful American land offensive continued the next month with victories at the Battles of Contreras and Churubusco. American troops finally took the Mexican capital after Chapultepec, a fortified castle on the western edge of the city, fell in September. "It is reported that Gen. Scott lost ninety-seven officers and eleven hundred men killed and wounded in the taking of the city of Mexico," noted Lieutenant Watson on November 14. "Santa Anna has not [been] heard from since he left the city."[46]

On February 2, 1848, the Treaty of Guadalupe Hidalgo formally ended the war. As a result of the negotiations, Mexico granted much of its territory—modern day California, Nevada, Utah, and parts of Colorado, Arizona, New Mexico and Wyoming—to the United States.

But less than ten days earlier, an event occurred that would affect both California and Joseph Warren Revere: gold was discovered at Sutter's Fort. "At the date of my departure from California, the vast deposits of gold had not been discovered," said Revere, who was about to set sail for Boston. "Had I any idea of the immense treasures I was unconsciously treading beneath my feet occurred to me, I might have easily amassed the wealth of Croesus."[47]

Revere realized that he had missed out on a tremendous opportunity to secure wealth, but he could do nothing except follow orders. "My ship now started on her long and tedious voyage home by way of Cape Horn, touching at Valparaiso," he said. "It was an uneventful voyage, and ended with our arrival at Boston in June, 1848."[48]

A month before reaching Boston, the *Portsmouth's* commander wrote a letter to Revere that was filled with praise. Captain Montgomery noted the lieutenant's "correct deportment" as "an officer and gentleman" and his "courage and skill" dealing with "the inhabitants" of Sonoma. There was no mention of Revere's suspensions.

Once gold was discovered at Sutter's Mill by James Marshall, one of John Sutter's workers, on January 24, 1848, a mad rush for the precious metal began. Hundreds of thousands of wealth seekers from the eastern states made the arduous overland journey to California; others sailed around Cape Horn and many others landed at the Isthmus of Panama, crossed the narrow jungle land mass, and continued their adventure by sea.

Despite being at sea for most of his early married years, Revere was eager to return to California, where economic opportunity beckoned. He may have contemplated resigning from the navy, but he probably realized that such a move jeopardized the financial stability of his family. To be sure, he might strike it rich, but the risks seemed to outweigh a decision to resign. He investigated various naval offices and duties which would allow him to continue his military obligation and also take advantage of civilian opportunities in California. And he found one. Revere offered his services as a timber agent for the navy and several months later on November 22, 1848, was given the authority to by Secretary of the Navy John Y. Mason to act in that capacity "for the protection of live oak and other naval timber on the public lands." The next day, Mason issued orders to Revere to "receive your instructions from the Bureau of Yards and Docks [and] proceed by the most practicable route to San Francisco." The instructions ordered Revere "to preserve from waste, destruction, removal and from every species of degredation, all timber suitable and valuable for Naval purposes growing on the public lands in Upper California."[49]

Revere prepared at once to return to the west coast. He sailed to Panama and landed at Chagres, where he secured the services of local boatmen who assisted him in his crossing of the isthmus. Arriving at Nueva Gorgona on the Pacific side of Panama, Revere could not help but notice the throng of humanity who had joined the search for gold in California. "Most of them, unused to hardship, instead of wealth found disease and death," said Revere, who came down with a debilitating fever.[50] Rather than remain in Nueva Gorgana, he pressed on. "To be sick at Gorgona, without friends, medicines, or doctors, was certain death," he said. "So I sallied forth, took the road on foot, and, by great good luck, met an *arriero* returning, with two pack-mules, which I secured at once."[51] Revere managed the difficult journey with the help of a "poor woman" who provided him with simple lodging, an acquaintance named Don Diego Feria, and a British surgeon who was serving on a royal navy vessel.

After his recovery, Revere boarded *The California*, a steamship which was bound for San Francisco. The ship arrived on February 28, 1849, and Revere was amazed at the number of "49ers" who populated the settlement. "The little idle place I had left, with its three or four houses and some twenty-five inhabitants, was now, by the potent power of gold, metamorphosed into a canvas city of several thousand people," explained Revere. "The harbor, formally only visited once a year by a trader in hides or an occasional whaler, was now crowded with merchantmen from every seaport in Europe, the United States and South America."[52]

Rosanna informed her husband of the birth of a daughter, Frances Jane, who had been born on March 26, 1849.[53] The Revere family had grown to four. But this pleasant news was replaced by sadness when Revere was informed that his firstborn, John, died a month later on April 22, 1849.[54]

Revere learned that small fortunes could be made quickly without ever looking for gold. He was informed that several of his fellow passengers on *The California* had purchased lots and promptly resold them before closing on their first real estate transaction. Within twenty-four hours, they had departed San Francisco with their riches. Revere confessed that he was amazed at the "wonderful vicissitudes of individuals [and] the tragical and amusing incidents" which he observed. He had certain duties to perform as a government agent, but wanted to join the economic boom.

The federal government promptly established its authority. "Gen. P. F. Smith of the United States Army came out with us to take command of the military department of the Pacific," wrote Revere, who also noticed the general's wife's "quite engaging Irish maid."[55] The maid quickly left Mrs. Smith's service in order to marry a local man of wealth. However, Revere's comment about the "engaging" woman provided a clue to the extent of his own matrimonial commitment. Revere was three thousand miles away from his wife, Rosanna, and he would soon be involved in scandal.

NOTES

1. Will Fowler, *Santa Anna of Mexico*. (Lincoln, NE: University of Nebraska Press, 2007), 176. Interestingly, twelve years after he fought Santa Anna at San Jacinto, Sam Houston visited Massachusetts Lieutenant Governor John Reed, Jr. at the Paul Revere House in Boston in April 1848.

2. Ibid., 177.

3. Joseph Warren Revere, *A Tour Of Duty in California; Including a Description of the Gold Region: and an Account of the Voyage Around Cape Horn; with Notices of Lower California, the Gulf and Pacific Coasts, and the Principal Events Attending the Conquest of California* (New York: C. S. Francis and Co., 1849), 2. Revere dedicated his book, which was edited by Joseph N. Balestier, to John Y. Mason,

who served as Secretary of the Navy under Presidents John Tyler and James K. Polk. On the dedication page, Revere said of Mason that his "able and upright discharge of his public duties has won for him the respect and applause of his countrymen and endeared him to the gallant service over which he so acceptably presides."

4. On December 22, 1847, Abraham Lincoln, a member of the Whig Party, questioned the location of the initial Mexican attack in 1846. Lincoln's "Spot Resolutions," deemed unpatriotic by some Democrats, were not adopted by the House of Representatives.

5. USS *Cyane* was launched in Boston on December 2, 1837. An earlier ship of the same name was formerly the HMS *Cyane*, a Royal Navy vessel that had been captured by the USS *Constitution* in February 1815. Later, the USS *Cyane* served in a convoy that carried the first African-Americans to Liberia, a free nation established with the assistance of the American Colonization Society.

6. Revere, *A Tour of Duty in California*, 3-4. The *New-York Spectator* reported in its July 2, 1845 edition that Revere received orders to report to the *Cyane*, which suggests that he may have seen brief service on another ship.

7. The ships that composed the Pacific fleet included a pair of frigates: the *Savannah*, the fleet's flag ship, and the *Congress*; four sloops: the *Cyane*, the *Portsmouth*, the *Levant*, and the *Erie*; two sloops-of-war: the *Warren* and the *Dale*; and two ships of the line, the *Columbus* and the *Ohio*.

8. Charles R. Smith, ed., *The Journals of Marine Second Lieutenant Henry Bulls Watson, 1845-1848* (Washington D.C.: History and Museum Division Headquarters, U. S. Marine Corps, 1990), [March 2, 1846] 82-83.

9. Ibid., [April 26, 1846], 104. Osborne's offense was not identified, although his punishment—which also included a dismissal from the service—was the decision of a court-martial.

10. Ibid., [May 17, 1846], 126. Mrs. Rachel Hobson Holmes, the wife of A. C. Holmes, a captain at sea, had an affair with Thomas O. Larkin aboard a ship during the spring of 1832. Aware of her pregnancy, she traveled to Santa Barbara, California, where she secretly gave birth. When she found out that her husband had died at sea, she and Larkin married. See Harlan Hague, "The Jumping Off Place of the World: California and the Transformation of Thomas O. Larkin," *California History*, Winter 1991/1992.

11. Revere, *A Tour of Duty in California*, 59.

12. Ibid.

13. Ibid., 61.

14. Fort Ross, in what is now wine-rich Sonoma County, was the base of Russia's influence in California. The Russian-American Company's primary commercial activities included the fur trade and agricultural produce, which was used to support Russia's Alaskan colonies. The Russian-American Company sold its California claim to John Sutter in 1849; Russia sold Alaska to the United States in 1867.

15. Revere, *A Tour of Duty in California*, 66.

16. Mariano G. Vallejo [To accompany Bill H.R.C.C. 92], February 11, 1860. Vallejo sought $12,600 from the United States for the use of his property.

17. Revere, *Keel and Saddle*, 143. At the time of his book's publication, painter John Gast created *American Progress* which depicted the mythical Columbia leading the nation westward.

18. Revere, *A Tour of Duty in California*, 64.

19. Ibid., 66.

20. Revere, *Keel and Saddle*, 144.

21. Ibid.

22. Revere to Montgomery in *Message from the President of the United States to the two Houses of Congress, at the commencement of the second session of the Twenty-ninth Congress*, Serial Set Vol. No. 493, 1846, 657.

23. Ibid., 145.

24. Revere, *A Tour of Duty in California*, 66.

25. Ibid., 67. Mare Island got its name from a prized white horse owned by Mexican General Mariano Guadalupe Vallejo that had survived a ferry wreck and swam ashore in 1835. Isla de la Plana was renamed Isla de la Yegua by Vallejo.

26. Ibid., 73.

27. Ibid., 79.

28. Ibid., 79-80.

29. Joseph B. Eaton [to accompany Bill H.R. No. 371], March 19, 1860. The House of Representatives' Committee on Military Affairs received the petition from Eaton, who requested payment for $653, the amount the United States was billed (via Revere's purchase on behalf of Frémont) for the horses and supplies from Carson. Eaton claimed that he secured the payment claim from Carson "in the regular course of mercantile transactions in California." The initial claim had been made in 1852, but two years later, a government board requested additional documentation before it could authorize payment. The board, however, dissolved before completing its task, so Eaton petitioned Congress in 1860.

30. Revere, *A Tour of Duty in California*, 80.

31. Ibid., 91.

32. Jack Mason, in collaboration with Helen Van Cleave Park, *Early Marin*, North Shore Books, Inverness, California, 1971, 140. Micheltorena served as governor and also held the rank of brigadier-general in the Mexican Army, positions given to him by Mexican President Antonio López de Santa Anna.

33. Revere, *Keel and Saddle*, 158. According to Jack Mason's *Early Marin*, Revere purchased the property from Cacho for "$1,000, plus his interest in a square-mile ranch he had acquired in Napa." Cacho and his wife, Encarnación, signed the property deed over to Revere; Jasper O'Farrell and Domino Sais witnessed the transaction and

signed the document. A listing in an 1880 *Report of the Secretary of State* identifies a "Conveyance, from J. W. Revere to Rafael Cacho."

34. Smith, *The Journals of Marine Second Lieutenant Henry Bulls Watson,* [Dec. 3, 1846], 251.

35. *Daily National Intelligencer,* May 26, 1847, 2. Revere's name was the first one listed in the newspaper. Revere and the other officers informed Beale that they had "ordered from England a pair [of] epaulets and sword, to be presented to you…" Beale later provided evidence of California's gold to the federal government, helped survey land for the first transcontinental railroad and other California roads, was appointed Superintendent of Indian Affairs in California and Nevada, participated in the Camel Corps pack animal experiment in the late 1850s, and served as President Ulysses S. Grant's ambassador to Austria-Hungary.

36. Smith, *The Journals of Marine Second Lieutenant Henry Bulls Watson,* [February 25, 1847] 300, [March 9, 1847], 305-306.

37. Ibid., [March 11, 1847], 307.

38. Montgomery to Revere, June 2, 1847. Revere Research Files.

39. Dr. Valentine Mott, the author of *Biographical Memoir of the Late John Revere, M. D.,* eulogized Revere with reverence. In his address to the faculty of the University of New York, where Dr. Revere had worked, Mott declared: "Both as a physician and a man, both in his *morale,* as well as in his profession proper, he was a model, gentlemen, that you might have good cause to remember."

40. Smith, *The Journals of Marine Second Lieutenant Henry Bulls Watson,* [June 16-18, 1847], 332.

41. Ibid., [August 27, 1847], 343.

42. Revere, *A Tour of Duty of California,* 287. The Aztec Club of 1847 was created on October 13, 1847, to establish a clubhouse resort for officers. American officers occupied the home of José María Bocanegra, the Mexican minister to the United States, and transformed the former eighteenth century palace into the home

of their new club. The medal issued by the organization featured an inscription: "Founded in Mexico City by officers of the United States Army who participated in the Mexican War, 1846-7."

43. Undated late nineteenth century or early twentieth century (photocopy) newspaper article in Revere Research Files. The article stated that the silk flag featured "California Battalion" and "Company B, Sonoma." Captain Henry L. Ford, who was a nephew of Mary Todd Lincoln, was elected by the men to command the company.

44. Santa Anna, who had served as President of Mexico ten times up until 1847, had lost his left leg battling the French at Veracruz in 1838 during the so-called Pastry War. Nevertheless, wearing a prosthetic cork leg, he managed to rally his troops during the Mexican War. His artificial leg, though, was seized by U.S. troops at Cerro Gordo. He was vilified in song during the Mexican War. Tunes like "Santa Anna's Retreat from Cerro Gordo" (1847), "The Leg I Left Behind" (ca. 1847), and "Santa Anna's Retreat From Buena Vista" (1848) were but a few of the compositions written about the Mexican leader. For more about the songs written about Santa Anna and the Mexican War, see William R. Chemerka and Allen J. Wiener, *Music of the Alamo: From 19th Century Ballads to Big-Screen Soundtracks* (Houston, TX: Bright Sky Press, 2008).

45. Smith, *The Journals of Marine Second Lieutenant Henry Bulls Watson,* [June 20, 1847], 333.

46. Ibid., (November 14, 1847), 367. American forces suffered over 1,600 casualties in the fight for Mexico City.

47. Revere, *A Tour of Duty in California,* 226.

48. Revere, *Keel and Saddle,* 147.

49. Mason to Revere, November 22, 1848, Revere Family Papers; Joseph Smith to Revere, November 22, 1848, Revere Research Files.

50. Revere, *Keel and Saddle,* 153. Revere may have originally contracted the fever during his time in Florida or Central America.

51. Ibid. An *arriero* is someone who transports goods with use of pack animals.

52. Ibid., 155. California's population continued at such a rapid pace that it qualified for statehood in 1850. Its 90,000-plus population figure of the 1850 census was dwarfed by the nearly 380,000 people count in the 1860 census.

53. Frances Jane Revere was named after one of Rosanna's sisters who had died in 1849.

54. It appears that the Reveres were temporarily residing in or traveling through New York when young John died.

55. Revere, *Keel and Saddle*, 156. Although this comment was printed in *Keel and Saddle* in 1872, the Irish maid clearly left her impression upon Revere.

CHAPTER FOUR

THE SAN GERONIMO SCANDAL

"It was generally believed that she was his mistress."

Revere wasted no time in his attempt to exploit the financial possibilities of the Gold Rush. He remembered the quick riches made by some of the passengers who sailed with him on *The California* and he wanted to follow in their fortunate paths. But Revere was willing to actually work for it. His plan was "to inaugurate measures for supplying provisions to the hungry crowd suddenly thrown upon these shores, instead of following the diggers to the mines."

Revere's base of operations was San Geronimo, which he stocked with "horned cattle and mares." He had hired a foreman to supervise the property in his absence; however, by the time he returned in early 1849, the man had "gone off to the bonanza." Fortunately for Revere, the foreman's departure did not diminish the size of his herds; in fact, quite the contrary. "In my absence the cattle had increased to about five hundred head of animals of all kinds, which roamed at will in a state of nature over my domain," stated Revere.[1]

The only capital improvement on his domain was "San Geronimo," a simple two-room wooden structure with a sloped roof that was named after the property. One room contained a bed, a table, a swinging naval-style cot, and a fireplace; the other had a bed, a bench, a table, a stove, and an area for his farming tools. Each room had its own entrance. There was probably some storage space above the ground floor level, but Revere did not describe or depict it in a primitive sketch he made of the place.

Revere joined with some neighboring rancheros to herd cattle to the mining areas, where beef prices were at a premium. Revere, now thirty-seven years old, enjoyed the profitable work and remarked that as a result of the cattle drives, his "physical powers were never greater" than any other time in his life. "Constant exercise, and sleeping in the open air—no hardship in that pure, dry atmosphere—hardened my body, invigorated my constitution, an induced an elevation of spirits, and confidence in my ability to endure privation, that I have never felt before or since."[2]

Revere didn't restrict himself to selling cattle. Although he devoted two months unsuccessfully digging for gold following a cattle drive, Revere spent most of his time buying and trading goods and selling them at inflated prices: "butcher-knives fetching twenty dollars apiece, common iron spoons five dollars, and ordinary wash-bowls and meaner vessels fifteen dollars."[3] Revere secured the service of twenty Native Americans, who helped him plow some of the land at his San Geronimo homestead. He later planted potatoes, which he secured from a ship's captain whose crew had abandoned him for the gold fields. "I then left the place in charge of my Indian servants, and addressed myself to the duties of my office as timber-inspector," said Revere, who devoted several weeks to inspecting government land.[4]

He returned to his ranch, where he continued to supply the daily needs of hungry prospectors. The increasing Gold Rush population's demand for food could not have come at a better time for Revere, who noted that his small seed potato crop produced "several hundred bushels" and generated a high financial rate of return. "The sale of the crop at one real (twelve and a half cents) per pound, which was the market price, fully repaid the expense and trouble of planting."[5]

Revere had a reputation as an employer who paid a fair wage. "Lieutenant Revere of the U.S. Navy had located there getting out timber for the Government and offered employment at higher pay than could be obtained in the mines," stated Andrew S. Church, who traveled to San Francisco from New York in search of gold in 1849.[6]

When he wasn't working, Revere enjoyed hunting–particularly deer hunting. And on many occasions, he was joined by Timothy Murphy, whom Revere described as a "Herculean, ruddy-faced, good-humored Hibernian." Revere was amused by Murphy, who brought a "splendid pack of grey-hounds" with him from Ireland.

Revere also devoted many hours to writing about his adventures, the people whom he encountered, the land, plants and wildlife–nearly everything that he observed. He assembled these writings into a manuscript which was published in 1849 as *A Tour Of Duty in California; Including a Description of the Gold Region: and an Account of the Voyage Around Cape Horn; with Notices of Lower California, the Gulf and Pacific Coasts, and the Principal*

Events Attending the Conquest of California, by New York's C. S. Francis and Company. Assisted by editor Joseph N. Balestier, the book traced his life from the summer of 1845, when he joined the Pacific Squadron, to the Gold Rush of 1849.

A Tour of Duty in California was more than a collection of personal essays on his experiences; it became a handy guidebook for those traveling to the west coast since its 305 pages contained many details about California's history, its people, and its environment. Included in the book are several lithographs based on Revere's illustrations: *Monterey–Capital of California, Quicksilver Mine–Near Santa Clara, Monte Diablo–From the Sacramento River, A Ranchero Feat,* and *A "Pui" Day,* which depicted a Native American feast celebration. The book also introduced Revere's submission for a California coat of arms. The vivid design included a wild horse and a bull supporting a crest that featured a star, mountains, ships, and a whale. The motto read: *Postera Crescam Laude* ("I shall flourish in the future"). The crest depicted a grizzly bear, holding a furled American flag and a Bowie knife, and the motto Tuebor ("I Will Defend"), a phrase that had already graced Michigan's state flag.

Revere expressed a number of concerns in the book. He strongly believed that the U.S. Navy should establish permanent ports in California since "about a year is consumed in going backwards and forwards, before and after a cruise, the officers and crew drawing their pay and rations the whole time. Thus one year out of three is wasted, and great expense and inconvenience incurred, which may hereafter be saved by the establishment of a Pacific navy."[7] Revere maintained the Manifest Destiny point of view that the "Anglo-Saxon race...seems destined to possess the whole of the North American Continent." But he rejected the extension of slavery in California–not on abolitionist principles, but on economic ones.

"The great expense and risk of transporting slaves to a country so remote, the vast number of Indians whose labor is so much cheaper than slave-labor can possibly be, the utter absence among the Spanish Californians of all prejudice with respect to color, the fact that the Indians are better herdsmen (vaqueros), than any African can ever become, and the ease with which any number of Kanakas from the Sandwich Islands, and Coolies, and other laborers from Asia can be procured, render it an absurdity that negro slavery will ever be established in California."[8]

In the final pages of the book, Revere cautioned the future settlers of California in a stern moral tone: "You go to a comparatively uncivilized country, where you will be beyond the reach of those salutary restraints, which are imposed at home by custom, religion, law, the example of all good men, and the benign influences of family and friends." He underscored those words with a warning: "If you meet with a lax system of public morals, be it your aim to elevate the tone of society."[9]

The book was well-advertised and well-received. Articles and advertisements in such newspapers as the *Boston Evening Transcript*, the *Charleston Courier*, and the *Richmond Enquirer* heralded the book for its vivid descriptions of California. "The work forms a neat volume of 305 pages, and cannot fail to have a large circulation at this time, when all authentic information in regard to the new land of promise, which has been so suddenly incorporated with our own, is sought for and read with the most lively interest," reported the *Boston Evening Transcript*.[10] *The Sun* of Baltimore remarked that the "style of the narrative is entertaining, and no one will rise from its perusal without a very sensible expansion of his ideas relative to California."[11] Two New York magazines, *The Living Age* and *The United States Democratic Review*, praised it. "Of all the books to which the California excitement has given being, this of Lieut. Revere is probably the most concise and comprehensive, as well as being of a lively and attractive style, abounding in anecdote and graphic scenery, noted the *Democratic Review*."[12] *The Living Age* called it a "much needed" work.[13]

Revere, no doubt, was pleased at the reviews, but he could not celebrate for long. He would soon be involved in a scandal.

Without naval barracks, private civilian housing allowed the officers to be conveniently based on land instead of being shuttled back to their ships every night. James Sawkins, a gold miner in San Rafael, had provided such quarters in his home for several naval officers, including Revere.

Revere soon met Octavia ("Rosa") Sawkins, a teacher and wife of James Sawkins. She was described as a "very handsome dark-eyed and black haired, well dressed young woman of about twenty years."[14] Whether she had the instant charm of the "engaging Irish maid" who had served General P. F. Smith's wife or whether it was her attractive looks, Sawkins quickly became an intimate part of Revere's world.

On the night of November 26, 1849, Sawkins returned home and climbed to the top of the stairs, where he saw Revere coming out of one of his wife's rooms. He greeted Revere with a handshake and noticed that he "was trembling and cold."[15] Upon entering the room, Sawkins observed that something was wrong with his wife. She was upset and told him not to come near her. And then she confessed that she had consumed a bottle of laudanum, an addictive opium-based drug. Sawkins left the room and asked another boarder, a Mr. Murphy, who the "author of this estrangement was?" Murphy tried to calm Sawkins, who returned to his wife's room—only to find it locked. With Murphy's assistance, the door was forced open. Rather than confront his wife, Sawkins left his wife and went downstairs with Murphy, where they joined a "Mr. Herron" and Revere. Sawkins thought it best to remove his wife from the house and explained that they would leave the next day.

The next morning, as Sawkins packed, his wife was restless and left her room. "I requested her to go to her room," said Sawkins. "This she refuse[d] to do on three different occasions. I then took her by the arm and led [as] far as the stairs.[16] She struggled with her husband and they both fell to the floor. "Then she said, 'You have thrown me to the floor,'" stated Sawkins, who believed that his wife was becoming suicidal. Octavia Sawkins' behavior grew increasingly erratic and she left the house without informing her husband. "She was not to be found," exclaimed Sawkins. "Lt. Revere mounted a horse and we both went in search for her. I had no doubt that she would destroy herself."[17] The search continued until 1:30 in the morning, but was resumed at dawn.

On Thursday, November 29, Sawkins led a search party into the woods. He was informed by a "cartman" that Mrs. Sawkins was at Pacheco, a settlement about five miles away. "I found her there and brought her back to the mission, promising to get her a lawyer, to see if she could obtain a divorce which she so much desired," remarked Sawkins.[18]

The next day, Sawkins had a revelation. "I suspected Lt. Revere was the author of her misconduct," he noted. His suspicion was confirmed when his wife later told him, "Swear by the Eternal God as you hope for your salvation injure not Revere, no not the hair on his head, for I am to blame."[19] "I gave myself up to Revere, what passed I scarcely know, but remorse was too great to bear. I flew to the Laudinum (sic) bottle and emptied it at one draught in the hopes of killing myself. Oh, that I had died, but now I love him; yes, James, to the bottom of my soul and will live for him alone."[20] Sawkins informed Murphy about what he had been told by his wife. Murphy went to his own room, retrieved a loaded rifle, and gave it to Sawkins. But Revere had left for San Geronimo.

On December 1, Sawkins and his wife boarded the *Vernon* in San Francisco Bay. They were bound for the Sandwich Islands, but she was reluctant to go. Her behavior became uneven. At times, she cursed and physically struggled with her husband and on other occasions she expressed remorse and even suggested that he engage Revere in a duel.

Eight days later, a writ was served to Captain Mac Kay of the *Vernon*. The document alleged that Octavia Sawkins "is now imprisoned and [forcibly] confined against her will...aboard the *Vernon*." The document was signed by Revere.[21] Mac Kay thought the writ to be "outrageous." Nevertheless, Octavia Sawkins left the ship and secured rooms at a boarding house on Pacific Street in San Francisco. But on December 30, she left the house and boarded the *Kit Carson*, a commercial vessel bound for San Rafael.

Days later, Revere and Octavia were together. But Revere deflected questions about their relationship when he suggested that he was escorting her in an effort to secure a teaching position for her. However, it was "notoriously the public opinion that Mrs. Sawkins was living there as J.W. Revere's mistress."[22] It was the last time the couple would ever see each other.

James Sawkins informed the navy of the affair and he received a reply: "A naval court of Inquiry composed of Commander James Glynn, Lieut. Chas. W. Pickering and William E. Levy, will convene on the U.S. sloop-of-war *Warren*, in the port of San Francisco, on Monday the 15th of April at 12 AM to inquire into the truth of the serious allegations lodged against Lieut. Joseph W. Revere of the U.S. Navy by James G. Sawkins, a citizen of the United States."[23]

The court of inquiry was hardly a secret military tribunal; as a matter of fact, next to the discovery of a new gold find on someone's claim, it was major news in San Francisco. Andrew S. Church called it "a famous Court Martial...at which the names of Lieutenant Revere and Rosa Sawkins were very important."[24]

Purser John N. Hamilton officiated as judge advocate for the court and asked the following question to every witness: "Lieutenant Revere is charged with having deprived Mr. James G. Sawkins of his wife. What do you know of this allegation?"

One unidentified naval officer told the court that he traveled to San Geronimo on or about February 22, 1850, in order to present Revere with orders. "I gave him the order and saw Mrs. Sawkins there," said the witness. "That is all I know of the affair."[25]

Initial testimony provided by Captain Elliott Libby added little to the case, but another witness described the frequency of Revere's visits to Octavia Sawkins' room. Another witness, an unidentified boarder in the Sawkins' house, remembered seeing Octavia and Revere in a room, sitting together on a hammock while two of her pupils worked at a nearby table.

The court resumed its proceedings the next day. Timothy Murphy's testimony included a statement that seemingly made the inquiry more complicated. He remarked that Mrs. Sawkins didn't want to live with her husband because he had another wife, one whom he had married when he was approximately eighteen years old and she was thirty-five. Their marriage resulted in the birth of two daughters. Murphy clarified that Sawkin's first wife had died and the story was not pursued by Judge Advocate Hamilton. Turning back to the case at hand, Murphy acknowledged that "Revere spent much of his time in the room of Mrs. Sawkins."[26]

The inquiry continued on Wednesday, April 17. Captain James C. Beck explained to the court that after word of the scandal spread, Mrs. Sawkins was denied a teaching position despite Revere's efforts to convince a potential employer. "Mr. Smith [the potential employer] would have nothing to do with her, as her character was gone and he, Lt. Revere, had taken her under his protection."[27]

The following day, James L. Poindexter, a boarder at Sawkins' home, answered numerous questions about alleged actions conducted by Revere while at San Geronimo and the house of Chapita Miranda, which was described by a member of the court as "a house of ill fame." The judge advocate asked the witness if "Revere on some public occasion stamped upon the miniature of his wife." Poindexter replied that he knew nothing of such behavior, but he did note that he characterized Chapita Miranda's house, a place where Revere allegedly rendezvoused with Mrs. Sawkins, as "an improper place." Poindexter added to the story of the first Mrs. Sawkins by suggesting that she wasn't dead and that James and Octavia Sawkins "believed she was still living."

After a recess, Captain Elliot Libby added to the polygamy story that was emerging in the inquiry. Perhaps Revere thought that the inquiry would turn in his favor if James Hawkins could be proved to have been polygamous. Libby explained that the story of Sawkins' first wife was "spoken of frequently" in San Rafael. Seth Sheppard, a resident of San Rafael, testified that he had seen Revere visit Mrs. Sawkins where she taught school and at San Geronimo. He also said that he believed that she was Revere's mistress. Later, William Urquahart, a San Rafael farmer, supported Libby's assertion about Mrs. Sawkins' relationship with Revere. "It was generally believed that she was his mistress," said Urquahart.[28]

The court resumed the next day and called Dr. Alfred Taliaferro, who had boarded at Murphy's house while Octavia was there. Taliaferro explained that she was briefly residing there "till

Mr. Sawkins returned from the mines." Under questioning by the accused, Taliaferro said that he believed Mr. Sawkins was a jealous man who "watched her closely." Taliaferro added that Mr. Sawkins was jealous towards him before Revere met Mrs. Sawkins. Before he could continue his testimony, Urquahart returned to the court and stated, "I have no reason to think Lieutenant Revere had any wish to deprive Mr. Sawkins of his wife." Although he did not testify, Andrew Church recalled Sawkins' jealousy. One night, Church was aboard a long boat that also carried Sawkins and his wife. "As we passed into the Bay, a light breeze sprang up with a northern chill in it," remarked Church. "I noticed she had no outer wrap, so I threw my overcoat around her shoulders, to which her husband objected."[29]

Revere sensed that the court had been unable so far to prove the allegations against him. Furthermore, the testimony about James Sawkins' jealousy and the possibility that he had another wife complicated the case to such an extent that it might influence the court to terminate the inquiry.

Taliaferro continued his testimony and mentioned that James Sawkins had papers which proved the illegality of his first marriage. The witness explained that Sawkins had told him that his wife and Revere had taken the papers. Taliaferro also explained that he believed that James Sawkins was trying to prove Octavia insane.

On Friday, April 26, the inquiry resumed with John Addison, a lawyer, providing testimony about his meeting with Mrs. Sawkins aboard the *Vernon*. "She told me she was anxious to obtain a divorce and she wanted it done immediately," said Addison. "She told me that she did not love her husband. He was odious to her and [she said that] she would rather die than live with him any longer." Addison explained to her that her reason for divorce was "not sufficient to initiate proceedings for a divorce."[30] Addison returned to the ship the next day when he learned that Mrs. Sawkins "made an attempt on her life, by cutting her arm with a razor, to open a vein." With her arm bandaged and in a sling, she told the lawyer that she was determined either to secure a divorce or die; in fact, she threatened to jump overboard. She admitted to Addison that she was in love with a married man, but refused to identify him. Then she added, "I'd rather be the mistress of the man I love than a king's wife." Mrs. Sawkins explained that she married her husband to get away from her life in the West Indies (her father served as a British consul) after a young British officer, who was in love with her, "had disobeyed some orders," was dismissed form the service, and subsequently committed suicide.[31]

Judge William B. Almond, who served on the Court of the First Instance in San Francisco, was the next to testify. Almond explained how he was approached by Henry T. Kyle, a lawyer, to approve a writ of *habeus corpus* which was designed to prevent Mrs. Sawkins from being taken away against her will while aboard the *Vernon*. At the time, the judge was unaware that Mr. Sawkins was on board the ship and admitted that had he known, he would not have issued it since he did not want to interfere in the couple's private life. Revere, of course, made the declaration upon which the writ was issued by Almond, but the judge said that he could not recognize that person in the court. "About that time, I was in the habit of taking so many affidavits in such a hurry and haste, that I cannot now recognize the features of that person," said Almond, who added that he believed that Kyle handled everything about the writ.[32] Revere must have been pleased that Judge Almond could not identify him.

The court continued on Saturday, April 27. Kyle was sworn in, but the court halted the proceedings because the lawyer's client,

Revere, had to first grant permission to allow the introduction of private counsel-client information. Revere agreed and the inquiry continued. Kyle detailed Revere's request about securing a writ to assist Mrs. Sawkins, who allegedly was being kept aboard the ship against her will. Kyle agreed to the request and went to Judge Almond, who asked the lawyer to write the writ himself since the clerk on duty was not competent enough to write it. Almond read the writ—which stated that Mrs. Sawkins was "imprisoned and forcibly confined against her will, without legal process on the board the barque *Vernon*"—and signed it.[33] Almond assumed that the ship's captain was responsible for Mrs. Sawkins' detention, not James Hawkins. Kyle dismissed a question from the court about why he did not mention in the writ that James Sawkins was on board the ship. The lawyer said that Mrs. Sawkins was aboard the vessel and it was under the authority of the captain, not her husband.

The alleged affair between Revere and Mrs. Sawkins was not the primary concern of the court. To be sure, Revere could be accused of violating his status as an officer and a gentleman, but the court had to consider whether Revere's premeditated writ declaration was made under false pretenses. And that would be a more serious charge.

On April 29, 1850, the court rendered its decision: "On or about the 9th day of December 1849, Lt. Revere did make an oath in the Court of the First Instance in San Francisco, upon which oath of 'habeus corpus' was issued to remove the person of Octavia Sawkins from on board the barque *Vernon* then lying in the Bay of San Franscisco, by which removal James G. Sawkins the husband of said Octavia was by violence separated from his wife, against his will and has in consequence thereof been deprived of his wife till the present time. And the Court are unanimous in the opinion, that Lt. Revere of the U. S. Navy, did from selfish motives and from personal consideration, swear falsely in the case, knowing at the time, that his declaration was false. And the Court are also unanimous in the opinion that there is a necessity for further proceedings in the case, till the innocence or guilt of Lt. Joseph W. Revere be fully established."[34]

On May 15, 1850, Revere was informed about what would happen next. "The findings of the Court is of a nature, involving high civil as well as military offense, which in the opinion of the Court demands further proceedings against you," wrote Thomas Catesby Jones, Commander in Chief, Pacific Squadron, aboard the flag ship *Savannah,* which was lying in port at Benicia, California. "I do not find it expedient to arraign you before a Court Martial on this Station, upon charges which might be founded on the findings of the court of Inquiry. You will therefore take passage onboard the U.S. storeship *Fredonia,* about to sail for New York; the full findings of the court of Inquiry will be sent to the Navy Department by the next mail."[35]

On May 20, Revere wrote a letter to the U.S. Navy Department and raised objections to the court of inquiry's findings. In a reply, the navy noted that Revere's objections were "well founded," but the court was merely assessing the alleged facts in the case. "Indeed the very words of the finding of the court of Inquiry are expressly that a Court Martial is necessary in your case to ascertain whether the charges are well founded or not, implying a doubt of the strongest kind—of which you are entitled to the full benefit—as to their truth which is only to be ascertained by the proceedings of a regular Court Martial. In conclusion, I have to state that upon mature reflection I am decidedly of the opinion that no fact has been distinctly proved affecting your character or your honor as an officer and gentleman."[36]

Jones, however, revoked his orders of May 15 to Revere in a letter dated June 12, 1850. "The proceedings of the Court of Inquiry, together with all other documents in your case will be submitted to the Hon. Secretary of the Navy for his decision," wrote Jones. "Until you are informed of the result of his revisal of the case, and decision thereon you have permission to remain in California."[37]

Despite not having to travel to New York for the court-martial, Revere was concerned that a decision was forthcoming and that he would have to eventually stand trial somewhere. The findings of the court of inquiry, like those of a civilian grand jury, did not determine guilt or innocence, but an unfavorable court-martial decision would be much more serious. If he was found guilty of the charge, Revere expected to be dismissed from the navy. And even if he were to be found not guilty, the humiliation of the court-martial experience and its impact on his marriage and family name would be a burden that he would bear for the rest of his life.

In order to avoid being dismissed from the navy and to prevent Rosanna from finding out about his affair with Octavia Sawkins, Revere resigned from the navy. He wrote his resignation letter on July 1, 1850. A "Graham" acknowledged Revere's letter with one of his own. Addressed to J. W. Revere, Esq., the letter read: "In reply to your letter of the 1ˢᵗ of July last, you are informed that your resignation had been received and accepted, and that your request to be restored to the service cannot be complied with."[38]

Years later in *Keel and Saddle*, Revere mentioned nothing of the court of inquiry. He concluded his twenty-second chapter with the following: "I remained at San Geronimo, attending to my duties both public and private; but, near the end of the year 1849, I resigned my commission as lieutenant in the United States navy, hopeless of promotion after twenty years of service, yet reluctant to abandon my profession."[39] It was hardly the honest explanation one would expect from an officer and a gentleman.

NOTES

1. Joseph W. Revere, *Keel and Saddle*, 158.
2. Ibid., 159-160.
3. Ibid., 160.
4. Ibid., 162.
5. Ibid., 165.
6. "Memoirs of Andrew S. Church," *Quarterly of the Society of California Pioneers*, Vol. III, No. 4, December 31, 1926, 157. Andrew Church, who was born in New York City on July 26, 1827, left his home for the Gold Rush on March 4, 1849. His 48-page "memoir" traced his interesting adventures in California until 1862.
7. Revere, *A Tour of Duty in California*, 278.
8. Ibid., 301.
9. Ibid., 303.
10. *Boston Evening Transcript*, February 13, 1849, 12. The newspaper added: "It is the opinion of Lieu R. that slavery can never exist in California."
11. *The Sun* (Baltimore, MD), February 23, 1849, 2.
12. *The United States Democratic Review*, Vol. 24, Issue 130, April 1849, 383.
13. *The Living Age*, Vol. 20, Issue 253, March 24, 1849, 575.
14. "Memoirs of Andrew S. Church," 158-159.
15. Case Number 1238, April 15, 1850, Testimony by James Sawkins in deposition, 1, in Revere Research Files.
16. Ibid., 2.
17. Ibid.

18. Ibid., 2-3.
19. Ibid., 3.
20. Ibid. In a letter to a "Mamie" on December 4, 1849, Octavia Sawkins wrote: "James is kinder than ever. I have done everything in my power to [have him] hate me and he will not. I can scarcely provoke him to anger...."
21. Ibid., 6.
22. Ibid., 9.
23. Ibid., 1. Commander Glynn was well known in naval circles. On April 26, 1849, while commanding the USS *Preble*, he successfully freed eighteen American sailors in Japan who had been held captive after a shipwreck. Following his return home, he recommended that the United States establish diplomatic relations with Japan.
24. "Memoirs of Andrew S. Church," 160.
25. Case Number 1238, April 15, 1850, Testimony by James Sawkins, 10.
26. Ibid., 14.
27. Ibid., 15.
28. Ibid., 25. Reflecting the mores of the era, the court asked Urquahart if Mrs. Sawkins drank champagne and smoked cigars. Urquahart replied that be believed she drank champagne. He added that he once gave her a cigarette, but he wasn't positive that she smoked it.
29. "Memoirs of Andrew S. Church," 159.
30. Case Number 1238, April 15, 1850, Testimony of John Addison, 34.
31. Ibid., 36-37. Addison did not explain if Octavia had described the nature of the "disobeyed...orders."
32. Ibid., 38-40.
33. Ibid., 41. Kyle charged Revere $500 for his legal services.
34. Ibid., 43.
35. Revere Research Files, "Letters Found in Revere's Library," 2. The commander's name, Thomas ap Catesby Jones, is Welsh for Thomas, son of Catesby Jones. Ironically, Jones, a naval veteran of the War of

1812 and the Mexican War, was found guilty in 1850 of oppressing junior officers. His was removed from command until President Millard Fillmore restored him to that position three years later.

36. Ibid., 3. The undated letter was signed by "Graham." The individual could be William Alexander Graham, who became Secretary of the Navy on August 2, 1850. However, if the letter was written by Graham, it was penned after Revere had resigned.

37. Ibid. William Ballard Preston was serving as Secretary of the Navy at this time. Appointed by President Zachary Taylor, Preston served from March 8, 1849 to July 22, 1850. Following Taylor's death on July 9, 1850, President Millard Fillmore replaced Preston with William Alexander Graham.

38. Ibid.

39. Revere, *Keel and Saddle*, 179. Although Revere stated that he resigned "near the end of the year," he had actually resigned on July 1, 1850.

CHAPTER FIVE

MORE ADVENTURES IN SAN GERONIMO

"A gentleman of high honor and integrity."

With his resignation behind him, Revere remained in California while Rosanna cared for their children on the other side of the country. He met Sandy McGregor, a rugged "Kentuckian born of Scotch parents" of considerable means who was fond of gambling. Revere was fascinated by McGregor, whom he called an "unlettered demi-savage" with an ability to engage in complex intellectual discussions.

In time, Revere described him as "the most remarkable man I have ever met."[1]

When Revere and McGregor learned that a shipwreck had occurred at Punta de los Reyes, "a bold promontory stretching into the Pacific," about a dozen miles from San Geronimo, the pair acted quickly. They organized a group of vaqueros who worked for Revere and quickly made their way to the coast.

When they arrived, the beach was littered with "casks, barrels, and boxes of merchandise of every description" and the local population was recovering everything that the tide washed ashore. Revere and McGregor were too late to secure any spoils of value. However, they were later invited to the nearby home of one Don Rafael, who hosted a fandango in honor of all those who had recovered items from the shoreline. The festive occasion, which featured "unlimited champagne" and fine wines, dancing by "light-hearted Spanish girls and their cavaliers," bull roping, and other activities, carried on for days.[2]

The captain of the wrecked ship even appeared at the grand festivities, where he met Revere and McGregor. The three soon engaged in conversation which resulted in a canoe ride to the wreck. "The captain told us that in the run, under the floor of the cabin, was a little iron safe, containing a small sum of money, some valuable articles, and a lot of papers; which last he was exceedingly desirous to recover," said Revere.[3] The captain offered Revere and McGregor the safe's money as payment for the recovery.

Revere and McGregor returned to San Geronimo and made plans for the recovery of the safe, which was underwater. Accompanied by "a native of the Sandwich Islands, who was a skilled diver," they returned to the beach and made a raft with some of the "empty casks and driftwood." The diver was able to place ropes around the safe and Revere and McGregor pulled it to the raft. Back on shore, they opened the safe's door with a charge of black powder. "We gave the captain his papers and half the money; the other half and the jewelry we divided between us," remarked Revere.[4]

Besides his adventures with McGregor, Revere developed a close friendship with Rodman Price, a fellow naval officer from New Jersey who had performed a number of diverse duties while stationed in California during the Mexican War. Active in the region's embryonic political scene, Price became a delegate at California's Constitutional Convention in Monterey in 1849.[5]

Revere invited Price to see how he had developed San Geronimo into a profitable ranch. Price was so impressed that he discussed with Revere the possibility of purchasing part of the property. On December 28, 1849, Price bought half the land for $7,500. Upon signing the agreement, Price paid Revere $2,500 and promised to pay the remainder no later than January 1, 1851. Both agreed to invest $2,500 in "stock improvements and expenses" in the property. Furthermore, the agreement stated that both would share equally of any profits earned from "the cutting and otherwise making use of the timber" at San Geronimo.[6] However, Price was not going to be an active partner, so he agreed to give Revere an additional fraction of future profits for his "management" of the property. San Geronimo proved profitable, but Revere soon divested himself from the property. However, the geographic details stated in the property agreement were not precise and over a half century later, a claim would be filed against a piece of Revere's land holdings.

On August 6, 1851, Revere sold the other half of Rancho San Geronimo to Price for $8,000. Besides the land, the agreement included half the livestock "consisting, more or less, of two hundred head of horned cattle, three yoke of oxen, and twenty horses and mules." The agreement stated that Price would immediately pay

Revere $2,500 and the rest in two payments: $3,000 on March 1, 1852, and $2,500 on September 1, 1852.[7]

With some of the money from the initial payment, Revere joined McGregor in another daring adventure. In September of 1851, the pair traveled to Mexico, where they purchased *La Golondrina*, a two hundred-ton Spanish brigantine which was armed with several artillery pieces, an ample supply of black powder, and various flintlock muskets and pistols.

Revere assembled a diverse crew of twenty that included an experienced chief mate from Truro, Massachusetts; a free black cook named Job; and "four Dutchmen and a Finn, two Italians, one Frenchman, two Spaniards, and five Kanakas."[8] The ship traveled along the coasts of California and Mexico, carrying goods from port to port. During a return trip from Guaymas, Mexico, Revere and his crew noticed a beached sailing vessel that was under attack from a "swarm of naked [Yaqui] Indians on the beach who were shooting their arrows and spears."[9] Revere immediately went into action. *La Golondrina's* anchor was dropped and the ship's launch and two whale boats were lowered. Revere commanded the launch, which carried a small-caliber artillery piece; McGregor led the other boats, which were filled with crew members armed with flintlock muskets and bayonets. Once the crew landed, Revere fired his gun, which was filled with grapeshot. McGregor, armed with a sword, and the crew charged the Indians while Revere maintained artillery fire. Although outnumbered, the superiority of Revere's weaponry eventually saved the day—and none of the crew were killed or wounded. Aboard the rescued vessel, the Spanish ship *La Hermosa Gaditana*, several men had been wounded, "while McGregor reported six bodies of the enemy left on the field, of which he grimly exhibited the scalps. He had acquired the Indian habit of preserving trophies."[10]

The rescued passengers—seventeen men and one woman—were cared for on *La Golondrina*. *La Hermosa Gaditana's* captain wanted to return to his ship to retrieve some property, but the vessel broke apart during the night's tide. Revere safely landed the captain, his crew, and the passengers at Mazatlan, Mexico, where representatives of the Spanish government expressed their appreciation and gratitude by granting him knighthood status in the Royal Order of Isabella. Mexico and Spain issued medals to him for his bravery.[11]

Unable to deposit his cargo in Mazatlan due to bureaucratic government whims and corrupt practices, Revere sailed on to San Blas, where he exchanged the Guaymas cargo at a counting house for $30,000 in gold which was "paid in golden ounces." Cognizant of Mexican laws that forbade the exportation of gold, McGregor supposedly concealed the bullion in a large handkerchief which he tied to his waist.[12] As the two left the dock with some crew members in one of their whale boats, a customs inspector and an armed guard ran towards them and demanded they return. Despite the penalty of a lengthy prison term, Revere ignored them and ordered his men to row quickly back to their ship, which was anchored about two miles away. Halfway to the safety of the ship, Revere noticed a Mexican harbor captain's gig, a harbor longboat, filled with inspectors and armed men, rapidly approaching. Revere told McGregor to throw the gold overboard because he feared being arrested and sentenced to twenty years in jail; however, McGregor had other plans. They had barely reached *La Golondrina* when shortly thereafter the Mexican vessel pulled alongside. Revere politely waited for the officials to board; McGregor seemingly disappeared. For two hours, the inspectors searched everywhere, but could not locate the gold. "The bland captain then took his leave, giving me to understand that he should return soon; and, if the money was not forthcoming, he should unship the rudder, and unbend my sails," said Revere. "The vessel would be libeled in the court of admiralty; and, meanwhile, he should leave an officer on board until he returned."[13] Meanwhile, McGregor emerged, but said nothing to the officials.

Later, at dinner, Job carried a kettle from the galley to the pantry, where he promptly removed the handkerchief filled with gold from its iron hiding spot. Everyone was amused, especially McGregor, who was proud that he had quickly thought of a way to hide the amount of precious metal from the experienced inspectors. But the Mexican officer left on board viewed the celebration. Revere and his crew quickly took action. "The angry inspector was quickly bundled into a boat, and transferred to a small vessel near us; our anchor was tripped, and sail made; and, in less than twenty minutes, we were gliding towards the entrance to the harbor," said Revere.[14]

However, the overnight tide and winds kept Revere from putting enough distance between his ship and the harbor. Also overnight, the bound officer had apparently managed to free himself and alert his superiors. The next morning three vessels–two Mexican boats and one from the British frigate HMS *Constance*– were in pursuit of *La Golondrina*.

"It [was] the practice of British ships abroad to mix up with the quarrels of others," explained Revere. "They seem to be a sort of self-constituted ocean-police for all nations."[15] Once again, Revere prepared his crew for action. The guns were loaded and "muskets, pistols, cutlasses, and boarding-pikes" were placed at the ready. The Mexican officer demanded surrender, but Revere replied by stating his maritime rights and threatening him. After the verbal exchange, the two Mexican boats approached Revere's ship from different locations; the British boat did not advance.

The Mexicans fired first. After a musket ball fired from a soldier's pistol passed through *La Golondrina's* mainsail, Revere gave the order to fire. An artillery piece filled with grapeshot raked one of the boats and sent its bloodied crew into the water. Intimidated by the accurate firepower of its antagonist, the other boat halted its advance and pleaded for mercy. Revere stopped his attack and sailed away.

Revere planned to take his ship to San Blas, but he realized that the port might be alerted in advance about his arrival. Instead, he sailed farther south to the Bay of Manzanilla near Colima, a small town situated next to an active volcano. At Colima, Revere was welcomed by the locals, who apparently knew nothing about the incident at Mazatlan. He deposited a partial cargo of "fine silk-goods" and then returned to his ship. Despite his earlier concerns about Mexican authorities awaiting his arrival in San Blas, he set sail for the port community. Upon his arrival, no officials questioned him or his crew. Revere was not only able to sell most of what remained of his cargo, but he and McGregor received an offer to buy their ship. And they sold it–to a group of British adventurers who were eager to exploit the Australia Gold Rush of 1851.[16]

Revere and McGregor removed a few remaining items from the ship and transferred them to a mule train which traveled to Tepic, Mexico, where they were temporarily stored.[17] Revere's reputation as *La Golondrina's* captain so impressed a local businessman that he wrote a letter of recommendation on his behalf. The letter, dated September 15, 1851, which he sent to another man in Chile, called Revere "a gentleman of high honor and integrity and a most skillful and sagacious seaman, deserving of confidence."[18] However, by the time the letter reached its destination, the ship had been sold.

Later joined by a former Prussian cavalry officer and his servant, whom Revere had met in Guadalajara, the men departed with the goods and headed to the annual commercial fair in San Juan de los Lagos.[19] But the journey was interrupted by highway robbers, who captured the Prussian's servant and demanded a ransom for him. The ransom was promptly paid and Revere and his companions continued on to their destination, where they sold the goods.

"We had disposed satisfactorily of our merchandise, and shared the profits," said Revere, who next joined McGregor in a demanding twenty-day journey to Chihuahua.[20]

While McGregor examined the possibility of exploiting the area's silver mine operations, Revere went duck hunting. But his hunt was interrupted by an approaching Apache war party that nearly found him hiding in a "thick clump of bushes."

Revere and McGregor parted ways in Chihuahua. McGregor returned to the United States; Revere remained in Mexico. They had shared more adventures in a year than many men had experienced in a lifetime; however, they were never to meet again. "Two years after our separation, he met his death at the hand of an assassin in New Mexico," said Revere, who continued his travels through Mexico.[21]

Revere arrived in Mexico City in 1851, where he met Robert P. Letcher, the American foreign minister, who introduced him to a number of prominent citizens, including President Mariano Arista, a veteran field commander at the Battles of Palo Alto and Resaca de la Palma during the Mexican War.[22] Arista explained to Revere that the Mexican military, especially the artillery, had been devastated during the recent war with the United States. Subsequent conversations between the two resulted in Arista's offer to Revere to assume the task of reorganizing and training the Mexican army's artillery. Furthermore, Revere would be given the rank of lieutenant colonel. Despite being on opposite sides during the Mexican War only several years earlier, Revere promptly accepted. "I was immediately charged with the work of organizing and drilling four light batteries; giving, at the same time, instruction to a class of officers twice a week in pyrotechny, and the science of projectiles, illustrated by target-practice, and work in the laboratory."[23]

He enjoyed the confidence President Arista had in him. As a staff officer, Revere was provided with his own quarters, servants, and horses. In February of 1852, he accompanied Arista to a mine inspection mission in Guanajuato and later that month, Revere participated in a major military operation led by the Mexican president against rebels in the state of Michoacan. The force of infantry, cavalry, and artillery numbered around 3,500 strong, but the rebels did not yield. On February 25, the rebels attacked the advance of the infantry column as it entered a rugged recessed roadway and forced the soldiers backwards in confusion. Due to the difficult terrain, Revere's artillery, located in the center of the column, was disassembled: the wheels, axles, gun tubes, and tools were mounted on horse-drawn wagons. Even under less rigorous conditions, it would take considerable time to assemble the guns and put them into service. But Revere had trained his men well and ordered them into action. "They took, one a wheel, another the trails and axles, a third another wheel, while four or five carried the pieces themselves between them with their lassos," said Revere. Within minutes, the guns were firing into the ranks of the rebels. "This sudden artillery attack shook the enemy, and gave time to our men to rally, who again pressed forward into the defile; while our cavalry, coming up in the rear, decided the event, and drove the rebels from the field."[24] The rebels reformed on a nearby plain, but

Revere's artillery scattered them, helping to end the fight. Upon his return to Mexico City, Revere was treated for a severe wound that he received during the campaign.[25] Soon thereafter, Revere resigned his commission and planned his journey back to his wife and family in the "spring of the year 1852."[26]

Although Revere's time in the Mexican military was brief, his services were appreciated. He earned the Order of Guadalupe, a badge of honor awarded to Mexican officers. Revere left Mexico and sailed for New Orleans, where he boarded a steamboat that was headed north on the Mississippi River. "Among my fellow passengers on the steamer was Lieut. Thomas J. Jackson of the United States army," wrote Revere, who explained that they engaged in a discussion about astrology. Revere told Jackson that he had an interest in the subject; as a matter of fact, he told him that he "sometimes, to amuse the idle hours of a sea-life, worked out the nativities of my shipmates."[27] To some, astrological forecasting was a meaningless exercise; however, Revere recalled that Jackson believed no one should be criticized for believing in the "occult sciences." They continued their conversations until the two went their separate ways after arriving in Pittsburgh. Several months later, Revere received a letter from Jackson which included an ominous astrological forecast: "Within some ten years, or during the first days of May, 1863; at which time the native ran great risk of life and fortunes: but, in case he survived that peril, the ominous period would never again recur."[28]

NOTES

1. Joseph W. Revere, *Keel and Saddle*, 180.
2. Ibid., 184-185. One of the most vivid events that occurred at the party involved a fight to the death between a grizzly bear and a bull.

The captured bear was tied to the bull with a lasso and both were placed in a corral. Although "dreadfully lacerated," the bull killed the bear. And the victor was "magnanimously liberated to rejoin his harem in the wild woods."

3. Ibid., 186.

4. Ibid., 187.

5. The delegates were elected on August 1, 1849, at Colton Hall, the home of Walter Colton, in Monterey. Robert Semple, a newspaper man from Kentucky who arrived in California in 1845, was selected as the president of the convention. Colton and Semple had published the first newspaper in California, *The Californian,* in 1846. Among the other delegates at the convention were John Sutter and Henry Wager Halleck, who would later gain fame during the Civil War.

6. Agreement between J. W. Revere and Rodman M. Price, dated and witnessed, December 28, 1849. Revere Research Files.

7. Agreement between J. W. Revere and Rodman M. Price, dated and witnessed, August 6, 1851. Revere Research Files.

8. Revere, *Keel and Saddle*, 188. Not counting himself or McGregor, Revere only identified seventeen of his "crew of twenty." The Kanakas were workers who came from various islands in the south Pacific, especially Hawaii.

9. Ibid., 190.

10. Ibid., 191. Revere noted that "four men [aboard *El Hermosa Gaditana*] had broken heads, and three had spear and arrow wounds."

11. Revere was acknowledged with two medals from Spain—one issued by the City of Cadiz for "having saved from death and captivity 14 of countrymen, 1850," and the other by the City of Sevilla in 1851 for "having saved the lives of 13 shipwrecked sailors"—and another from the Tayleur Fund for the Succour of Shipwrecked Strangers for "distinguished gallantry in saving life at Sonora, Mexico, 1850." The fund was established in honor of the RMS *Tayleur,* an impressive clipper ship of the British White Star Line which ran aground and

sank off the coast of Ireland during its maiden voyage in 1854. Fewer than 300 of the ship's nearly 700 passengers, who were bound for Australia to join the Gold Rush, survived. The Tayleur Fund assisted the survivors and paid for the burials of those passengers whose bodies were recovered. The remaining monies in the fund were later used for medals of bravery. Although the specific information regarding date and the numbered of rescued individuals on the three medals does not match, all are in agreement regarding Revere's courage and bravery. The medal issue by Mexico "For Valor" has sometimes been associated with the rescue of *La Hermosa Gaditana's* crew and passengers, but it may have been issued later to Revere for his service as an artillery officer in the Mexican army.

12. Revere, *Keel and Saddle*, 192. Revere must be mistaken. The approximate price of an ounce of gold in 1851 was $20 an ounce, which meant that Revere and McGregor's $30,000 would translate to 1,500 ounces or nearly 94 pounds of gold. How such an amount could be concealed and carried in a handkerchief is beyond belief.

13. Ibid., 193.

14. Ibid., 194.

15. Ibid., 195.

16. The Australia Gold Rush of 1851 began as a result of the rare metal being found in multiple locations. Gold had actually been discovered earlier in Australia; as a matter of fact, some gold had been found in a few places in 1848, the same year as the discovery of the precious metal at Sutter's Mill in California. Like the California Gold Rush, the Australia Gold Rush attracted tens of thousands of precious metal seekers.

17. In *Keel and Saddle*, Revere did not identify what these unsold items were.

18. Letter from [illegible signature] to Don Manuel Moutt, September 15, 1851. Revere Research Files.

19. In *Keel and Saddle,* Revere did not identify the names of the two men.

20. Revere, *Keel and Saddle,* 205.

21. Ibid., 211.

22. Robert P. Fletcher, who Revere identifies as Robert F. Fletcher in *Keel and Saddle,* arrived in Mexico in early 1850 and attempted to negotiate a treaty that would allow American investors to construct a transportation route on the Isthmus of Tehuantepec. His efforts proved unsatisfactory and he returned to the United States in the summer of 1852.

23. Revere, *Keel and Saddle,* 224. A battery consisted of a group of two or more artillery pieces. Light artillery pieces were maneuverable field guns–as opposed to larger siege guns–that worked in conjunction with the infantry.

24. Ibid., 233-234.

25. Ibid., 235. Revere claims to have been "severely wounded," but he did not explain how or where he received the wound.

26. Ibid., 252. Revere states that he resigned his commission following the "retirement of my excellent patron and friend, Don Mariano Arista, from the presidency." Revere is mistaken in his chronology. By the time Arista, a victim of Mexico's internal political turmoil, was forced to resign on January 6, 1853, Revere was living in Morristown, New Jersey. There is also a problem of chronology involving Revere's recollection of his February 1852 military expedition. According to the February 9, 1852, edition of the New Orleans *Daily Picayune,* Revere left Vera Cruz aboard the *Hercules* and arrived in New Orleans. On February 6, 1852, Revere was one of eighteen passengers who signed a "thank you" card to the ship's captain that appeared on page one of the newspaper. This placed in him in the United States at the same time President Arista battled the Michoacan rebels.

27. Ibid., 254.
28. Ibid., 257.

CHAPTER SIX

THE WILLOWS

"She was lovely in death as in life."

His worldly adventures seemingly behind him, Revere searched for property where he could build the house of his dreams. And he found it in Morristown, New Jersey.[1] Rodman Price may have told him about New Jersey during their frequent conversations at San Geronimo. In fact, Price returned to his home state, where he became active in local politics. In 1852, he was elected as a Democrat to the House of Representatives. During his term in Congress, Price maintained ownership of San Geronimo, but secured the services of Lorenzo E. White, a cattle drover, to manage the property in his absence.

Morristown was rich in history. It was the place where George Washington's Continental Army camped in 1777 following the patriot victories at Trenton and Princeton and later during the Revolutionary War's "Hard Winter" of 1779-1780. General Henry Knox, the Continental Army's chief artillery officer, established his headquarters in a barn on property that Revere would own seventy-two years later.[2] Morristown was also the home of George P. Macculloch, an entrepreneur who initiated the idea for the creation of the important Morris Canal, which linked the Delaware River to Newark Bay, in the 1820s. And on January 11, 1838, Samuel F. B. Morse publicly demonstrated the telegraph for the first time in Morristown.

But Morristown–and Morris County–was more than just a place of historic importance: it was a pleasant rural retreat for those who lived in densely populated Manhattan and other nearby urban communities. The fresh air, the lush trees, and farmlands attracted many wealthy city dwellers later in the nineteenth century. "With the dawn of the Gilded Age Americans who could afford it showed a disposition to live in the country for more than a few summer months, and to take more pleasure in the characteristic occupations of country life."[3] But for Revere, Morristown was more than just a comfortable place where he could finally settle down with his family: it was place where the temptations of the past would be replaced by a marital obligation to his wife.

In the December 11, 1851 issue of *The Jerseyman*, Revere read the following real estate advertisement: "Pleasantly situated with fine southern exposure and contains 88 acres of land. There is upon it an excellent two-story dwelling house with kitchen attached; good barn, cow house, wagon house, and other outbuildings; never failing spring run of water passing near the house and through lawn; wood land. Title indisputable."[4] The property was conveniently located only a few miles away from the Morristown Green, the center of the town.

Financing the purchase would not be that difficult because Revere believed he had adequate funds. Furthermore, he was expecting the second San Geronimo sale payment from Price on March 1, 1852, and the final payment on September 1, 1852. But the March payment didn't arrive. Months passed. Revere finally received a payment from Price on July 10, but it was for only $1,000. "I hope you will be able to get by on this sum until September," wrote Price from his office in the House of Representatives. "My private affairs are suffering very much from my confinement in this place."[5] Revere, though, had enough money for his next real estate investment.

On November 20, 1852, Revere purchased Morristown property from landowner Platt Rogers for $6,000. He quickly made plans for his new house, which would be located on a rise several hundred feet away from the existing farm house. The new house's front door would face southeast. Revere's planned home would reflect his appreciation for the Gothic structures that he witnessed during his European travels, but he understood that it was impossible to duplicate the size of the enormous buildings. Still, Revere wanted to incorporate the Gothic style into his house plans. Fortunately, he had found the ideal compromise of Gothic tradition and economic practicality in *Rural Homes*, an 1851 publication created by architect Gervase Wheeler.[6] *Rural Homes* featured a $3,000 home designed by Wheeler for Henry Olmstead in East Hartford, Connecticut. "Wheeler, who apprenticed under Richard Carpenter of England, a strong proponent of Gothic architecture, produced an arresting expression of exaggerated verticality with the use of steeply-pitched roofs and an arcade of five pointed arches across the front façade. Additionally, the side gables of the modified Greek cross plan framed an articulation of the interior structure with beams mimicking the second floor vaulted ceiling."[7]

Revere was impressed with the Connecticut house design, but he was not content to replicate the Olmstead house with its gingerbread trim, floor to ceiling windows, and dramatic two-story porch tracery. He wanted more and he wanted it built quickly. And his family was growing: Thomas Duncan Revere was born on November 22, 1853. He contracted local builder Ashbel Bruen of Chatham to make his house larger by adding a library, a bathroom, an attached kitchen, and a second-floor balcony. Although the finished product was asymmetrical, it retained a sense of esthetic balance.

In back of the house, Revere added an ice house and storage shed to the construction plans. The construction contract of August 7, 1854 stated that Bruen "shall and will on or before the first day of February next erect, build, setup and finish one dwelling house" for $7,125.15. During construction, Revere and his family lived in the house that came with the Rogers property. Bruen, however, died before the year was out and the work was completed by his business partner, Lewis Carter.[8]

Once the house was built, Revere oversaw the landscaping that featured Norway spruces strategically planted near the ends of the front porch. Orchards filled with apple and pear trees and open fields created an idyllic and relaxed setting.

He called his new home "The Willows." Perhaps the name was inspired by some of the "gracefully drooping willows" on his property.[9] The Willows became a prime example of the Gothic Revival movement that had been gaining popularity in the United States since the 1830s. Abandoning the Greco-Roman Classicism that had dominated American architecture for generations, the new style was championed by British architect Richard Upjohn, who designed Manhattan's Trinity Church, and American architect Alexander Jackson Davis, who published *Rural Residences* in 1837 and designed the "Lyndhurst" estate in Tarrytown, New York.[10] And Revere embraced the movement with his own personal flair.

The Willows today. Photo by Ralph Iacobelli.

Inside The Willows, Revere embellished his house with several tromp l'oeil paintings, which were faux creations depicting three-dimensional-like images.[11] Guests who entered his home would stand upon imported British tile and gaze at an intricately carved wooden fireplace mantel with unique finials and Gothic motifs. The arch details in the balustrade were particularly impressive. For a moment, visitors would be fooled when they looked at the "wooden" gothic arches since they were actually painted on the walls.

Revere's library, located in the rear of the first floor, was a Gothic retreat of tall, dark wood bookcases, a handsome desk, black walnut wainscoting, a fireplace, tromp l'oeil embellishments, and an alcove with a window seat that faced the trees. The room reflected Gervase Wheeler's concept of what a library should be: "a sort of snuggery, half-library, half-saloon, but wholly comfortable."[12] Revere, an avid reader, filled the shelves with hundreds of books.

Revere may have had some of the tromp l'oeil murals commissioned, but he painted the main one over the dining room's fireplace himself, which he signed with his initials. The large dining room mural features the Revere family crest, food and wine, canned goods, a glass vase filled with flowers, and a banner which reads, "Praise God from whom all blessings flow," a lyrical phrase from Thomas Ken's popular seventeenth-century hymn.[13] He added a playful touch to the mural when he strategically featured a knife and a peeled lemon which appeared to dangle off the creation's bottom frame. Although Revere was certainly artistic, he was not proficient in the tromp l'oeil style; his artistic effort came across more as two dimensional than three-dimensional. Another mural on the dining room wall, which Revere may have painted, features the head of a bull, a reflection of his cattle enterprise in California and his knowledge of astrology–Revere was born under the sign of Taurus, the bull. Additional paintings of animals, which were successfully hunted, are strategically placed on every wall of the room. One wall painting features a cluster of baked breads.

Two large bedrooms, connected by a common fireplace, which feature Gothic-inspired curved ceilings, dominate the second floor of The Willows. The main bedroom features two large windows that face the front of the house and a door that leads to a sitting room and a balcony. A third floor, with single arched windows at the front and back, was designated for storage.

The construction plans included a plumbing system that "was very progressive for its time." An attic cistern supplied water to the house through gravity; its water supply originated from an underground cistern that was pumped to the attic.[14]

While Revere was involved in his house's construction and decorating, he wrote to the navy about the issue of back pay and the findings of the court of inquiry. Although he had resigned his commission on July 1, 1850, he felt he was owed additional pay because he did not receive the navy's acknowledgment of his decision until months later. As a result, he believed he may have been kept on the navy's roles and was entitled to the pay. Furthermore, Revere felt that his final title in the navy should have been lieutenant commanding—a rank higher than lieutenant, but lower than commander—since he had led troops on land and had been prize master aboard the *Admittance*. The second issue was important to him and he pursued it.

Revere expressed his concerns in a letter to the navy on August 24, 1852. On April 4, 1853, the navy replied: "It has long since been settled that the commander of a military post on shore, or of a prize vessel, does not give a lieutenant the right to receive the pay of a 'Lieutenant Commanding.'" The navy acknowledged that Revere had been credited with $128.91 in pay to November 8, 1850, but that the amount "was credited to him on the settlement of his account as Timber Agent."[15] However, upon further investigation by the Treasury Department's Fourth Auditor's Office, Revere was informed that an additional "sum of fourteen hundred and forty five dollars and forty seven cents" was owed him, primarily for "serving in the Pacific."[16] On June 24, 1854, a letter from the Secretary of the Treasury, transmitting an account of the receipts and expenditures of the government for the year ending June 30,

1853, stated that Revere was actually owed $1,752 in extra pay for his service "in the Pacific, on the Coast of California."[17]

He also asked the new Secretary of the Navy, John P. Kennedy, for information that would help clear his name regarding the findings of the court of inquiry. On October 3, 1852, Kennedy wrote Revere and informed him that a decision based on the opinion of two highly regarded San Francisco lawyers "completely exonerates you."[18] Surprisingly, the good news was addressed to Revere in Canton, Massachusetts, the home of his namesake uncle. Perhaps Revere wanted to keep mail from the navy away from his wife.

Revere attempted to eradicate the case by requesting that the papers in the court of inquiry be withdrawn. In a follow up letter several months later to Revere at his Canton address, Kennedy informed him that while he appreciated the "sensibility on the subject," it was not the policy of the Department of the Navy "to allow papers upon which proceedings [have] been founded, to be withdrawn."[19]

Disappointed in the navy's responses, Revere focused his energies on his new home and family—except for a brief international sojourn. Although there is limited documentation about Revere's activities during the 1850s, "a British medal... issued for the Indian Mutiny campaign of 1857-1858, indicates he may have spent some time as a military consultant to various European governments."[20] He also "served as brigadier-general of the Morris County Militia."[21]

The Committee on Naval Affairs contacted Revere in 1856 during an investigation into the dismissal of Lieutenant Washington A. Bartlett. The officer, who had served on the USS *Portsmouth*, was removed from the rolls of the navy because he engaged in "fraudulent and dishonest conduct," among other charges, including one in which involved the "illicit" selling of a ladies' shawl. Bartlett believed that the Board of Naval Officers' decision of dismissal was "illegal and unjust." Revere, who had enough of naval courts, wrote to Bartlett on April 29 and expressed outrage. "The further persecution of you, to which I was a witness on board the Portsmouth, in the many small ways in which naval tyrants show their malignity, I not only did not approve, but spoke freely of, among those of my messmates with whom I was on intimate terms, as petty and ill-natured in the extreme," wrote Revere. "Finally, I have to state that I consider you, among other many others, as the victim of a most despotic, tyrannical, and despicable law, unconstitutional in its enaction, and under which I would not hold a commission."[22] Less than a decade later, Revere would confront what he considered an "illegal and unjust" court decision.

Revere's Mexican War compatriot John C. Frémont, who had briefly served as one of California's first U.S. Senators, became the new Republican Party's candidate for president in 1856. Although Revere was somewhat sympathetic to Frémont's anti-slavery platform, as a loyal Democrat, he supported Pennsylvania's James Buchanan, who won the election.

Tragedy entered Revere's life. Young Thomas, who was not quite three years old, died on September 18, 1856. Ten days later, though, Rosanna gave birth to another son, Paul. Three years later, Frances became seriously ill. She developed a severe fever and pneumonia and died on September 25, 1859. Revere and his wife were heartbroken. Rodman Price, who had left Congress after one term and served as New Jersey's governor from 1854 to 1857, wrote a poignant letter of sympathy to Revere. On October 1, 1859, Revere replied to his good friend in a three-page letter.

"I received your kind note sympathizing with us in the dreadful affliction God has seen fit, for my sins, to bring upon us and we feel truly grateful to you and your wife for your kind feelings towards us," wrote Revere. One wonders if Revere was confessing the sins of his behavior in California or merely the sins that all Christians acknowledge. Revere informed Price that Frances–who was affectionately called Fannie–seemed to be recovering just prior to her death. "The dear child was not reduced in flesh in the least, and got up out of bed but a few moments before it came. She was lovely in death as in life, and we have the melancholy pleasure of knowing that she did not suffer in the least."[23]

Revere explained that his wife was "suffering seriously from nerves and grief" and that it would be best if they spent some time away from home. They departed for Europe in November and returned home the following year. Their sojourn marked a time in their marriage when they seemingly became closer to one another. For once, it was just the two of them. For Rosanna, it may have been more like the early days of their courtship or, perhaps, it was the way a dutiful Victorian husband was expected to behave in a time of family grief. In any event, they were together. But it would not last long.

While in Strasburg, Germany, Revere engaged in conversations with veterans of the recently completed Second Italian War for Independence.[24] In Paris, he met Major Philip Kearny, a celebrated veteran of the Mexican War, who warned Revere about the inevitability of "a long and sanguinary civil war" back in the United States.[25]

Revere was well aware of the tensions that had developed between the free and slave states. Although a lifelong Democrat, he was highly critical of Democratic President James Buchanan. "The conspiracy grew and strengthened in the Southern States; while the imbecility of the administration encouraged the secessionists to perfect all their plans for a vast insurrection, until the attack on Fort Sumter aroused the sleeping North to a sense of the real condition of national affairs," said Revere.[26]

NOTES

1. Morristown included the town and the nearby districts that were not part of any other municipality. On April 6, 1865, it was incorporated as its own municipality separate from Morris Township, which surrounds Morristown.

2. The winter of 1779-1780 was the one of the coldest seasons of the eighteenth century. Washington and his beleaguered force of approximately ten thousand soldiers suffered through more than twenty documented snowstorms and severe shortages of food, supplies, and equipment while encamped at Morristown. Part of Henry Knox's artillery park was located in what is now Morristown's Burnham Park.

3. John W. Rae and John W. Rae, Jr., *Morristown's Forgotten Past–The Gilded Age: The Story of a New Jersey Town, Once a Society Center for the Nation's Wealthy* (Morristown, NJ: John W. Rae, 1979), 2-3. The authors noted that by 1896, Morristown "had 54 millionaires with a total wealth of $289,000,000."

4. *The Jerseyman*, December 11, 1851. The property's original owner, Jonathan Ogden, had died in 1825 at the age of eighty-two. The land was passed to his wife and later to his son, who sold it in 1826 to Henry Mooney. In 1835, Mooney sub-divided the property and sold it, except for an eighty-eight-acre parcel which was bought by Isaac Storm of Brooklyn, New York. It was Storm who placed the ad in *The Jerseyman*. Platt Rogers saw the ad and purchased the property

on March 21, 1851, for $5,000. Less than a year later, Rogers sold the land to Revere for $6,000.

5. Price to Revere, July 19, 1852. Revere Research Files. Price later sold his interests in San Geronimo to his brother, Francis Price.

6. According to Renee Elizabeth Tribert's 1988 University of Pennsylvania thesis, *Gervase Wheeler: Mid-Nineteenth Century British Architect in America,* Wheeler's name is "seldom found in architectural history texts…because he worked in an era when the profession of the architect was not yet firmly established in America."

7. Nancy E. Strathearn, "The Willows." *Nineteenth Century*, Vol. 10, No. 2, [1990], 9. Strathearn served as curator/historian at The Willows and chaired the Historic Preservation Committee of Morris Township, New Jersey.

8. *Biographical and Genealogical History of Morris County, New Jersey*, 210. Bruen is sometimes identified as being a resident of nearby Madison. The builder had moved to Madison prior to his death on October 8, 1854. His wife, Mary, lived at the Madison home until she died on April 24, 1889, at age eighty-five.

9. Strathearn, "The Willows," 10.

10. Revere was probably familiar with other influential writers whose periodicals and books heralded the Gothic Revival movement. Alexander Jackson Downing teamed up with Andrew Jackson Davis, the editor of *The Horticulturist* magazine, and wrote *Cottage Residences* in 1842. Eight years later, Downing wrote *The Architecture of Country Houses*. Both books included dozens of house plans as well as landscape designs.

11. Tromp l'oeil is a French term that means "trick the eye." Tromp l'oeil's illusionary three-dimensional style was popular in the mid-nineteenth century, but was out of vogue near the end of the century. Originals were often painted over.

12. Strathearn, "The Willows," 9. Revere's first attempts at painting tromp l'oeil were located on the library's walls, but because they were rather elementary, they were subsequently covered with wallpaper.

13. Ken, an Anglican Bishop, wrote the doxology in 1764: "Praise God, from Whom all blessings flow; Praise Him, all creatures here below; Praise Him above, ye Heavenly Host; Praise Father, Son, and Holy Ghost. Amen."

14. Paula Sagerman, *The Willows: Restoration Manual,* 1991, 16. Sagerman prepared the manual while serving as a summer intern in the University of Pennsylvania's Graduate Program of Historic Preservation.

15. Dayton to Wallach, April 4, 1853. Revere Research Files. Wallach, who resided or worked in Washington, D.C., may have represented Revere as his legal counsel. A copy of a Treasury Department, Fourth Auditors Office document dated September 7, 1852, indicates the $128.91 figure along with other amounts.

16. Dayton to Wallach, May 11, 1853. Revere Research Files.

17. Letter from the Secretary of the Treasury to the House of Representatives, Thirty-third Congress, First Session, June 24, 1854, 347.

18. Kennedy to J. W. Revere in Canton, Massachusetts, dated October 3, 1852. Revere Research Files.

19. Kennedy to J. W. Revere, Esq. in Canton, Massachusetts, dated March 1, 1853. Revere Research Files.

20. Russell E. Belous, "A Revere in California," Los Angeles Museum Association *Quarterly*, Vol. 17, #1, winter 1960-1961, 8. A photocopy of the article is located in the Revere Research Files.

21. *Biographical and Genealogical History of Morris County, New Jersey,* 97.

22. Revere to Bartlett, April 29, 1856, in Senate of the United States, July 22, 1856, submitted to Mr. [John] Bell of Tennessee, 61.

23. Revere to Price, October 1, 1959. Revere Research Files. Another typed document in the files suggested that "she died in a riding accident at the Willows."

24. Revere, *Keel and Saddle*, 258.

25. Ibid., 269. During the Battle of Churubusco on August 27, 1847, a blast of grapeshot from a Mexican artillery piece ripped into Kearny's left arm, which was subsequently amputated.

26. Ibid., 270.

CHAPTER SEVEN

THE SEVENTH NEW JERSEY

**"The general condition of the army at this time
was deplorable."**

The election of Abraham Lincoln, the Illinois Republican who championed an end to slavery's extension in the new territories, was repudiated by South Carolina when the rebellious state seceded in December 1860. By the time of Lincoln's inauguration in March 1861, six more southern states–Mississippi, Florida, Alabama, Georgia, Louisiana, and Texas–had left the union and formed the Confederate States of America.

New Jersey wasn't fond of Lincoln, either. Fifty-two percent of its voters cast their ballots for Northern Democrat Stephen Douglas in the 1860 election. Lincoln barely managed to win a majority of the state's Electoral College votes–four of the seven votes. But New Jersey was unique in a number of ways. For example, it was the last Northern state to adopt an emancipation law. Although its 1804 legislative act provided for the gradual abolition of slavery, eighteen slaves were still listed in New Jersey's 1860 census. Furthermore, the state's largest cities–Newark, Paterson, and Camden, among others–had strong economic ties with the South, providing antebellum customers everything from leather saddles to locomotives. And several New Jersey newspapers criticized Lincoln, Republicans, and abolitionists at every opportunity. One, the *True Democratic Banner*, heralded the Democrats as the "white man's party."[1]

In his inaugural speech, Lincoln tried to reassure the South of his position on slavery: "I have no purpose, directly or indirectly, to interfere with the institution of slavery in the States where it exists," said the president on March 4, 1861. But his words failed to persuade the Southern states. In the following months, Virginia, Arkansas, Tennessee, and North Carolina joined the Confederacy.

In his address, Lincoln added that he held the authority to "hold, occupy, and possess the property and places belonging to the government" that were located in the states which had seceded. But that authority was severely challenged on April 12, 1861, when Confederate artillery batteries fired at Fort Sumter, a federal stronghold in the Charleston, South Carolina harbor. Thirty-four hours later, Fort Sumter surrendered. The "long and sanguinary civil war" that Philip Kearny had warned of had begun.

Revere believed that the war resulted, in part, from the federal government's complacency. "The people of the North could not or would not then believe that any danger was threatened to themselves by the state of affairs, and to the last hour went on with their business and social enjoyments in perfect confidences that they would be left undisturbed to pursue the even tenor of their way," he wrote. "They were confirmed in this security by the politicians intrusted with the government, who assured their constituents that there would be no war, or a very little one. The conspiracy grew and strengthened in the Southern States; while the imbecility of the administration encouraged the secessionists to perfect all their plans for a vast insurrection, until the attack on Fort Sumter aroused the sleeping North to a sense of the real condition of national affairs."[2]

On April 15, 1861, three days after the shelling of Fort Sumter began, President Lincoln called for 75,000 troops. New Jersey was supposed to supply a brigade of four regiments totaling 3,123 men.[3] Patriotic events were quickly organized throughout the state to encourage enlistments. The citizens of Morristown expressed their support to "sustain the Government" by purchasing a new U.S. flag which they planned to raise on a special Liberty Pole during a grand ceremony on the evening of April 18, coincidentally the eighty-sixth anniversary of Paul Revere's legendary ride. Joseph Warren Revere, as brigadier general of the Morris County Militia, wanted to make the ceremony memorable. *The Jerseyman* reported that "Gen. Revere ordered out our military companies to add to the interest of the occasion."[4] Revere formed the companies on the Morristown Green, where speeches were delivered and a band played patriotic songs. And many of the young men answered President Lincoln's call.

Many teenage boys who were too young to enlist sought out military training wherever they could secure it and some went to Revere. Jacob William Miller, 14, "recalled how much 'Captain Revere was to us school boys on 1861. I shall remember his yarns and sympathetic interest as we youngsters confided to him, at his place on the Mendham Road, our desire too become soldiers and sailors. It was there that he drilled us, laughing at our awkward manual of arms.'"[5]

Following the First Battle of Bull Run on July 21, an embarrassing Union defeat, Lincoln quickly realized that many more soldiers would be needed to suppress the Confederate rebellion and he increased the number of volunteers that each state would have to provide. Revere was critical of Lincoln's early assessment of the war in which the president suggested that the existing federal forces and short-term state militia units could check the Southern rebellion. "The administration resorted to feeble and uncertain measures for defense, while continuing to assure the world, through the medium of the State department, that the war would be a trivial affair of sixty or ninety days at farthest," remarked Revere.[6]

Revere was also concerned about the contrasting quality of the opposing ranks on the battlefield. "But it must be remembered, that, in [the South] there flourished a higher martial spirit; for in the war with Mexico, fourteen years before, the Southern States furnished more than forty thousand men to the general service, while only about half that number was contributed by the more populous North," he noted.[7]

Eventually, President Lincoln authorized the recruitment of ten infantry regiments from New Jersey. A typical regiment would be composed of about 1,000 men arranged in ten companies. Each company would be commanded by a captain. Governor Charles Olden selected the regimental commanders, who would be given the rank of colonel.

Once the war began, Revere felt obligated to serve his nation again. He believed that his many years of experience in the navy would be acknowledged with an appropriate rank. Revere sought reactivation; however, Gideon Welles, the Secretary of the Navy, did not approve the request. In a letter dated May 30, 1861, Welles bluntly told Revere: "The Department could not appoint you a Commander in the Navy without doing injustice to those already in the service." Revere acknowledged the secretary's letter without any bitterness. "I had already offered my services to the General Government; but was assured they would not be required, as no increase of the navy was contemplated," he remarked.[8] Undaunted, Revere approached New Jersey Governor Olden, a Republican, for a commission in the volunteer infantry.

Despite Revere's interest to command an infantry regiment, Olden favored others, especially the highly regarded Philip Kearny. President Lincoln also sought Kearny's service. The forty-six-year-old veteran was soon appointed a brigadier general and given the command of the First New Jersey Brigade, which was organized in the spring of 1861.[9] Revere thought that Kearny's new federal command assignment provided him with an opportunity to be selected by Olden as a regimental commander on the state level.

On June 10, Governor Olden wrote to Revere and described the difficulties in raising regiments that fulfilled federal expectations. "I have on the part of this state offered one or two regiments to the Secretary of War in addition to those called for which they declined to receive," stated Olden. "Since declining to receive the regiments offered on the part of the State of New Jersey the authorities at Washington have accepted several bodies of troops offered for service as I understand it by individuals–for instance Sickles Corps from New York."[10] However, Olden concluded his letter with some encouraging words for Revere: "Should I receive an intimation that any further call is to be made of this state I will advise you of it and should be rejoiced to have a regiment go from New Jersey under your command."[11]

New Jersey raised additional regiments in the months that followed. Finally, the Seventh New Jersey Volunteer Infantry was authorized by Congress on July 22, 1861, and mustered into federal service at Camp Olden in Trenton on September 3, 1861; Revere was appointed as its commander. Lieutenant Colonel Ezra Carman of Newark was the Seventh New Jersey's second in command; Francis Price, son of Revere's friend, Rodman Price, served as the unit's adjutant. Unlike the early war units that only served for several months, the new regiments were obligated to serve for three years.

Ezra Carman and Francis Price.
Courtesy of the John W. Kuhl Collection.

"Recruits came rapidly in, all men of the best class, young, patriotic, and athletic, principally from the agricultural districts, and all eager to begin their new career, and to acquire a knowledge of the duties of a soldier," Revere pointed out.[12] But they didn't arrive rapidly enough.

The enlisted men were a diverse group. Over 200 men in the Seventh New Jersey were born in foreign countries; Ireland and Germany represented seventy percent of the total. Holland, Austria, Canada, Russia, Poland, and Italy were also the birthplaces of some of the men in the regiment.[13] But most were native-born and they hailed from nearly every area of the state–from Burlington County, Newark, northern Atlantic County, and Hudson County to western Essex County, Passaic County, and Warren County.

The soldiers of the Seventh New Jersey came from all walks of life. John Bettenbender, 30, was a mason; Edward Fanning, 24, worked as a carpenter; Samuel Rhodes, 19, was a wheelwright; Thomas Derkin, 35, made umbrellas; Aaron Hayward, 28, painted coaches; Jacob Herr, 31, was a baker; Curtis Dangler, 21, tended gardens; Heyward Emmell, 19, was a store clerk; Peter Meuman, 20, finished hats; and David Halloway, 19, was a stone cutter. Coincidentally, the quartermaster sergeant of Company K was Merritt Bruen, whose father, Ashbel Bruen, built The Willows. And there were blacksmiths, tobacconists, glassblowers, shoemakers, teachers, students, waiters, machinists, and farmers among the ranks of Revere's regiment.[14]

Revere was not the only grandson of the legendary Paul Revere who was serving in the Civil War; in fact, he had two first cousins in the Union army: Edward Hutchinson Robbins Revere and Paul Joseph Revere. Edward Hutchinson Robbins Revere (born September 23, 1827) was the son of Joseph Warren Revere (born in 1777), Paul Revere's eleventh child. Edward Revere became a surgeon in the Twentieth Massachusetts, a unit led by his brother, Colonel Paul Joseph Revere (born September 10, 1832). During the war, all three Reveres would meet, but they would suffer in one way or another before the great rebellion came to an end.

While at Camp Olden, Revere received some wonderful news from Rosanna: Augustus LeFebre Revere was born on August 8, 1861. Paul, who was nearly five years old, was no longer an only child. Unlike their three other siblings who had died, the two brothers would live into the twentieth century.

Like other regiments, the Seventh New Jersey was designed to be composed of ten hundred-man companies. But pressing Union demands for soldiers in the field forced the regiment to depart from Trenton under strength. Instead of ten companies, Revere led only seven to Washington, D.C. on September 19. And they were under-armed. As an alternative to being issued 1861 Springfield rifle muskets or such new imports as the Enfield rifle muskets, the soldiers in the Seventh New Jersey were initially given Model 1842 Springfield muskets, relatively inaccurate smooth-bore weapons that had seen prior service in the Mexican War. "Our muskets are not very serviceable as the nipple holes need widening which causes them to clog," lamented Revere.[15]

Despite deficiencies of men and weapons, Revere carried on. The unit traveled by train from the state capital to Camden, where New Jersey's first railroad, the Camden and Amboy, made its trial run debut thirty years earlier. The men boarded ferries and crossed the Delaware River, landing at Philadelphia, where they boarded another train. After a relatively short run, the train stopped at the banks of the Susquehanna River at Perryville, Maryland. Like the Delaware River, the Susquehanna River had no bridge capable of supporting a train. But the *Susquehanna*, a novel railroad-car ferry that began its service in 1836, carried the train's cars to the other side of the river at Havre de Grace, Maryland. The men of the

Seventh New Jersey continued by rail until they passed through Baltimore and reached Washington, D.C.

Revere received complimentary press coverage. The *Atlantic Democrat* reported: "The Regiment is well officered, having for its Colonel Joseph Warren Revere, of long service in the Navy, having been appointed midshipman in 1828. During the Mexican war he was a Captain of mounted rifles serving with distinction."[16]

Revere eagerly awaited the arrival of the rest of his regiment. On September 26, Revere wrote a letter to Lieutenant Colonel Carman, who remained in Trenton where he was supervising the new recruits. "I think it decidedly best to have all the companies of the regiment come even if not quite full," stated Revere.[17] Several weeks later, the remaining three companies, having completed rudimentary training at Camp Olden, left for the nation's capital on October 3. One of the new companies, Company K, was recruited in Morris County, Revere's home county, and sent off to battle following a formal meeting at the First Presbyterian Church of Morristown.[18] One newspaper described the company's patriotism: "But love of country drowned every other consideration, and impelled them to rise above every obstacle that stood in their way, and go forth with the swelling hosts to maintain the honor of their country's flag, or die in its defense."[19] Upon the arrival of the three companies, Colonel Revere's regiment consisted of 920 men: 882 enlisted men and 38 officers. The Seventh New Jersey was briefly attached to General Silas Casey's Provisional brigade, but in the autumn it was assigned to the Third Brigade, Hooker's Division, Army of the Potomac.[20]

Revere and his regiment camped on Meridian Hill in Washington, D.C. Nearby, other units formed camps. He observed that "the general condition of the army at this time was deplorable" and he intended to do something about it. Revere, who had "an eye for the beautiful," according to Francis Price, established his camp with care. "The tents were pitched upon a sidehill affording most excellent drainage and kept the company streets in most excellent condition," remarked Price. "At one end of the encampment we had a beautiful log chapel named Saint John's in the Wilderness, and services were always held on Sundays and sometimes during the week. We had a large bakery and baked about 1,500 loaves of bread per day, pies and cakes. Each company had a tailor, a shoemaker and a barber. Having over one hundred horses, we had a large blacksmith shop, and, to complete the list, a French restaurant."[21] Price added that Revere's camp also "had a large general store where the men were allowed to trade in the matter of $5.00 per man." The store not only provided the men with assorted sundries, but it curbed the nefarious efforts of anti-Union peddlers who sold tainted food and beverages which occasionally resulted in illness or death. As a result, Revere "banned peddlers from his camp as a precaution against further trouble" and posted guards "near all sources of drinking water... and food from sources outside the army."[22]

Once the company streets had been organized and the tents erected, Revere promptly initiated daily drills–three two-hour sessions–although they were carried out by the competent Lieutenant Colonel Carman, who had graduated from the Western Military Institute in 1855 and later served as an assistant professor of mathematics at the University of Nashville. "[Revere] rarely appeared on review because he could neither master regimental or brigade evolution, and I was not long in discovering the hard work and drill of the regiment was to fall upon my shoulder," said Carman.[23] Despite Revere's absence from the drill field, he was depicted in *The Jerseyman* as an involved and highly regarded regimental commander–"our gallant townsman, Colonel Revere."

Revere reinforced Carmen's instructions in a martial style that he was familiar with. "Instruction now began in earnest; and in a few weeks I had the satisfaction of seeing my raw recruits transformed into tolerably proficient soldiers," recalled Revere. "I applied at once the principles of discipline I had learned in a hard school–the United States navy–firmly and uncompromisingly; as I knew, that, once taught, they would never be forgotten."[24] And they were not, much to the dismay of the men.

Revere applied the harsh discipline to both his officers and the enlisted men. "It was very hard for these young men to stand sentinel for eight hours together with loaded knapsacks, to be made a 'living statuary' on a pork-barrel for a pedestal, and to endure other penalties know to military discipline; but the lessons of such experience were lasting, and the recruit who had gone once through the course enjoyed immunity ever afterwards," said Revere.[25] Lieutenant Colonel Carman even felt the wrath of his commander's discipline when Revere had him arrested "for some unknown reason."[26]

The rigorous drilling continued. Each soldier learned how to march as part of a larger unit, how to load and fire his musket in unison, how to "charge bayonet," and execute numerous other martial tasks. And when a soldier failed at one of his duties, swift punishment followed. Earlier in the year, Revere used to laugh at the young teenage boys who awkwardly drilled at home. The situation was very different now.

"Persons are punished very severely for small offenses," said Private Heyward Emmell of Company K, who, like the other enlisted men, soon referred to their training area as Camp Revere. "I have seen a man have to wear a barrel with a hole in the top for his head to stick out and holes in the sides for his arms. He had to run all the afternoon around camp. He fainted after a while. You can see men with large logs on their shoulders running around every day for slight offences."[27] Revere creatively combined prayer and punishment when he "insisted that the chapel built by his troops also serve as a guardhouse."[28]

In Revere's defense, some of the men–including officers– were unable to adjust to military life. He was able to weed out unsatisfactory officers after Major General George B. McClellan, the commander of the Army of the Potomac, "ordered all regimental commanders to place before a review board the names of all officers thought to be unfit for command." When Revere named Captain John Craven of Company B to appear before the review board, the twenty-nine-year-old resigned. A few other officers left the service after the review board found them "unfit."[29]

George B. McClellan.

While Revere was responsible for schooling the men of the Seventh New Jersey, McClellan was responsible for the coordinated training of all the combined regiments and brigades. Revere had high praise for his thirty-five-year-old commander. "Gen. McClellan was charged with reducing this mass of heterogeneous elements to order; and he accomplished his task in about three months, converting the mob into an efficient and disciplined army," said Revere. "To say that McClellan acquitted himself credibly in this colossal work is to accord him scant justice: for the fact is, that his achievement was one which entitles him to a place in the first rank of soldiers."[30]

On October 19, Revere and his regiment participated in a grand ceremony in which Governor Olden presented them with the flags of the United States and New Jersey. "[Revere] wore a variety of medals on his person and when he appeared on grand occasions he was most fearfully and wonderfully made up and bedizzened," remarked Carman sarcastically.[31]

A few weeks later, Revere received his first orders for action. But he and his regiment were not sent to battle against Confederate soldiers; instead, the Seventh New Jersey was ordered to protect Maryland polling places during the upcoming state elections. Some in the ranks may have dismissed the mission as an easy assignment; however, there was a cause for concern. On April 18, 1861, five Pennsylvania militia companies traveling to Washington, D.C. were assaulted in Baltimore by a mob of Confederate sympathizers and dock toughs. A day later during a march between two train stations on Pratt Street, the Sixth Massachusetts Regiment was attacked by even a larger mob. When the so-called Pratt Street Riot came to an end, several soldiers and a number of civilians lay dead and dozens of soldiers and civilians were wounded.

Maryland's allegiance to the United States was under question. It was a slave state whose voters cast fewer than 2,300 ballots for Lincoln in the 1860 election. Lincoln understood that Maryland could not be lost to the Union since a Confederate Maryland and Virginia would surround Washington, D.C. Although Maryland's House of Delegates voted 53-13 against convening a secessionist convention on April 29, 1861, the issue remained unresolved. Nevertheless, on September 17, a secession convention convened, but it lacked a quorum and no vote was taken. Eligible voters would make the final decision about Maryland's allegiance in the state elections.

In order to prevent known secessionists from voting or disrupting the polls, Union soldiers were sent to various polling places. Brigadier General George Sykes ordered four New Jersey regiments to their assigned locations. "I detached Colonel Revere, Seventh New Jersey, to Chaptico, on an intent (sic) of the Potomac, 10 miles distant," wrote Sykes. "The villages in possession of the troops were election precincts, and on the following day (6th) the polls were opened and the elections held without trouble or disturbance."[32] Revere's men were glad that nothing occurred that remotely resembled the Pratt Street Riot. However, Lieutenant Colonel Carman sensed that the Chaptico citizenry were "extremely bitter against the Union" and Private Emmell noted of the 488 votes that were cast, "only seventeen of these are for the Union."

Although the assignment at Chaptico only lasted a few days, it had an impact on Revere's health. "The weather was very inclement and the regiment suffered greatly, especially on the last day when, owing to the very heavy rain and almost impossible roads, it was obliged to camp for the night and camp fires could hardly keep lighted," said Adjutant Price. "That for several days after this exposure Colonel Revere complained of rheumatic pains in his limbs."[33]

Following the election, Revere led his regiment back to camp, where they settled for the upcoming winter. But the daily drills continued. The Seventh New Jersey also participated with other regiments in battalion drills, which were designed to prepare the men for the movement of large bodies of men in a quick and efficient manner. The Seventh New Jersey was joined by the Fifth, Sixth, and Eighth regiments to form the Second New Jersey Brigade.

In November, the men of the newly formed brigade were paid for the first time; they received two months' pay. *The Jerseyman*, a weekly newspaper, reported that a "large portion of the money has been sent home by the soldiers." The publication also boasted that the brigade would "pollute the sacred soil of South Carolina."[34]

Daily drilling continued. Operating within the larger structure of a brigade, the men of the Seventh New Jersey soon mastered the martial skills which would allow them to smartly move into an "order of battle" and execute more complex battlefield maneuvers with other regiments.[35] Despite the daily drills and the threat of severe discipline for infractions of any sort, Revere gave the men a day off in order to celebrate Thanksgiving on November 27.[36]

But Revere was not in the holiday spirit as Christmas day approached. He ordered an unannounced nighttime formation of the regiment just to see how quickly all the men could to fall into ranks with their weapons, accoutrements, and knapsacks. He also scolded a sergeant for an infraction during the exercise. When the non-commissioned officer sarcastically asked his commander if he should kneel before him, Revere became outraged and promptly took action. "The Sergeant has been court-martialed and his sentence is to carry a log of wood on his shoulder from sunrise to sunset for twenty days, and to live on bread and water, and to have his stripes taken off his arm before the whole regiment, and have $10.00 of pay taken each month for four months."[37]

In December, "being exposed to bad weather and snow and sleet…Revere again complained of rheumatism."[38] Besides his personal health concerns, Revere was also having a problem with Company B, the unit which was formed from the greater Newark area. Its original commander, Captain John Craven, had been discharged on October 22, 1861; Lieutenant William Fitzgerald resigned nine days later and Second Lieutenant Gardner Green resigned on November 6. Louis B. Tenner, formerly of the Thirty-ninth New York, became the new company commander. Without continuity among its officers, Company B's performance on the drill field and on dress parade suffered and disciplinary problems increased.

A nighttime alarm drill put Company B to the final test. "The whole line formed in nine minutes after the first alarm," stated Lieutenant Carman. "[However,] Capt. Tenner could not find his company."[39] When the company finally joined the rest of the Seventh New Jersey, Revere punished the entire regiment by having the men "remain under arms for one and half hours."[40]

The situation became so deplorable that Revere proposed to disband the company. He informed Governor Olden, who replied to Revere's request in a letter on March 31, 1862. "I have the pleasure to inform you that arrangements have been made and are in progress to raise a company for your regiment to supply the place of the one you propose to disband," wrote Olden from Trenton. "You will be informed soon, when the company being raised may be expected to leave here."[41] In the letter, Olden also agreed with Revere's request that Adjutant Price be promoted as major of the Seventh New Jersey.

Although Confederate forces were stationed nearby on the other side of the Potomac, Revere and the other officers did not expect any significant military operations until the spring. But the winter encampment of 1861-1862 was difficult enough. Disease and illness were widespread. "Seventeen boys are sick with the measles, three from Company K," recalled Private Emmell, who had noted that as early as mid-October "two or three soldiers die every day." On February 22, Revere again "complained of rheumatism" after "attending [a] general court-martial."[42]

Confederate artillery batteries on the other side of the river periodically fired shells at the Seventh New Jersey and the other regiments, but their guns suddenly went silent in early March. By March 11, the rebel troops had evacuated their positions and moved south. In the weeks that followed, the Army of the Potomac underwent reorganization. The Fifth, Sixth, Seventh, and Eighth New Jersey regiments composed Brigadier General Francis Patterson's Third Brigade–the so-called Second New Jersey Brigade–in Brigadier General Joseph Hooker's Second Division. Hooker's division and Brigadier General Phil Kearny's Third Division composed Major General Samuel P. Heintzelman's Third Corps, one of two corps that composed the Army of the Potomac's infantry. McClellan's army also included cavalry units and batteries of artillery. It was an impressive force that grew to over 120,000 men, nearly 15,000 horses and mules, hundreds of artillery pieces, and endless wagons filled with ammunition and various supplies. And Richmond, Virginia, the capital of the Confederate States of America, was its goal.

Lincoln was eager for McClellan to initiate his campaign, but the cautious commander moved slowly. Finally, by early April,

McClellan was ready to advance. "In anticipation of seeing action, Revere requested 75,000 rounds of buck and ball."[43] McClellan planned a circuitous route to Richmond, first establishing a base of operations at Fort Monroe on the Virginia coast and then moving inland. It took an entire day for Brigadier General Francis Patterson's Third Brigade to board two transport ships. Revere and four of his companies, along with the Sixth New Jersey, were crammed aboard the *Arrowsmith*; the rest of the unit was aboard the *John Brooks*. It took several days for Revere and his men to reach their destination, an unpleasant journey that caused a number of them to get seasick while traveling on the Chesapeake Bay.[44]

McClellan's first objective was Yorktown, the site of George Washington's important victory over Lord Charles Cornwallis during the Revolutionary War in 1781. As Revere's regiment passed a home near the coast, a Southern woman made a prediction to some of the soldiers. "She says we will never take Yorktown," noted Private Emmell.[45]

Confederate Major General John B. Magruder commanded the Army of the Peninsula, a force about one-tenth the size of McClellan's. Although outnumbered, Magruder's men had created an extensive earthworks line north of the Warwick River that extended from Yorktown to the James River. Fort Magruder was the line's most formidable position. McClellan planned to send the Third Corps against the defenses near Yorktown while Brigadier General Erasmus Keyes' Fourth Corps turned the other end of the Confederate defenses.

While he waited for re-enforcements, Magruder, a flamboyant officer who loved the theater, deceived his Union adversaries with histrionic flair by marching the small units of his men many times past small openings in his defenses. He also supplemented his artillery with Quaker guns, trimmed tree trunks that were painted black to look like real artillery pieces. From McClellan's view, the Confederate force appeared large, formidable, and well armed.

Meanwhile, the spring rains turned McClellan's advance into a "Mud March."[46] Nature's creatures added to the misery. "Ticks, spiders, snakes and bugs of all kind abound night and day, crawling over bed and bedding," stated Carman.[47]

Revere's men moved slowly to their designated encampment location, which, ironically enough, was Magruder's home. The Seventh New Jersey and the rest of the brigade set up their tents "thoroughly packed" in the Confederate general's peach orchard while the Union medical staff turned his house into a hospital.

Some of Revere's men almost became the first Confederate prisoners of the Yorktown campaign. Captain Louis Raymond Francine, 24, of Company A, the youngest company commander in the regiment, got lost leading his entrenchment detail near Confederate lines. Fortunately, another Union soldier alerted Francine in time and the men returned safely to camp. "The rebels saw us coming and did not fire expecting to get us a little nearer and then capture us," said Private Emmell.[48]

Disease and illness—primarily dysentery, typhoid, and respiratory infections—affected many of the men. Mid-April of 1862 was particularly deadly. Private Charles Drake of Company I died of disease on April 11; Private Martin Wilson of Company E died two days later. Private Jonathan Woolson of Company A and Denmark Courtwright of Company I died on April 14; Private James Kent, of Company C died on April 16. Private John Tillotson of Company K died on April 18; Private Sapfford Sanders of Company K died the following day. Private John Denis of Company I died on April 22.[49] By the time the war ended, 123 men of the Seventh New Jersey died of disease.[50]

Revere "again complained of rheumatism and became so sick as for some time [became] to[o] unfit...for active duty."[51] He was sent back to the hospital at Fort Monroe. In his absence, Lieutenant Colonel Carman, who had been primarily responsible for drilling the men at Camp Revere, once again assumed command of the Seventh New Jersey. Carman, no doubt, enjoyed Revere's temporary absence. But he wanted a permanent separation from Revere. When Carman heard that Colonel James T. Hatfield, commander of the Sixth New Jersey, had resigned on April 27, he requested command of the unit.

Though still ill, Revere was eager to return to his regiment. He left the hospital briefly only to return. One enlisted man observed that he "heard him groan and complain, his knees and ankles were swelled and he could not walk."[52] Carman remained in command of the Seventh New Jersey as the unit prepared to advance on Yorktown's defensive lines. However, the Confederates quietly abandoned their lines and strategically retreated on the night of May 3. The befuddled McClellan quickly ordered cavalry and infantry units, which included the Seventh New Jersey, to chase after the rebels.

On May 5, the opposing forces clashed in the rain-soaked Battle of Williamsburg. General Hooker sent Brigadier General Patterson's New Jersey troops to reinforce Brigadier General Cuvier Grover's brigade, which was being threatened near Fort Magruder. The Seventh New Jersey was engaged for hours in bloody combat.[53] "Gen. Hooker was in [the] thickest of it giving orders; he had a horse shot from under him," said Private Emmell. "Gen. Paterson [sic] commanding our brigade rode up and down behind our brigade when fighting saying 'give it to them Jersey Blues.'"[54] Superior Union numbers and brave actions by a number of federal officers, including Lieutenant Colonel Carman, forced the rebels to suspend their attack in the afternoon. "There was 30 shot dead in our regiment and 100 wounded a good part of them mortally so, and we lost a few by being taken prisoner," noted Private Emmell. "It is a horrible sight to see the wounded with a leg or arm taken off with a shell, or see the piles of legs and arms around the Doctors field amputating table."[55] Carman suffered from minié ball wound to his right arm, but it was not severe enough to be amputated. Some of the wounded were sent back to the hospital at Fort Monroe, where the bedridden Revere saw some of his men for the first time in days. But Revere was so "very sick" that a soldier had to "lift him and carry him." He was soon escorted to The Willows to recover.[56]

Revere arrived home on May 9 and eight days later, he turned forty years old. He remained at The Willows until June 6. Feeling much better, Revere returned to Camp Lincoln on the Virginia peninsula. On June 18, Revere was pleasantly surprised to be visited by his cousins Paul and Edward, officers in the Twentieth Massachusetts. His cousins' unit–part of the Third Brigade, Second Division, Second Corps in the Army of the Potomac– had also participated in the fighting on the peninsula. Revere's cousins probably described their time as Confederate prisoners after being captured at the Battle of Ball's Bluff on October 21, 1861. They were later released after a complicated exchange.[57] This family reunion of sorts no doubt lifted the men's spirits, but soon all three returned to their respective regiments for the advance to Richmond. It was the last time that the three cousins would ever see each other together again.

Revere soon took command of his undersized regiment. "Three captains, one acting adjutant, five lieutenants, and 280 non-commissioned officers and privates," he reported.[58] On the morning of June 25, he led them into combat against General

Benjamin Huger's Division of General Robert E. Lee's Army of Northern Virginia at The Battle of Oak Grove, the so-called first of the Seven Days Battles. "Revere, who was the only officer on horseback," advanced to the front of the Seventh New Jersey, but did not notice the rebels at the edge of the nearby woods. After some of the men began firing at will, "Revere rode back to the Regiment and ordered them to cease fire and lie down."[59]

Later, the Seventh New Jersey advanced through the woods at the Williamsburg Road. "There we dressed on line, somewhat augmented by some 30 of the Second Brigade, who were lost in the woods, and commenced a heavy and well-directed file fire against the enemy in our front, which was hotly returned by them," stated Revere, who ordered his left-flank companies to engage another regiment on the Williamsburg Road.[60] The Nineteenth Massachusetts stood in reserve as the Seventh New Jersey continued the fight. At 10:30 a.m., "General Hooker ordered us to retire, which we did in good order, carrying off our dead and wounded and leaving the Nineteenth Massachusetts on the ground, at 11 a.m.," noted Revere.[61] The fighting continued until dark. Union forces had advanced about 600 yards with a casualty rate of about one man killed, wounded, or captured per yard.

The next day at Camp Lincoln, Revere wrote his report to Captain C. M. Prevost, the assistant adjutant general of the Third Brigade in Hooker's Division. He praised "the gallant and skillful conduct" of Capt. H[enry] C. Bartlett [of Company C] and also cited the efforts of Captain Frederick Cooper [of Company F]; Acting Adjutant Lieutenant W. J. Evans; Dr. Julius D. Rose, the regimental chaplain; surgeon Dewitt Hough, and assistant surgeon Alvin Satterthwaite.

Revere was praised as well by Second Lieutenant Michael Mullery of Company K. "Of the courage and daring of Col. Revere, none can speak to highly," noted Mullery. "I always thought him the highest type of soldier, but it now seems to me that I never half appreciated his soldierly qualities."[62] Colonel Joseph Carr, the commander of the Third Brigade in Hooker's Division, was impressed by Revere and his unit. "I refer to you the accompanying report of Col. J. W. Revere for a detailed account of the part that the Seventh New Jersey Volunteers took in the engagement, and as they were immediately under the eye of General Hooker he is enabled from actual observation to indorse [sic] the praises which Colonel Revere bestows upon the coolness and bravery of his officers and men," noted Carr in his headquarters report.[63] Under Revere's leadership, the Seventh New Jersey had "become the pride of the State."[64]

On the day he wrote his wrote his report to Prevost, Revere's fever returned. It was later reported as "an attack of tyhoid."[65] He became so ill that he was incapable of leading the regiment. Revere removed himself from the front and sought medical attention once again.

NOTES

1. *True Democratic Banner*, May 22, 1862, in *Gone to Wear the Victor's Crown: Morris County and the Civil War*, a Documentary Account, Comp. and edited by David Mitros (Morris County Heritage Commission, 1998), 65.

2. Joseph W. Revere, *Keel and Saddle*, 270.

3. *The War of the Rebellion: a Compilation of the Official Records of the Union and Confederate Armies, Vol. I*, Correspondence, Orders, Reports, And Returns of the Union Authorities From November 1, 1860, To March 31, 1862.

4. *The Jerseyman,* April 20, 1861. One of Revere's militia companies, the Morris Greys, volunteered to become one of the four regiments that Lincoln requested from New Jersey, but the federal government rejected the unit's offer since the regiment was undermanned. See Mitros, *Gone to Wear the Victor's Crown,* 28-29.

5. John Brett Langstaff, *New Jersey Generations: Macculloch Hall, Morristown* (New York: Vantage Press, 1964), 117. Young Jacob "Jack" Miller became the captain of the Brewerton Zouaves, a juvenile drill unit. He later graduated from the United States Naval Academy.

6. Revere, *Keel and Saddle,* 270-71.

7. Ibid., 271.

8. Ibid., 272.

9. The First New Jersey Brigade was initially composed of the First, Second, and Third New Jersey Volunteer Infantry regiments. Joined by the New Jersey Militia, a 90-day unit, in late June, the brigade marched to Virginia, where some of its units fought during the retreat phase of the First Manassas on July 21, 1861. A month later, the Fourth New Jersey Volunteer Infantry joined the brigade.

10. Olden to Revere, June 10, 1861. Revere Research Files.

11. Ibid.

12. Revere, *Keel and Saddle,* 272.

13. John Hayward, *Give It To Them, Jersey Blues!, A History of the 7th Regiment, New Jersey Veteran Volunteers in the Civil War* (Longstreet House, Hightstown, New Jersey), 291. According to the author's examination of the unit's muster rolls, one enlisted man was born "at sea."

14. Ibid., 256-282.

15. Letter from Revere to Carman, September 26, 1861. The original letter is part of the Ezra Ayers Carman Papers, 1860-1903 collection at the New Jersey Historical Society.

16. *Atlantic Democrat,* September 28, 1861, 2.

17. Revere to Carman, September 26, 1861.

18. *Morristown – History – Civil War*, Program of meeting held in the First Presbyterian Church, Morristown, NJ to bid farewell to Company K, Seventh NJ Vol., October 1, 1861. Each member of the company was given a Bible.

19. *Jerseyman*, Oct. 5, 1861, in Mitros, *Gone to Wear the Victor's Crown*, 41.

20. Frederick H. Dyer, *A Compendium of the War of the Rebellion* (Des Moines, IA: Dyer Publishing Co., 1908), 1359.

21. Francis Price to Tillie Price, March 23, 1895, 3. Revere Family Files, Collection of the Morris County Park Commission.

22. Rebecca Kirkman, "Revere's Involvement in the Civil War 1861-1863," 1999, [3]. Kirkman's 14-page overview was designated as "In house information" to be used by the staff and volunteers at Fosterfields. Revere Research Files.

23. Ezra A. Carman, *Seventh New Jersey Infantry to Battle of Williamsburg*, 1873, 7. New Jersey Historical Society.

24. Revere, *Keel and Saddle*, 273. In his September 26, 1861 letter to Lieutenant Carman, Revere told his second-in-command, "You can do much with the regiment."

25. Ibid.

26. Hayward, *Give It To Them, Jersey Blues!*, 11.

27. *Heyward Emmell Journal*, October 19, 1861. Madison Historical Society, Madison, New Jersey. See also *The Civil War Journal of Private Heyward Emmell, Ambulance and Infantry Corps: A Very Disagreeable War*, edited by Jim Malcolm (Fairleigh Dickinson University Press, Madison, 2011), 4.

28. Kirkman, "Revere's Involvement in the Civil War 1861-1863," 1999, [4].

29. Hayward, *Give It To Them, Jersey Blues!*, 12. Captain John Clark of Company A resigned on October 13; Lieutenant Francis Dubois of Company A resigned on November 19. Rather than face the review

board, Captain Cravan, whom Revere called "generally inefficient and unfit," resigned on October 31, 1861.

30. Revere, *Keel and Saddle*, 273. Abraham Lincoln and most historians do not concur with Revere's 1872 assessment of McClellan as a "first rank" soldier.

31. Carman, *Seventh New Jersey Infantry to Williamsburg*, 7.

32. *War of the Rebellion*, Vol. 5, Chapter XIV, 387. Maryland remained in the Union, one of four border states—Delaware, Kentucky, and Missouri were the others—which maintained the institution of slavery during the war. Approximately 25,000 Marylanders joined the ranks of the Confederacy.

33. Francis Price 1887 pension claim on behalf of Mrs. Rosa[nna] D. Revere. Revere Research Files.

34. *The Jerseyman*, November 23, 1861, 2.

35. At first, the Seventh New Jersey utilized the 1861 *United States Infantry and Rifle Tactics*, originally published as [William J.] *Hardee's Rifle and Light Infantry Tactics* in 1855. However, Hardee was a Georgian who resigned his commission in the U.S. Army. Avoiding the awkward situation of using a Confederate publication, the next year the United States adopted Brigadier General Silas Casey's *Infantry Tactics for the Instruction, Exercise, and Manœuvres of the Soldier, a Company, Line of Skirmishers, Battalion, Brigade, or Corps D'Armée Vol. I*, which became the principal guide for infantry instruction in the Union Army. Casey' publication, which relied on *Hardee's School of the Company and School of the Battalion*, was approved by President Lincoln and endorsed by Secretary of War Edwin Stanton on August 11, 1862. Casey revised his work in volumes II and III, which were also published in 1862.

36. November 27, 1861, fell on a Wednesday. Until 1863, each state determined the day to celebrate the holiday. President Lincoln's proclamation stated that the last Thursday on November would

mark Thanksgiving. In 1941, President Franklin D. Roosevelt moved Thanksgiving to the fourth Thursday of November.

37. Emmell *Journal,* December 25, 1861; *Civil War Journal of Private Heyward Emmell,* 11.

38. Francis Price 1887 pension claim. This was written on behalf of Rosanna Duncan Revere, who sought a widow's pension following the death of her husband.

39. Carman, *Seventh New Jersey Infantry to Williamsburg,* 41.

40. Hayward, *Give it to Them, Jersey Blues!,* 19.

41. Olden to Col. J. W. Revere, March 31, 1862. Revere Research Files.

42. Seventh New Jersey Returns [1862], Revere Family Papers. The document, which stated that Revere attended the court-martial while on "detached duty" in January and February, did not identify any additional information about the legal proceeding. Another Seventh New Jersey Field and Staff Muster Roll in the Revere Family papers states that Revere was "present" during January and February.

43. Hayward, *Give it to Them, Jersey Blues!,* 19. The buck and ball cartridge for the Model 1842 Springfield Musket contained a .69 caliber lead ball and three smaller lead buckshot pellets.

44. *Emmell Journal,* April 7, 1862.

45. *Emmell Journal,* April 11, 1862.

46. Frederick H. Dyer, *A Compendium of the War of the Rebellion,* 1359.

47. Carman, *Seventh New Jersey Infantry to Williamsburg,* 63.

48. *Emmell Journal,* April 23, 1862.

49. Hayward, *Give it to Them, Jersey Blues!,* 256-291.

50. Ibid., 253. On page 250, the author states that 105 men in the regiment died due to disease. Of all the early war (spring 1861-summer 1862) New Jersey units, the Seventh New Jersey had approximately the same number of deaths caused by disease as most other units. The Tenth New Jersey had the highest number of deaths caused by disease: approximately 190. Of those regiments mustered later in the war (late summer and autumn of 1863), the Thirty-fourth

and Thirty-fifth New Jersey both lost approximately 130 and 165 men, respectively, to disease.

51. Francis Price 1887 pension claim.

52. Draft of unsigned letter from Francis Price to Commissioner of Pensions, June 13, 1887. Revere Research Files. The draft was written on the commercial stationery of Edward Fanning, a Paterson carpenter who had first served in the Seventh New Jersey as a corporal and later rose to the rank of first lieutenant. Fanning was wounded at the Battle of Spotsylvania Court House in May 1864 and left the service two months later due to a disability. He returned to Paterson and became a successful "carpenter and builder" who provided "estimates given on all kinds of buildings" and work "neatly and promptly done." Price also wrote on behalf of Rosanna Duncan Revere, who attempted to secure a widow's pension for herself.

53. For an excellent account of the regiment's participation in the Battle of Williamsburg, see John Hayward's *Give It To Them, Jersey Blues!, A History of the 7th Regiment, New Jersey Volunteers in the Civil War,* 28-41.

54. *Emmell Journal,* May 7, 1862.

55. *Emmell Journal,* May 7, 1862. Emmell emerged from the Battle of Williamsburg without a scrape, but was later hospitalized. "I have now got the jaundice and my skin is all yellow," wrote Emmell in his diary on July 26, 1862.

56. Letter from unknown to Commissioner of Pensions, June 13, 1887.

57. Paul Joseph Revere, who was wounded in the foot, and Edward Hutchinson Robbins Revere were initially imprisoned at John L. Ligon's Tobacco Warehouse in Richmond, the first building in the city to be used to hold Union prisoners. On September 3, 1861, the *Richmond Whig* reported: "In the four prisons on Main Street, the number of Federals confined is 1,375. At the hospital, where those more desperately wounded are treated, are 350 more. The captured officers number about 60." After the federal government threatened

to try a group of captured rebel seamen as pirates, the Confederacy threatened retaliation. If the seamen were convicted and sentenced to death, Judah Benjamin, the Confederate Secretary of War, threatened to execute the same number of Union prisoners–and the Revere brothers were part of the group. While both sides exchanged threats, the brothers and the other four Union captives were sent to another prison. The federal government succumbed to Benjamin's protestations and agreed to treat the captured Confederates as prisoners of war, not pirates. Upon that decision, the Revere brothers were released and sent home to Boston, where they awaited exchange for Confederate prisoners of equal rank. Not content to wait for the official paperwork which would send the brothers back to the front with their regiment, Paul Joseph traveled to Fort Warren in Boston harbor and sped the exchange process by selecting their Confederate counterparts.

58. Revere to Prevost, June 26, 1862. Revere Research Files.

59. Hayward, *Give It To Them, Jersey Blues!*, 47.

60. Revere to Prevost, Revere Research Files; *War of the Rebellion, Series I, Vol. III* (part II), Ch. XXIII, 156.

61. Ibid.

62. Hayward, *Give It To Them, Jersey Blues!*, 47. Mullery was later promoted to captain and assigned the command of Company I.

63. *War of the Rebellion, Series 1, Vol. 11* (part II), 149.

64. "New Jersey and the Civil War (1861-1865)," *The County Circular*, Vol. 13, No. 1, (Morristown: Morris County Heritage Commission, Spring 1991), 2.

65. Untitled document of August 1, 1862, Revere Family Papers.

CHAPTER EIGHT

ON THE ROAD TO RICHMOND

"Col. Revere is back and in command of the regiment again."

While Revere slowly recovered from his fever, the Seventh New Jersey participated in several engagements with Confederate forces on the peninsula. On June 29, 1862, the Jersey Blues fought at the Battle of Savage's Station, a makeshift Union supply depot on the Richmond and York River Railroad. The following day, the regiment was involved in the Battle of Glendale and on July 1, the Seventh New Jersey was part of the Union defenses at the Battle of Malvern Hill. But on July 2, McClellan yielded to his Confederate antagonists; he gave up on his plan to take Richmond. The Peninsula Campaign was over and the Army of the Potomac made a strategic retreat to the safety of Harrison's Landing on the James River.

During the Seven Days Battles, the Union had suffered nearly 16,000 casualties, including men who had been captured or missing. The Seventh New Jersey was more fortunate with only "three wounded and two captured."[1] But Union morale plummeted. Less than a month earlier, Private Heyward Emmell had confidently noted in his journal: "On the road to Richmond. We are now 7 or 8 miles from Richmond."[2] But Richmond would not fall until April 1865.

By the time Revere had recovered in August, the Army of the Potomac was ordered to join with Major General John Pope's Army of Virginia. Once again, Union and Confederate forces would face each other at Bull Run. However, the makeup of Revere's regiment was quite different from its roster of a year earlier. Death, desertions, resignations, transfers, and disability discharges greatly altered the ranks of the Seventh New Jersey. Furthermore, additional men had been mustered out of service while still others had been listed as missing or captured. Revere's regiment was less than one-third its original size.

Among its officer ranks, Lieutenant Colonel Ezra Carman had been promoted as colonel of the Thirteenth New Jersey. Captain Louis Francine, a highly regarded commander of Company A, was elevated to Carman's previous position on July 8. Francine had been enthusiastically recommended for the position by his men. "Our boys are in perfect love with him, and will follow him through 'thick and thin,'" wrote First Sergeant George W. Smith of Company A.[3] In a letter to Captain Frederick Cooper of Company F, Revere also endorsed Francine.[4]

Revere and the Seventh New Jersey were on the move. They left Harrison's Landing and arrived at Alexandria on August 24.

**Louis Francine.
Courtesy of the John W. Kuhl
Collection.**

Two days later, Revere and his unit boarded trains on the Orange and
Alexandria Railroad. After arriving at Warrenton Junction, Revere
and his men camped for the night. At dawn the next morning, the
men prepared for battle. "We marched 14 mile[s] through a very
hot sun [and] several of the regiment were sun struck," said Private
Emmell.[5] The Seventh New Jersey and its companion Union units
were on the same ground where a year earlier Confederate General
Thomas Jackson earned his "Stonewall" nickname during the First
Battle of Bull Run. And Jackson had returned to the same ground.
On August 27, Jackson's men captured a Union supply depot at
Manassas Junction and awaited their Union adversaries. Instead
of General Irvin McDowell, General John Pope commanded
the men in blue. But McDowell had also returned—as the major
general who commanded the Army of Virginia's Third Corps.
Jackson was ready, as was his commander: General Robert E. Lee,
who headed the Army of Northern Virginia.

Revere and the Seventh New Jersey were part of Colonel Joseph B. Carr's Third Brigade in Major General Joseph Hooker's Third Division, one of two detached divisions from the Army of the Potomac's Third Corps. On August 27, Revere's men encountered rebel forces near Bristoe Station. "When we ran across the field the rebels throw grape and canister at us," recalled Private Emmell.[6] The fight was a preliminary action which foreshadowed the upcoming major battle.

On August 28, brutal fighting erupted on the property of a civilian farmer named John Brawner, but Revere's regiment was not engaged in the battle; instead, the Seventh New Jersey was assigned to guard duty "on one of the principal roads [with orders to] not let any wagons…pass…."[7]

The next day, Revere and his men were involved in combat. After he sent Captain Thomas Thompson and Company A out as skirmishers, a company of Confederate skirmishers began firing. But the Seventh New Jersey did not return fire. Captain Thompson requested permission to fire back, but Revere preferred "to wait until the rebel[s] commenced" firing.[8] The awkward command became meaningless as the men of Company A initiated fire on their own. Soon, the entire regiment was engaged in combat. After firing a dozen rounds or so, the men's weapons became more difficult to load. The residue of black powder (fouling) in the barrel built up to such an extent that the ramrod was unable to force the lead projectile against the breech. To complicate matters, the men's ammunition was getting low. Revere ordered his men off the battle line. "We were then taken a little ways back to clean our muskets having been relieved by the Sixth New Jersey," explained Private Emmell.[9]

After Revere's men had cleaned their weapons and secured ammunition, Colonel Carr kept them briefly as a reserve force. But the Seventh New Jersey was soon ordered back to the front. The regiment "was now located on the extreme left of Hooker's division and was coming under fire on its front and left flank."[10] But overwhelming Confederate firepower forced Revere's unit back. When other Union soldiers panicked and fled past the Seventh New Jersey, Revere rallied the ranks and held the line against the oncoming rebels. "Our soldiers went into the action greatly fatigued from the hot pursuit of the enemy in the forenoon and the previous day, but fought with great courage and determination, and held their ground until relieved against three reliefs of the enemy in front successively," explained Revere.[11]

By the early evening, the fighting had stopped. The men who had survived the day's fight on both sides of the battlefield had earned their rest. Private Emmell remarked that he had a good night's sleep except when Colonel Revere's horse kicked "over a stack of muskets and one of them went off close by me and woke me up."[12]

The next morning, Revere and his men prepared for battle, but they were not engaged until late in the afternoon. General Pope misread Robert E. Lee's strength and position. The Union commander believed that the Confederate right under Jackson was vulnerable to an assault and ordered Major General Fitz John Porter to attack. But Pope was unaware that the entire right wing of the Army of Northern Virginia under Major General James Longstreet had arrived and extended the Confederate right. Porter, aware of Longstreet's presence, did not engage his force the previous day. But on August 30, Porter reluctantly followed Pope's order to attack. Porter's 10,000-man force was repulsed by

Jackson's infantry, supported by Longstreet's artillery. Longstreet's 30,000 infantry then advanced in a massive counterattack on Pope's left flank, resulting in intense fighting south of the Warrenton Turnpike.

Pope ordered Hooker to reinforce a Union artillery position near Henry House Hill, the site where the "Stonewall" legend began a year earlier. "Our brigade was sent to support the battery about 5 o'clock," recalled Private Emmell. "The rebels had a cross fire on this battery and it had to limber up and change positions several times, and we had to go on a double quick after them."[13] A blast of rebel gunfire dropped Revere and he was removed from the battlefield.

The next day, in the field near Centreville, he was examined by John Freeman, the Third Brigade's acting surgeon, who observed that Revere was "suffering from fever and nephritis, inguinal hernia and lacerated wounds of the right groin from gunshot wound, and contusion of the lumbar region from shell wound, all received in the action of yesterday, and there being no shelter, medicines or hospital accommodations here within reach, he is authorized and recommended by me to proceed to Washington without delay."[14]

Upon his arrival in the nation's capital, Revere was examined by the medical staff and Dr. J. C. Fisher, the medical director of Hooker's division. Fisher concurred with Freeman's assessment.

> Colonel Joseph W. Revere, 7th New Jersey Infantry, Vols. has been carefully examined by me and I find he is suffering from fever and nephritis caused by a gunshot wound in right groin; minie bullet; and contusion of right side, from a fragment of shell; and that in my opinion he is unfit for duty. Said wounds were inflicted at Battle of Manassas, Aug. 30, 1862, while

commanding his regiment. I therefore recommend him
for a leave of absence.

J. C. Fisher, Med. Director
Hooker's Division
Washington, D.C. Sept. 3, 1862[15]

In an additional document, Fisher noted: "I further declare my
belief that he will not be able to resume his duties for fifteen days
and that permanent disability is immenent."[16] On September 6,
the Adjutant General's Office granted Revere thirty days' leave.[17]

On the same day that Fisher described Revere's medical
condition, the Seventh New Jersey arrived at Camp Lyon, an
earthwork fort located outside Alexandria, after an eighteen-mile
march. They were issued a paltry ration of six pieces of hardtack
and "a piece of pork." The next day, the battered regiment was
issued full rations. "Our feet are blistered and a good many are
without shoes and a good many sick," stated Private Emmell.[18]

As Revere prepared to return to Morristown, he learned that
Major General Phil Kearny had lost his life days earlier at the
Battle of Chantilly. One development that Revere was not aware
of at first was that General Porter was relieved of command
for insubordination at the Second Battle of Bull Run. Porter
was subsequently arrested in November and court martialcd.
He was defended by lawyer Reverdy Johnson, who had served
in Maryland's House of Delegates. Two charges were brought
against him: disobeying a lawful order and misbehavior in front
of the enemy. Each charge contained multiple specifications. In a
widely documented public trial that was covered by the *New York
Times*, Porter was found guilty of both charges, although not all of
the specifications. He was dismissed from military service. Porter
would spend years trying to clear his name.[19] Revere, of course,

became aware of the court-martial, but little did he know that one day he would experience Porter's unfortunate circumstance.

During the early part of his recuperation at The Willows, Revere learned that his cousin, Edward, a surgeon in the Twentieth Massachusetts, was killed on September 17, 1862, during the Battle of Antietam "while in the discharge of his duties." Dr. Revere was thirty-five years old. Rosanna continued to care for her husband for the next five weeks. By the third week of October, Revere felt strong enough to return to the Seventh New Jersey.

Revere had seen death during his years in the navy, but never had he witnessed carnage on such a large scale and the death of his cousin, Edward, was tragic for the entire family. Revere was also reminded of life's fragility as he battled periodic fevers and severe rheumatism. Perhaps these concerns led to a questioning of his faith. In any event, Revere became a Catholic on October 19, 1862, at the Basilica of the National Shrine of the Assumption of the Blessed Virgin Mary in Baltimore, Maryland. The Reverend H. B. Caskery performed the baptism.[20]

On October 26, 1862, Private Heyward Emmell proclaimed in his journal: "Col. Revere is back and in command of the regiment again."[21] When Revere returned, he found many new faces in the ranks, including scores of raw recruits. Besides the demands of preparing the new men for combat, Revere had to deal with several officers who argued among themselves about seniority issues and promotion concerns. One of the officers, [First] Lieutenant William Ferris, a transfer from the disbanded Twelfth Virginia, a Union unit, was eventually cashiered out of the military.[22]

Revere's military status was soon elevated as a result of a rather unpleasant circumstance. Brigadier General Francis Patterson, the commander of the Second New Jersey Brigade, had ordered a strategic withdrawal without orders at Catlett's Station on the

Orange and Alexandria Railroad between Warrenton Junction and Bristoe Station during operations in early November. Division commander Brigadier General Daniel Sickles removed Patterson from command and initiated an investigation against the officer who had served in the artillery during the Mexican War. Revere was promoted to brigadier general on October 25, 1862, and was designated to replace Patterson. On November 22, 1862, a gunshot rang out from Patterson's quarters. He was found dead with a pistol at his side. It was not known whether Patterson died as a result of an accidental or deliberate discharge of his weapon. The enlisted men, however, believed he had committed suicide. "There is a report that the reason Gen. Paterson (sic) shot himself was on account of Gen. Sickles calling him a coward for not remaining at Catlett Station," wrote Private Heyward Emmell in his journal on November 28. "Gen. Revere received his commission as brigadier the night before and so took command of our brigade."[23] One newspaper heralded Revere's promotion: "This is a well merited promotion of one of the bravest and most accomplished officers in the service."[24] However, some men in the ranks "believed Revere was involved in Patterson's removal. [Revere's] welcome by his brigade was a cold one."[25]

Although Revere no longer commanded the Seventh New Jersey, he was still concerned about the unit. Since the regiment was severely undersized, Revere learned "informally" that Governor Olden was considering consolidating the Seventh New Jersey with another unit. On November 30, Revere wrote Olden and officially offered his resignation as the Seventh New Jersey's commander. He also pleaded with the governor to retain his former unit's identity. "The history of these gallant regiments… and the names of battles inscribed in the war worn and tattered regimental standards belong exclusively to the numbers which designate those decimated battalions, the heroes of this war," wrote Revere. "To wipe out and utterly destroy those numbers is to degrade and disgrace them in a military point of view. New Jersey must never be allowed to go backwards in the path of military distinction to which her sons have won for her so proud a title."[26] Revere suggested that "voluntary enlistment, by conscription or draft, or to consolidate them with those new regiments as yet entirely unknown to fame" should be utilized first.[27] He concluded his letter by recommending that Lieutenant Colonel Francine should be named his replacement. On December 9, 1862, Francine was promoted to colonel and became the new commander of the Seventh New Jersey.

Brigadier General Joseph Warren Revere commanded the Third Brigade in Brigadier General Dan Sickles' Second Division, which was part of Brigadier General George Stoneman's Third Corps in Major General Joseph Hooker's Grand Center Division of the Army of the Potomac. Major General Ambrose Burnside had replaced Major General George McClellan on November 9, 1862, as the commander of the Army of the Potomac. Revere's brigade consisted of the Fifth, Sixth, Seventh, and Eighth New Jersey regiments and the Second New York and the One Hundred Fifteenth Pennsylvania.

Like his predecessor, Burnside was determined to capture Richmond. But first, he and his 120,000-man army would have to cross the Rappahannock River and defeat Lee's Army of Northern Virginia. In mid-November, Lieutenant General James Longstreet's First Corps awaited Burnside on the other side of the river at Fredericksburg. Although more aggressive than McClellan, Burnside took too long to move most of his force across the river. The pontoon boats that would support makeshift bridges over the Rappahannock did not arrive on time and when they did, Burnside didn't use them as quickly as he should have. In the meantime, Robert E. Lee massed his army–including Stonewall Jackson's Second Corps–on the high ground west of the town. Approximately 75,000 well-entrenched Confederates–some protected by an extensive stone wall at Mayre's Heights–prepared to stop the Federal advance.

Ambrose Burnside.

Like the Southern woman who predicted in April that the Union would "never take Yorktown," Confederate pickets shouted similar warnings. One rebel picket yelled to his Union counterpart on the other side of the river that Burnside would "have to go through Longstreet and over a big hill and over a stone wall." Private Emmell explained the threat: "We had Gen. Longstreet and Gen. A. P. Hill and Gen. Stonewall Jackson to whip before we could take Fredericksburg."[28]

Burnside planned to attack Lee's flanks with two of his grand divisions. Hooker's division, in which Revere served, would be held in reserve. Each man was supplied with four days' worth of rations and twenty extra rounds of ammunition. On the morning of December 13, 1862, the Federal attack began—and so did the slaughter of Union troops. Wave after wave of Burnside's men were cut down by relentless artillery and musket fire. By the afternoon, Hooker's Center Grand Division was sent across the Rappahannock and was soon engaged in the attacks against Mayre's Heights. Revere's brigade crossed the river. "[I] formed a line of battle in a sunken road in the rear of the First and Second Brigades and the battery in our front," noted Revere. "During this time a heavy action was progressing on our right at Fredericksburg, and on our left, while the enemy appeared to be massing troops in our front."[29] But the major fighting soon ceased, although "very heavy" skirmishing continued.

Joseph Hooker.

Skirmishing continued the next morning. The cost of the previous day's fighting was horrific. Over 12,000 Union soldiers had been killed, wounded, or reported missing; some 5,000 Confederate soldiers were casualties. Like the other brigade commanders, Revere awaited for Burnside's next order to resume the assault. Persuaded by his officers not to launch another attack against the well-defended Confederate lines, Burnside ordered a retreat back across the Rappahannock. Picket lines were established to protect the retreating units. Revere instructed Colonel William J. Sewell of the Fifth New Jersey to "remain in support of the picket line until further instructions."[30] But Sewell's unit became vulnerable to an attack when it was not informed that the pickets on its right had been withdrawn from their position twenty minutes earlier. Fortunately for the unprotected Fifth New Jersey, the Confederates had had enough fighting and the unit managed to cross back over the river without incident. "If Burnside had pontoons to cross the river when he first arrived at Falmouth he could have taken Fredericksburg," reasoned Private Emmell.[31]

Burnside established a camp on the other side of the Rappahannock at Falmouth and Stafford Heights. Revere expected that he and his brigade would settle in for the winter, but Burnside had other plans. One month later, the commander of the Army of the Potomac had his men on the march again. Fredericksburg was the goal, but Burnside wanted to reach the town by crossing the Rappahannock several miles away.

On January 19, 1863, the first Union units were on the march. Revere led his brigade out of camp the next day, but a cold rain interfered with the move. The dirt roads were transformed into a muddy quagmire. "The mud is so awful you can hardly move your feet to walk," remarked Private Emmell. "The artillery is all stuck in the mud, to[o]."[32] Revere and his men plodded in the rain and mud for days, but got nowhere. By January 23, the entire operation was called off. "So ends Burnside's stick in the mud," quipped Private Emmell.[33] On January 26, President Lincoln removed Burnside from command and replaced him with Major General Joseph Hooker.

Other leadership changes occurred in the Army of the Potomac. Brigadier General Daniel Sickles was elevated from his division command to that of major general of the Third Corps. Revere was transferred from his Third Brigade command to the Second Brigade, which was composed of the Seventieth New York, the Seventy-first New York, the Seventy-second New York, the Seventy-third New York, the Seventy-fourth New York, and the One Hundred Twentieth New York. Revere's new unit had an older name: the Excelsior Brigade. It was originally formed by Sickles, who recruited the first five regiments in New York. [34] The ranks of the Excelsior Brigade were not made up exclusively of New York men; New Jersey volunteers from Newark, Paterson, and Morris County, among other places, enlisted in the unit. Sickles probably "had a high regard for the ability of Joseph Revere…to command his pet brigade."[35]

Although Revere was no longer directly associated with the Seventh New Jersey, he returned to his unit on March 7, 1863, in order to witness a wedding. Revere and the other major officers were invited to the ceremony of Captain Daniel Hart of Company E and Ellen Lammond of Phillipsburg, New Jersey. Revere and nineteen other officers signed the Harts' wedding certificate. "Since Captain Hart was unable to obtain a furlough to go to Phillipsburg to be wed, Miss Lammond came to him bringing ten bridesmaids and ten groomsmen."[36] Hart's fellow soldiers creatively constructed a church-like scenario around a tent fly for the bride and groom. "An arch of pine boughs was built and a

**Daniel Sickles.
Courtesy of the Robert
Jones Collection.**

pyramid of field drums was to be used as an altar."[37] Weeks later, Hart "wandered beyond the lines and [was] 'gobbled up' by the rebels."[38]

On April 5, 1863, Revere had a will drawn up and witnessed in Falmouth, Virginia. The document's introduction reflected his recent initiation into Catholicism and his standing in the Union Army.

"In the name of the Most Holy Trinity, Amen, I, Joseph Warren Revere, Brigadier General, commanding the 'Excelsior ('Second')' Brigade, Second Division, Third Corps, Army of the Potomac, do make a publish and declare this to be my Last Will and Testament."[39]

In the will, he ordered that "a sum of money be set apart from my estate sufficient to have two masses said by a priest of that church annually for the repose of my soul." He left all his property—The Willows, the farmland, and livestock, including estate property from his parents that was held in trust—to his wife. Upon Rosanna's death, the estate would "be equally divided" between his sons Paul and Augustus. Revere added that if his sons died "childless leaving no widow," the estate would be divided equally between "Mary Revere, the daughter of my cousin Assistant Surgeon Edward H.R. Revere, Twentieth Mass. Infantry, killed at the battle of Antietam, and Pauline Revere, daughter of my cousin Colonel Paul Joseph Revere, Twentieth Mass. Infantry." If the girls had died prior to receiving the remains of the estate, Revere left his estate for "the educational fund of the Holy Roman Catholic Church in the state of New Jersey, under the direction of the Bishop of the diocese of Newark."

Revere was one month away from the event which would indelibly mark his military career.

NOTES

1. John Hayward, *Give It To Them, Jersey Blues!*, 56.
2. *Heyward Emmell Journal*, June 6, 1862. See also *The Civil War Journal of Private Heyward Emmell*, 23.
3. Smith letter, September 28, 1861, in the *Cape May Ocean Wave*, October 10, 1861. *Louis Raymond Francine, Brevet Brigadier-General U.S. Volunteers*, 1910. Reprint, 2000; New Introduction by Paul J. Lader, iv-v.
4. Ibid., viii. Revere's letter of July 18, 1862, was printed in the August 13, 1862 issue of the *West Jersey Press*.
5. *Emmell Journal*, August 27, 1862.
6. Ibid.
7. Ibid.

8. Ibid. Revere probably wanted his skirmishers to return to his regimental line, where the Seventh New Jersey would wait for the first Confederate company or battalion to initiate volley fire.

9. Ibid.

10. Hayward, *Give It To Them, Jersey Blues!*, 64.

11. Report of Colonel J. W. Revere, Seventh New Jersey Volunteers, Carr's Brigade, Hooker's Division, Heintzelman's Corps in *Proceedings and report of the board of Army officers, convened by special orders No. 78, headquarters of the Army, Adjutant General's Office, Washington, April 12, 1878, in the case of Fitz-John Porter* (Washington: Government printing Office, 1879), 517.

12. *Emmell Journal*, August [29], 1862.

13. Ibid., August 30, 1862.

14. John Freeman certificate #1, August 31, 1862. Revere Research Files. The illness could have been rheumatic fever, which may have damaged his heart.

15. J. C. Fisher certificate, September 3, 1862. Revere Research Files.

16. J. C. Fisher certificate, undated. Revere Research Files.

17. Assistant Adjutant General E. D. Townsend of the War Department, Special Orders No. 224, September 6, Revere Family Files, Collection of the Morris County Park Commission.

18. *Emmell Journal*, September 5, 1862.

19. Porter was dismissed from the army on January 21, 1863. Porter spent years gathering evidence which would be used to challenge the court-martial's findings. On March 19, 1879, a special commission headed by Major General John Schofield recommended that the sentence of the court-martial be set aside; however, it would take another seven years before he was absolved of the charges. He retired from military service on August 7, 1886.

20. Certificate of Baptism, Revere Family Papers.

21. *Emmell Journal*, October 26, 1862.

22. For a more complete story about the infighting among the officers of the Seventh New Jersey, see John Hayward, *Give It To Them, Jersey Blues!*, 71-73.

23. *Emmell Journal*, November 28, 1862. Several days later, Revere received a letter from Frederick Koch, a former enlisted man of the Seventh New Jersey who had resigned. "I forever shall remember the position you placed me in after the last Bull Run Battle," wrote Private Koch on December 3, 1862. Koch never explained the "position," but said "it was a small affair" and he informed Revere that he subsequently enlisted in the One Hundred Seventy-third "Pencilvinea."

24. Washington *Daily National Intelligencer*, December 1, 1862, 3. The article was reprinted from similar piece in the *Newark Advertiser*.

25. Rebecca Kirkman, "Revere's Involvement in the Civil War 1861-1863," 1999, [7]. Revere Research Files. According to the New Jersey States Archives, a $300 voucher to Joseph Hopkins for transportation "services rendered as wagon master" was authorized by Revere and Brigadier General Joseph Hooker. The bill was finally paid on February 23, 1863. The charges, however, were not explained. The amount seems excessive for the shipment of Revere's tentage and equipment from the Seventh New Jersey's camp to his new headquarters.

26. Revere to Olden, November 30, 1862, New Jersey State Archives.

27. Ibid. Revere's suggestion of conscription came a year before the United States adopted a national draft in 1863. The Confederate States of America enacted a conscription law in 1862.

28. *Emmell Journal*, December 6, 1862.

29. *War of the Rebellion*, Vol. XXI, 389.

30. Ibid., 390.

31. *Emmell Journal*, December 21, 1862.

32. Ibid., January 21-22, 1863.

33. Ibid., January 23, 1863. A day before, the *Albany Evening Journal* announced that the U.S. Senate had confirmed Revere's appointment–along with Phil Sheridan, John Buford, and others–to the rank of brigadier general.

34. The name Excelsior comes from the state's motto, which means "ever upward." Brigadier General David B. Birney, the First Division commander in Sickles' Third Corps, considered giving Revere command of the First Brigade. "The First Brigade is without a Field Officer," wrote Birney in an "unofficial" letter to Revere on March 8, 1863. The First Brigade, composed of the Fifty-seventh, Sixty-third, Sixty-eighth, One Hundred Fifth, One Hundred Fourteenth, and One Hundred Forty-first Pennsylvania regiments, was commanded by Brigadier General Charles K. Graham during the Battle of Chancellorsville. Like Revere, Graham had served in the navy during the Mexican War.

35. Carl B. Scherzer, "Morris County's Role in the Civil War," *Morristown Daily Record,* May 11, 1961.

36. Malcolm, ed., *The Civil War Journal of Private Heyward Emmell,* 54.

37. John Hayward, *Give It To Them, Jersey Blues!,* 85. See also *Hartford Daily Courant,* March 13, 1863, 3.

38. *Springfield Republican,* March 23, 1863, 2. The newspaper reported that Hart "has been missing for several days." However, he eventually rejoined the Seventh New Jersey.

39. Joseph Warren Revere, Last Will and Testament. Revere Research Files.

CHAPTER NINE

THE BATTLE
OF CHANCELLORSVILLE

**"I at once concluded that I was the commanding officer
of the Second Division."**

The Army of the Potomac's drive "on to Richmond"
continued in the spring of 1863, but its commander,
"Fighting Joe" Hooker, wanted to do more than capture
the enemy capital: he wanted to destroy Robert E. Lee's Army
of Northern Virginia. Like McClellan before him, he prepared
and supplied his army well. But unlike the former commander
of the Army of the Potomac, Hooker was more aggressive.

Lincoln appreciated that. Revere, of course, had thought highly of McClellan and he was ready to follow the orders of Hooker and his lieutenants—as long as they were clear and precise.

The spring of 1863 marked the third year of the war. Hooker believed that if he could crush Lee's troops, the war's end could be hastened and the nation could return to its traditional season of planting and growing.

With over 130,000 men, Hooker outnumbered the ranks of the Army of Northern Virginia two to one. But Hooker wanted to defeat Lee without depending exclusively on numbers: he wanted to strategically earn the victory. His plan involved sending Major General George Stoneman's cavalry of nearly 10,000 men north of Lee's position to cut off railroad lines which provided supplies to the Army of Northern Virginia. Unfortunately, like Burnside's "Mud March," the heavy spring rains halted Stoneman's mid-April advance and Hooker's plan could not be implemented. Lincoln was disappointed, but Hooker quickly organized another plan. The new strategy involved a double envelopment of the Confederate position by utilizing both Stoneman's cavalry and three infantry corps: Major General George G. Meade's Fifth Corps, Major General Oliver O. Howard's Eleventh Corps, and Major General Henry W. Slocum's Twelfth Corps. Hooker's new plan involved over 50,000 of his men, a group that was nearly the size of the entire Army of Northern Virginia. And Hooker had an additional force of 80,000 men at his disposal. Once the three corps attacked Lee from the west, Stoneman's cavalry would ride around the battle zone and proceed "on to Richmond." Once Hooker's right wing was in position to secure the U.S. Ford, a strategic crossing, elements of Major General Darius N. Couch's Second Corps would cross the Rappahannock and join the Fifth, Eleventh, and Twelfth Corps concentrating at Chancellorsville.

The second part of the double envelopment involved Major General John F. Reynolds' First Corps and Major General John Sedgwick's Sixth Corps, a force 40,000 strong. Sickles' Third Corps, which included Revere's brigade, remained near Falmouth, supporting Reynolds and Sedgwick. Hooker believed that Lee could not escape the trap of superior numbers—and strategy. However, Robert E. Lee was about to create his most memorable masterpiece of the war, a strategy so unconventional and risky that it defied battlefield logic.

Revere's brigade left camp at 3:30 p.m. on April 28 and "bivouacked for the night near the Rappahannock, below Fredericksburg, near Skinker's Bend." The following day, Revere and his men advanced another mile closer to the river and established a camp for the night.[1]

About ten miles west of Fredericksburg was Chancellorsville. A structure rather than a town, the place was George Chancellor's grand multi-level brick house, which had also seen service as an inn. It was ideally located for travelers since it was situated near the intersection of four roads. The structure became Hooker's headquarters when the Union commander arrived on April 30.

On the morning of Friday, May 1, fighting erupted between Meade's Fifth Corps and rebel units along the Orange Plank Road, one of the principal roads near Chancellorsville. Meade believed his offensive was developing satisfactorily along a ridge line near the Zoan Church. He believed if he could hold the higher ground, Union forces would hold a stronger position against Lee's men, who were still threatened by Sedgwick's Sixth Corps to the east. But Hooker quickly ordered Meade back to Chancellorsville, where he was to join the other corps commanders in establishing a new line. In a matter of hours, Hooker had transformed a promising Union offensive into a static defensive one. "Fighting

Joe's" decision shifted the momentum of the battle to Lee and the Confederate commander would take advantage of it. Sickles' Corps began crossing U.S. Ford at 7:30 a.m. on May 1. Revere's brigade was on the march towards Chancellorsville.

"We crossed the river on the pontoon bridge, and proceeded about one and a half miles from the ford, where we were placed to the right of the road, with a strong picket-guard of the brigade in our front facing westwardly, but before we had completed the disposition of the troops, were ordered to proceed immediately to the front at Chancellorsville, which we did, reaching that place about 5 p.m., and finding our forces hotly engaged with the enemy in the advance," said Revere.[2]

Despite not being engaged in combat, Revere was concerned about the readiness of his men. "The operations in which my brigade took part, during the few days preceding the battle of May 3rd, at Chancellorsville, were peculiarly harassing and fatiguing," he pointed out, although his unit suffered no more than other federal troops. "After several days continuous marching and countermarching, near Falmouth, on the north bank of the Rappahannock, the brigade crossed the river on Friday, the first of May and moved to the front at Chancellorsville, where they were stationed as a reserve, to support the troops then hotly engaged, and where, that night, they bivouacked under arms."[3]

Overnight, Lee and Jackson held a meeting about a mile south of Hooker's headquarters. With information provided by the proprietor of nearby Catharine Furnace and maps created by Lee's trusted cartographer, Jed Hotchkiss, the two discovered a route around the Union right flank. Jackson planned on leading his entire Second Corps–minus Jubal Early's division–of some 28,000 men on a twelve-mile march behind Hooker's lines. Although outnumbered, Lee agreed with Jackson to divide his force again.

Of course, Lee's segmented army was even more vulnerable during Jackson's march. But if Jackson's corps could move without being detected by Union pickets, Lee would be able to inflict a devastating strike against the Army of the Potomac.

"It will be recollected, that during that night and the following day the enemy were busy in cutting a road through the forest, around our left flank and along our front, and in marching by it immense masses from our left to our right, in preparation for the furious attack made from the westward towards Saturday evening, the 2nd of May," recalled Revere.[4]

On the next day, Revere's brigade was placed in reserve just east of the Ely's Ford Road. In front of the Excelsior Brigade were elements of Brigadier General Joseph Carr's First Brigade. To the west was Major General Oliver Otis Howard's Eleventh Corps, arguably the "weakest link in Hooker's defensive chain."[5] Jackson's flank march did not go undetected; as a matter of fact, several reports of Confederate movements were forwarded to Howard, including one from Hooker, who warned that "the enemy is moving to our right."[6]

Although Howard failed to react to the warning, Hooker ordered elements of Sickles' Third Corps to engage Confederate forces at Catharine Furnace. Revere and his brigade remained positioned east of Ely's Ford Road. Joined by units in Slocum's command, Sickles' advance left a gap between Howard and the rest of Hooker's army. Still, Howard remained unconcerned. After all, he reasoned, the thick growth of the Wilderness area to the west would slow any adventurous attack upon his flank.

As the afternoon wore on, Jackson positioned his men for the attack. Not all had arrived by the late afternoon when he ordered the attack, but it mattered little; he believed he had enough men to carry out the plan. Shortly after 5 p.m., Brigadier General Robert

Rodes led the first line of some 10,000 Confederate soldiers against Howard's outnumbered ranks. A tidal wave of butternut and gray rolled through the Eleventh Corps over the next two hours. When Hooker discovered what had happened, he shifted his forces to meet the oncoming rebel advance.

Revere was ordered to a new location about a half mile to the west of his previous position. "The Second Division, after being under arms the whole of Saturday, were hurried forward about 5 p.m. to check this assault, and to restore the battle, which was fast turning into a rout, from the repulse of the Eleventh Corps, which had given way on the extreme right," said Revere.[7] "We were hurried up to intercept their fugitives and repel the enemy. We moved forward on the road, this brigade leading, and the major-general commanding the division at our head, first brigade in our rear, meeting fugitives, ambulances, batteries, caissons, limbers, etc., hurrying to the rear, of the troops which had broken."[8]

The chaos of the battlefield affected the exchange of messages among the major field commanders. "The last communication I had with General Sickles was through [Major] General [Hiram] Berry, about two o'clock on Saturday afternoon, and the only food my men received was at noon that day–rest they had none."[9] However, Revere exaggerated the exertions of his brigade.

Joined by First Brigade units under Brigadier General Joseph Carr, Revere's right flank was situated near the Bullock Road and his left near the Orange Turnpike "in a semicircular form from the plank-road to a woods road on the right, in the following order, commencing on the right: 26th Pennsylvania, 3rd Excelsior, 1st Excelsior, 2nd Excelsior, 120th New York, 5th Excelsior, 1st Massachusetts, and a Maryland regiment resting on the plank-road to Orange Court House."[10] John S. Poland, Second U.S. Infantry, Acting Assistant Inspector-General and Chief of Staff, stated in his report of May 13, 1863, that "the Twenty-sixth Pennsylvania Volunteers were also taken from the First Brigade and posted on the right of the first line, but by direction of General Revere, commanding Second Brigade, this last regiment, with the Fifth Excelsior, was thrown nearly perpendicular to the rear."[11]

Once Revere established his line—whether it was in a semicircular or perpendicular form—no Union troops were in front of him. He awaited the Confederate advance. "During the night between Saturday and Sunday, the brigade, while kept constantly on the alert from frequent alarms and the driving in of pickets, managed to throw up a line of log breastworks, expecting a renewal of the attack, for which we knew the enemy were massing their forces," stated Revere.[12]

At night, the victorious Jackson led a small group of mounted men towards the east to examine the terrain for the following day's attack. Heading back on the Old Mountain Road, shots rang out and Jackson fell with wounds to his right hand, his left forearm and his upper left arm. His horse galloped away amidst the gun shots. Other men in Jackson's party were killed or wounded. Ironically, the shots were fired by members of the Eighteenth North Carolina, who believed that they caught an unsuspecting Yankee patrol.

At the same time, Revere was inspecting his picket lines in the moonlight. "I began my inspection on the right of the picket-line, progressing gradually to the left, where I stopped to rectify the post of a sentinel not far from the plank-road," recalled Revere, who later heard gunshots and "rode towards the confederate lines" because "there was a danger of our firing upon friends."[13]

Once the shots stopped, Revere heard the sound of an approaching horse. "A riderless horse dashed past me towards our lines; and I reined up in presence of a group of several persons gathered around a man lying on the ground, apparently badly wounded," he said. "I saw at once that these were confederate officers, and visions of the Libby [Prison] began to flit through my mind; but reflecting that I was well armed and mounted, and that I had on the great-coat of a private soldier such as were worn by both parties, I sat still, regarding the group in silence, but prepared to use either my spurs or my saber, as occasion might demand."[14]

Revere stated that one of the Confederates ordered him to see what troops had fired on them. "I instantly made a gesture of assent, and rode away slowly in the direction indicated, until out of sight of the group; then made a circuit round it, and returned within my own lines," said Revere.[15]

Revere later believed that he had been an "involuntary witness" to the death of Robert E. Lee's most trusted officer. "About a fortnight afterwards, I saw a Richmond newspaper at the camp at Falmouth, in which were detailed the circumstance of the death of Stonewall Jackson. These left no doubt in my own mind that the person I had seen lying on the ground was that officer, and that his singular prediction [that the first days of May 1863 would be marked by 'great risk of life and fortunes'] had been verified."[16]

However, the ominous time that had been forecast years earlier was about to come true for Revere.

"Going towards the rear during the night, I discovered that we had no second line there, and that our right was uncovered–a distance of half a mile, unoccupied by troops, intervening between it and the next force, at White House," said Revere.[17] "That night we took prisoners a captain and some twenty privates of the enemy, from whom we learned that General A. P. Hill commanded a large force directly in our front, intending to attack and gain possession of the cross-roads at Chancellorsville." Revere promptly sent the information to his division commander, Major General Berry.

Despite Jackson's bold flank attack, Hooker was not as vulnerable as he thought. Major General John F. Reynolds' First Corps arrived and strengthened Hooker's defenses. Lee's army remained divided and the ranks of the Army of Northern Virginia had thinned after several days of fighting. Major General J. E. B. Stuart now commanded Jackson's Second Corps. Hooker, though, remained poised to halt an attack; he was not ready to initiate one.

"At daylight on Sunday, May 3rd, the enemy drove in our pickets, and opened the battle with a heavy fire of artillery and musketry," said Revere, whose right flank now extended north of the Bullock Road.[18] Revere expected the small arms fire, but the massive Confederate artillery was surprising. Hooker had ordered Sickles to abandon Hazel Grove, the only significant clearing in the Wilderness where artillery could be used effectively. It was a major mistake, an "inexplicable blunder."[19] Prior to the retreat, Hooker's control of Hazel Grove gave him an advantage over Lee's separated army, but that advantage quickly deteriorated when over two dozen Confederate guns quickly moved into position and opened fire.

Revere's brigade moved into its new position. "The brigade fought steadily for several hours, until the enemy turned our left flank, and enfiladed the breastwork, when they were forced by numbers to retire," remarked Revere, who did not explain why his flank had been turned.[20] But the Confederate attack led by Brigadier General E. L. Thomas' Georgians—the Fourteenth, Thirty-fifth, Forty-fifth, and Forty-ninth regiments—threatened his right flank.

To the right of Thomas were brigades in Major General A. P. Hill's Second Corps, commanded by brigadier generals William D. Pender, Henry Heth, and James H. Lane. And behind them were the advancing units of Brigadier General Raleigh E. Colson's

Division: the brigades of Francis T. Nicholls (commanded by Colonel Jesse M. Williams), E. F. Paxton, Edward T. H. Warren (commanded by Colonel Titus V. Williams), John R. Jones (commanded by Colonel Thomas S. Garnett), and Samuel McGowan. And Brigadier General James Archer's men were positioned further south. It was a determined Confederate force; Hooker needed all of his men to remain steadfast.

The scene became chaotic as stragglers from other Union units passed through Revere's ranks. As tens of thousands of shots rang out, one struck Major General Berry and killed him; another wounded Brigadier General Joseph Carr.

"I at once concluded that I was the commanding officer of the Second Division, Thirds Corps; and in that capacity I directed all the officers of my division who could be found, personally and through my staff, to rally and report to me," stated Revere.[21] One of the officers who reported was Colonel Louis Francine, the commander of the Seventh New Jersey. Francine had earlier been informed that Third Brigade commander Brigadier General Gershom Mott and the unit's second ranking officer, Colonel William Sewell, had been wounded. But the information was only true regarding Mott; Francine "assumed command as senior ranking officer" of the Third Brigade.[22]

The situation was sardonically chaotic: Revere incorrectly assumed command of a division that included at least one brigade commander who also incorrectly assumed command. "And as this new position devolved upon me both the responsibility of directing the division and the enlarged discretion which every general officer in such circumstances is supposed to possess, I determined upon my course of action," said Revere.[23]

Revere's "course of action" was hastened by the aggressive advance of Thomas' Georgians, who were augmented by the

Thirteenth North Carolina. Revere acknowledged that the "need of some action was urgent." He reasoned that "his men were worn with the marches and battles of four days, with want of rest and food for the last twenty-four hours, and with sharp fighting for the last four, and were nearly out of ammunition."[24] To be sure, Revere's men had been on the march, but so had thousands of other Union soldiers. He also explained that he could best reorganize the many Union stragglers "by retiring." Revere also believed that the "front of the battle had... shifted to the right" and that his brigade could be of most use somewhere else–"anywhere along the road to the ford" where additional fighting was underway. But he was wrong about the location of the battle's "front." He was moving away from it. Perhaps there was more to his explanation–something more personal, the will to live or some other rationalization to survive–but he never revealed it except in the printed testimonies which would follow after the battle. In any event, around eight o'clock in the morning, Revere promptly ordered his men to the rear. "Revere, to the bewilderment of his men and everyone nearby...marched his New York brigade right off the battlefield."[25]

Revere and his men passed between the ranks of Colonel Hiram Berdan's U.S. Sharpshooters and Brigadier General Samuel Carroll's regiments and continued to march north-northeast. The result of this action was obvious. "Portions of the line commenced to crumble...hastened by the somewhat less than courageous action of...Revere," noted one historian.[26] Another wrote, "The gap left in the line by this retrograde movement helped to ensure federal failure on the field, to which Revere never returned."[27]

Revere's flight was a quick one. His men hastily left muskets, bayonets, accoutrements, knapsacks, haversacks, tents, canteens, and tools behind. Despite Revere's explanation that his men were nearly out of ammunition, nearly 30,000 rounds were left behind. Revere's retreat left a gap in the Union lines, but it was not immediately exploited by the Confederates. Fortunately—at least for the time being—other units stepped forward, notably Brigadier General Erastus Tyler's First Brigade in the Third Division of Meade's Fifth Corps.

"Striking a direct course by compass through the woods, I moved a mile and a quarter towards a point on the main road about midway to the United States Ford, and then marched a short distance down the main road, to a position where the stragglers on both sides of it might be intercepted and rallied, and where orders from either flank might reach us with equal ease," said Revere.[28] "Strange to say, he started off towards the river with a portion of the Division and with no orders to do so," remarked Colonel Robert McAllister of Eleventh New Jersey.[29] As a result of Revere's move, Brigadier General William D. Pender's brigade of five North Carolina regiments "made substantial inroads" on the Union's line. Meanwhile, Revere and his men "sat out the rest of the battle."[30]

While Revere marched away from the battlefield, the fighting continued in the area he had abandoned. Hooker filled the void by sending in Major General William H. French's Third Division from Major General Darius Couch's Second Corps. Revere crossed paths with French and the major general instructed him to occupy "a line of abatis." "But on arriving at them I found them lined with troops, and to put more there would be superfluous," said Revere. "In fact, the whole place was covered with troops; and a constant stream of stragglers was going to the rear by the main road."[31] Revere essentially joined the stragglers' flight—but in a more organized manner. French's determined counterattack exploited Thomas' Georgians, who were also running low on ammunition, but the Third Division commander could only advance so far.[32]

160

Later, an artillery projectile smashed into one of the Chancellorsville house's columns that Hooker was standing next to. The impact thrust Hooker to the ground. Though not severely wounded, Hooker was dazed and was immediately cared for. But the fight–what there was left of it–had been taken out of him.

Revere's former regiment, the Seventh New Jersey, now in Brigadier General Gershom Mott's Third Brigade in Berry's division, was heavily engaged in the day's fighting. At dawn, the unit was positioned near the Orange Plank Road and engaged a number of North Carolina regiments. Fighting valiantly throughout the early morning, the Seventh New Jersey captured several rebel flags and killed Colonel Thomas J. Purdie, the commander of the Eighteenth North Carolina. Purdie's overcoat, which was riddled with "19 bullet holes," was retrieved by Colonel Francine, who later "brought it to camp as a trophy."[33] At one point during the battle, the Seventh New Jersey advanced farther westward than any other Union unit in the immediate area. "We repulsed brigade after brigade of rebels unsupported, and with other Union troops breaking and falling back all around us, maintained our position til all our ammunition was expended and our muskets clogged and hard to load," said Captain William Hillyer of Company K.[34]

Francine was informed that Mott had been wounded and as senior officer, he assumed command of the brigade. He was met by Revere, who ordered him and his men to the rear. Brigadier General Carr later questioned the move. "[He] left the line without proper authority, and proceeded, with about 400 of his men, to the United States Ford," noted Carr, who did not mention Revere's orders regarding Francine's actions. "At this critical period of the engagement, he could illy be spared, and the loss of his men was severely felt."[35] Carr requested an explanation for Francine's action, which the regimental commander provided. "Francine defended himself by saying that he did not withdraw but simply gathered in one spot those men in the Brigade who were already in the rear."[36] His explanation was accepted.

Carr said that the Second Division "held its position for over four hours...until its ammunition was entirely expended." He retired from his position and reformed the remaining elements of the First and Third Brigades near the White House. "Here I learned that Brig. Gen. J. W. Revere had marched his command, with two regiments of the First Brigade, to the United States Ford," said Carr.[37] Colonel William Blaisdell, commander of the Eleventh Massachusetts and second in command of Carr's brigade, concurred that "part of the command had been taken some miles to the rear by General Revere, with his command."[38] Major Robert L. Bodine of the Twenty-sixth Pennsylvania added: "we were marched by General Revere down the road toward the ferry and back again the same day."[39]

When Revere reached a point several miles from the battlefield, he "halted the column [and] sent out patrols in all directions, to collect stragglers, and obtained from the river, and distributed food and ammunition."[40] Above all, the distance between the battlefield and Revere's position exacerbated the developing situation. Revere engaged in a brief conversation with Lieutenant Colonel O. H. Hart, Sickles' adjutant general, and at noon tallied his men: "1,715 officers and men, in the aggregate, were reported present for duty."[41] However, there were approximately 5,000 men in Berry's division who were not with Revere. He may have described his retreat in an orderly fashion, but Revere had abandoned a large number of men in the field.

Nevertheless, Revere was ready to return to the battlefield. "Anxious to avoid delay, I gave the men little time to prepare their food, and then led the division towards the front again, increasing

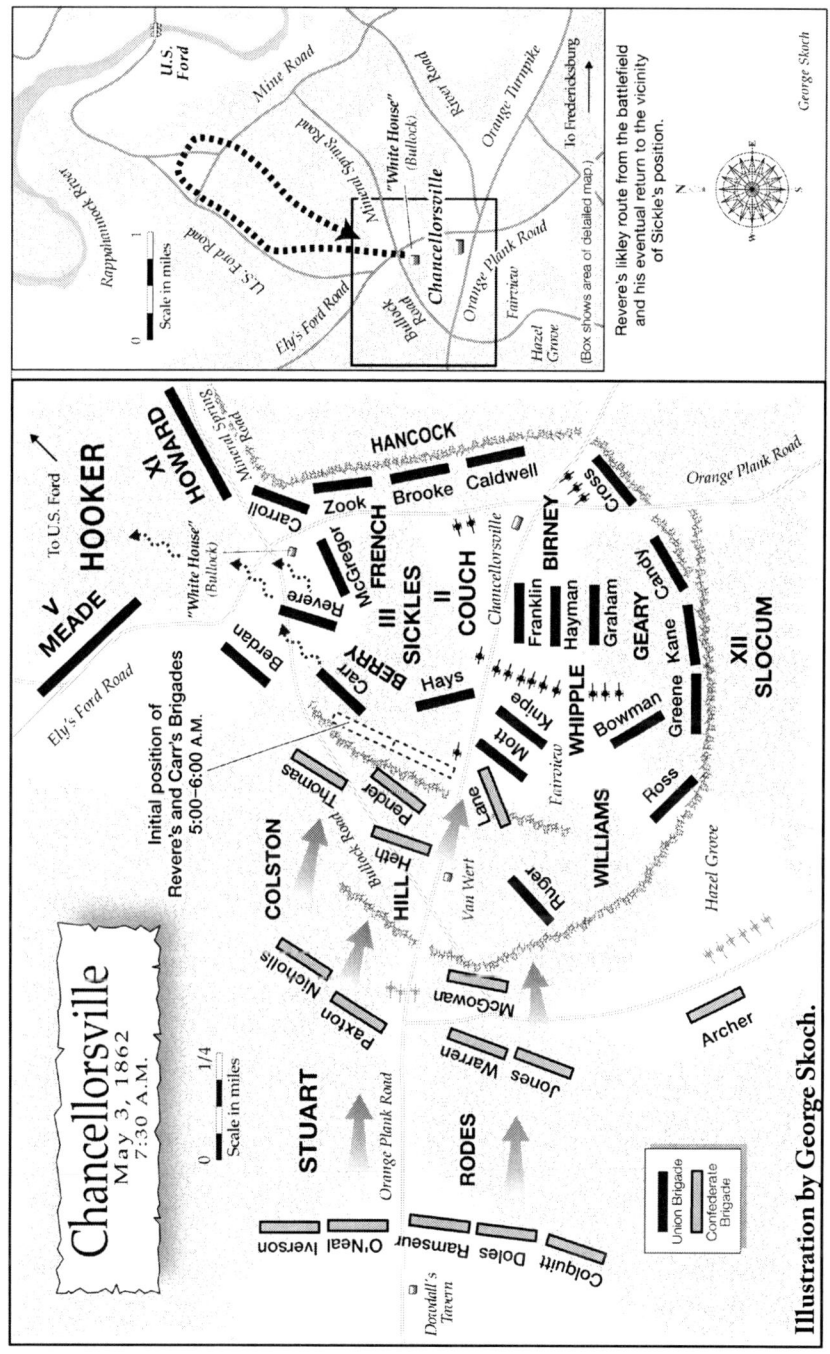

Illustration by George Skoch.

our force at every rod."[42] Clearly, Revere had no intention of permanently leaving the scene of action. While on the return march, Revere's ranks were augmented by several hundred stragglers from the Third Corps.

An aide from Sickles reached Revere and ordered him to return to the corps commander. "I reached the front at the head of about 2,000 men of the division, at half-past two in the afternoon, by my watch," stated Revere, who seemed oblivious to the circumstance he had created for himself.[43] As soon as Revere reported to Sickles, he was promptly relieved of his authority on the field.

Sickles was furious.

"After the fall of the lamented Berry, some confusion occurred in the withdrawal of the Second Division, owing to the assumption of command by Brigadier General Revere, who, heedless of their murmurs, shamefully led to the rear the whole of the Second Brigade and portions of two others, thus subjecting these proud soldiers for the first time to the humiliation of being marched to the rear while their comrades were under fire," wrote Sickles to Brigadier General Seth Williams, Assistant Adjutant General, Army of the Potomac. "General Revere was promptly recalled with his troops, and at once relieved of command."[44]

Sickles demanded an explanation from Revere and sent Lieutenant Colonel J. Hayden, his assistant adjutant general, to him with a message: "General Sickles directs that you report immediately the authority under which you moved your brigade to the rear this morning."

Revere responded to Hayden:

"Colonel: I have the honor to state that after my brigade had left the field this morning, I found myself the senior officer of the division present; and after rallying and forming the broken command, who were almost without ammunition and quite out of rations, I moved them down the road for the purpose of reorganizing and bringing them back to the field comparatively fresh, after consulting the commanding officers of the regiment present. I did not act under any orders, but did as seemed best to me under the circumstances.

"This movement commenced about eight a.m., and I returned at two p.m., with parts of nearly every regiment in the division, having received numerous augmentations on the march, and with renewed ammunition."[45]

Colonel J. Egbert Farnum, commander of the Seventieth New York and Revere's second in command of the brigade, was promptly informed of the situation. "At about 3 p.m. the same day, I was officially informed that General Revere was relieved from duty, and then command of brigade devolved upon me, whereupon I assumed command, and Lieutenant Colonel [Thomas] Holt took command of the regiment," explained Farnum.[46]

Sickles said that "the claim of Revere to command... lost us precious moments of time," but "Colonel [William O.] Stevens of the [Seventy-second New York in the] Second Brigade, in the absence of General Revere, changed front to repel the advance of the enemy on the flank."[47]

Although Revere had lost his command, the fighting continued. In Slocum's Twelfth Corps, division commanders Alpheus Williams and John W. Geary maintained their positions until a lack of ammunition and overwhelming Confederate numbers forced them off the field.[48] But not all in the Union ranks stood their ground. Some additional units—particularly several companies in Brigadier General Joseph Knipe's brigade—were prematurely led off the field.[49]

After forcing Major General Jubal Early's troops to retreat from Fredericksburg, Major General John Sedgwick's Sixth Corps moved west to join Hooker. Sedgwick's slow pace was halted by Confederate forces at Salem Church. The following day, Lee resumed his attacks on Sedgwick, forcing him to retreat over Bank's Ford. Hooker held a council with his corps commanders. Some wanted to resume the offensive; others, like Sickles, did not. Hooker had seemingly had enough. On May 5, the Army of the Potomac began its retreat. The next day, a sub-headline in the *Boston Daily Advertiser's* report on the battle stated: "Stonewall Jackson Checkmated!"[50] Hooker and every man under his command knew otherwise; in fact, Major General Couch noted simply that Hooker had been "outgeneraled by Lee."

The Battle of Chancellorsville cost the Army of the Potomac nearly 1,700 dead and 10,000 wounded. Another 6,000 were missing or captured. In the Third Corps, Revere's Second Brigade in Berry's Second Division suffered 317 casualties: 27 killed, 159 wounded and 131 missing.[51]

The Army of Northern Virginia totaled approximately 1,700 dead and over 9,000 wounded. Another 2,500 Confederates were missing or captured. But Robert E. Lee had lost nearly one-fourth of his infantry. Nevertheless, the victory emboldened the Confederate commander. Lee next planned to move into Pennsylvania.

Back at Falmouth, the Army of the Potomac buried its dead, tended to the wounded, prepared its captured Confederates to be sent to Union prisons, and conducted courts-martial. A week after the retreat from Chancellorsville, Special Orders, Number 128 were issued: the court-martial of Brigadier General Joseph Warren Revere. Word of Revere's predicament quickly spread through camp. "Revere… has been put under arrest for bad conduct in the late fight," noted Private Emmell of the Seventh New Jersey.[52] Colonel McAllister of the Eleventh New Jersey was sympathetic to Revere's situation. "He went without orders and is still under arrest for it," he said. "It is a most unaccountable thing, for we consider him a good and brave officer."[53]

NOTES

1. Revere to Lieutenant Colonel O. H. Hart, Revere Family Papers. See also Joseph Warren Revere, *A Statement of the Case of Brigadier-General Joseph W. Revere, United States Volunteers* (New York: C. A. Alvord, 1863), 41.

2. Revere to Hart; Revere, *A Statement*, 42.

3. Revere, *A Statement*, 9.

4. Ibid.

5. Stephen W. Sears, *Chancellorsville* (New York: Houghton Mifflin Co., 1996), 237.

6. Gary W. Gallagher, *The Battle of Chancellorsville* (Eastern National Park and Monument Association, 1995), 23.

7. Revere, *A Statement*, 9-10.

8. Revere to Hart; Revere, *A Statement*, 42.

9. Ibid., 10.

10. Revere to Hart; Revere, *A Statement*, 42. The First Massachusetts was situated left of the One Hundred Twentieth New York; the Fifth Excelsior (Seventy-third New York) was positioned to the left of the First Massachusetts. The unidentified Maryland regiment was the Third Maryland, which was placed behind the Fifth Excelsior.

11. *War of the Rebellion*, Series I, Vol. XXV, 449.

12. Revere, *A Statement*, 10.

13. Joseph W. Revere, *Keel and Saddle*, 276.

14. Ibid., 277.

15. Ibid.

16. Ibid. Rumors circulated within the Confederate ranks about Jackson's condition. For example, A. L. Peel of the Nineteenth Mississippi noted in his diary that "Jackson had his arm shot off by his own men." However, Dr. Hunter McGuire amputated Jackson's left arm hours after he was shot. Lee stated that Jackson "has lost his left arm but I my right." Jackson appeared to recover; in fact, his condition improved during May 5 and 6, but deteriorated on the following day. The May 8 edition of the *Richmond Whig* reported: "His wound is by no means serious, and he will doubtless be ready for duty in the course of a month or two." On May 10, Jackson succumbed to complications associated with pneumonia. His amputated arm was buried separately on the property of J. Horace Lacy in the Wilderness; his body was buried in Lexington, Virginia. Despite Revere's belief that he had witnessed a wounded Jackson, there is no corroborating evidence. Furthermore, the "Thomas J. Jackson" who Revere had met on a steamboat years earlier could not have been the celebrated Confederate commander. "Stonewall" Jackson was a deeply religious man who would have dismissed any serious thoughts of astrology or the "occult sciences." Also, it is difficult to imagine someone unfamiliar with the Wilderness to be able to successfully negotiate its dense brush on horseback. Clearly, Revere was mistaken. In 1999, Fosterfields' employee Rebecca Kirkman wrote an in-house article, "Revere's Involvement in The Civil War, 1861-1865," that provided a possible explanation for the story. "In Revere's favor, there was a Lieutenant Thomas K. Jackson in the army in 1852," wrote Kirkman. "It is possible that General Revere met this officer on the Mississippi and later presumed that he was the gentleman who became known as Stonewall. It is possible that Revere witnessed another man's wounding at Chancellorsville and again mistakenly assumed it was Stonewall."

17. Revere, *A Statement*, 10.
18. Ibid.

19. Vincent J. Esposito, ed., *The West Point Atlas of American Wars, Vol. 1, 1689-1900* (New York: Frederick A. Praeger, 1959), 91. Esposito also criticized Hooker for "his failure to coordinate properly the two wings of his army so that their attacks would be mutually supporting."

20. Revere, *A Statement*, 10. Revere noted that the makeshift breastworks served their purpose: "Owing to the practice of the enemy firing so low, the breastwork was a great protection…."

21. Ibid., 12.

22. John Hayward, *Give It To Them, Jersey Blues!*, 102. According to the author, Francine's assumed command included elements of the Fifth, Sixth, Seventh, and Eighth New Jersey, and the Second New York.

23. Revere, *A Statement*, 13.

24. Ibid.

25. Sears, *Chancellorsville*, 325.

26. Edward J. Stackpole, *Chancellorsville: Lee's Greatest Battle* (Harrisburg, Pennsylvania: The Stackpole Company, 1958, 293.

27. Robert C. Krick, *Chancellorsville: Lee's Greatest Victory* (Civil War Preservation Trust, 2010), 166.

28. Revere, *A Statement*, 14.

29. James I. Robertson, ed., *The Civil War Letters of General Robert McAllister* (New Brunswick, NJ: Rutgers University Press, 1965), 306.

30. Edward G. Longacre, *The Commanders of Chancellorsville* (Nashville, Tennessee: Rutledge Hill Press, 2005, 234-235.

31. Revere, *A Statement*, 43. South of the intersection of Mineral Springs Road and Ely's Ford Road, Major General Winfield Scott Hancock, commander of the Second Corps' First Division, positioned brigades assigned to Brigadier General Samuel K. Zook, Colonel John R. Brooke, and Brigadier General John C. Caldwell. Brooke, however, had been severely wounded the previous day.

32. Evert A. Duyckinck had high praise for French in his multi-volume *National History of the War for the Union* (New York: Johnson, Fry and Company, 1861-65. "It was General French who charged and drove the enemy on the flank," noted Duyckinck in Vol. III, 128. French, a West Point graduate (Class of 1837), spent much of his adult life in the military. In his early sixties, French assumed command of the historic Fort McHenry, which stood at the harbor of his hometown–Baltimore, Maryland.

33. *Heyward Emmell Journal*, May 3, 1863. The May 30, 1863 edition of *The Jerseyman* heralded the capture of the flags, which the newspaper reported were being "sent to the Governor of New Jersey." Dr. Albert Phillip Francine noted in a 1910 biographical sketch–*Louis Raymond Francine: Brevet Brigadier-General U.S. Volunteers, 1837-1963*–about the banners: "The colors were taken from the Twenty-first Virginia, Eighteenth North Carolina, First Louisiana, Second North Carolina, and the fifth from some Alabama regiment." See also *History of Morris County, New Jersey*, 81; Watertown, New York's *New-York Daily Reformer*, May 5, 1863, 3; St. Johnsbury, Vermont's *The Caledonian*, 1.

34. *The Jerseyman*, May 10, 1963, 2. William Hillyer, who is listed as a first lieutenant in John Hayward's *Give it to Them, Jersey Blues!*, probably exaggerated the size of the rebel units that the Seventh New Jersey countered. However, the unit's bravery has never been in question.

35. *War of the Rebellion*, Series I, Vol. XXV, 445.

36. Hayward, *Give It To Them, Jersey Blues!*, 103.

37. *War of the Rebellion*, Series I, Vol. XXV, 446.

38. Ibid., 452.

39. Ibid., 459.

40. Revere, *A Statement*, 14.

41. Revere to Hart, May 7, 1863, Revere Family Papers. The following regimental totals were submitted by Revere: First Excelsior (210),

Second Excelsior (150), Third Excelsior (204), Fourth Excelsior (282), Fifth Excelsior (137), One Hundred Twentieth New York (224), First Massachusetts (80), Fifteenth Massachusetts (74), and the Twenty-sixth Pennsylvania (354).

42. Revere, *A Statement*, 14.

43. Ibid., 15.

44. Sickles to Williams, May 20, 1863, *War of the Rebellion:* Series 1, Vol. XXV, Chapter 37, 392.

45. Revere, *A Statement*, 47.

46. *War of the Rebellion*, Series 1, Vol. XXV, Chapter 37, 464.

47. Sickles to Williams, May 20, 1863, 392.

48. Slocum's brigades under Colonel Samuel Ross and Brigadier General Thomas H. Ruger suffered over 1,100 casualties. The number of men killed, wounded, and missing in the ranks of Brigadier General Thomas Kane, Colonel Charles Candy, and Brigadier General George S. Greene's unit numbered nearly 1,200. The casualties varied from unit to unit. Nearby, Colonel Edward Cross of the Second Corps suffered over one hundred casualties while Colonel Samuel M. Bowman of the Third Corps tallied nearly six hundred killed, wounded, or missing.

49. Sears, *Chancellorsville*, 331. Knipe's men were also involved in a "friendly fire" exchange. The author also noted that Colonel Samuel B. Hayman in Birney's division was aware "that the fire [came] from friend as well as foe."

50. *Boston Daily Advertiser*, May 6, 1963, 2. The battlefield report, which was filed on Sunday night, May 3, noted boldly that the Union "position is impregnable if our troops continue to fight as they have." The Augusta, Georgia, *Daily Constitutionalist* was more accurate with its May 6, 1863 headlines: "The Yankees Renew The Fight. They Are Whipped At Every Point."

51. Sears, *Chancellorsville*, 481. Besides one wounded staff officer, Sears provided the following statistics (killed, wounded, missing, total) for each regiment:

Seventieth New York (4k, 11w, 17m, 32), Seventy-first New York (1k, 15w, 23m, 39), Seventy-second New York (12k, 30w, 59m, 101), Seventy-third New York (3k, 31w, 4m, 38), Seventy-fourth New York (3k, 22w, 15m, 40), One Hundred Twentieth New York (4k, 49w, 13m, 66). Revere's original document, "Recapitulations of Casualties in the 2nd Brigade 2nd Division, 3rd Army Corps in the operations near Chancellorsville, VA," offers a more detailed description of the casualties. See Appendix C.

52. *Emmell Journal*, May 9. This passage, which was crossed out in the journal, was not reproduced in Malcolm's *The Civil War Journal of Private Heyward Emmell*.

53. Robertson, ed., *The Civil War Letters of General Robert McAllister*, 306.

CHAPTER TEN

THE COURT-MARTIAL

"Was this a breach of duty?"

Two days before Revere's court-martial, the *New York Times* published an article titled "A Review of the Recent Operations of the Army of the Potomac," which included the sub-headline: "Arrest of Gen. Revere." The article read like an indictment.

"On Monday morning, after we had successfully repelled the attack of the rebels on our front, Gen. Revere, commanding the Excelsior brigade, marched his men out of their position, back to the United States Ford. This proceeding on his part seemed entirely incomprehensible to his officers and men. They never before received orders to retreat before an enemy, and they looked upon this as a mistake of some one. Who that some one was they could not tell, but like true soldiers, who obey the mandates of their superiors, they wended their way to the ford, with hearts sinking with them. The disgrace of a retrograde movement had never yet fallen upon their noble escutcheon. 'Excelsior' was not a motto for a rear guard to have engrossed upon their banners. Their battle-torn and tattered flags, remnants of what had once been as bright and beautiful as the colors of a rainbow, appeared to them steeped in disgrace; but their absence from the front was of short duration. As soon as General Sickles heard of the ignoble course of their commander he dispatched all his available Aids with the most peremptory orders for their immediate return to the front, and in a little time back came the old veterans with hearts full of pride, at the thought again sharing with their comrades the fortunes of the field. On hearing of their return, Gen. Sickles sent immediately for Gen. Revere, and inquired of him his reasons for this strange procedure. Gen. Revere had no particular excuse to make, save that his men were out of ammunition–(when there was plenty within a stone's throw of his former position.) His frivolous apologies for his conduct, Gen. Sickles would not accept, and he ordered him under arrest to report at Falmouth. The expression of indignation on the face of Gen. Sickles, as he addressed Gen. Revere when placing him under arrest, was a study for a painter. Gen. Sickles had always been a friend of Revere's. He (Revere) had been placed in command of Sickles' old brigade. Gen. Sickles thought a great deal of him, but Sickles has no friends on the battle-field who fail to discharge their duties. In the flashing eyes of Sickles, when he relieved Revere, you could have read: 'Cassio, I love you–But never more be officer of mine.'"[1]

The article also praised General Hooker and suggested that he was not responsible for the loss at Chancellorsville. Instead, the newspaper placed various levels of blame on other high-ranking field officers like General Stoneman.

Prior to the court-martial, Revere probably recalled his unpleasant experience during the naval court of inquiry which resulted in his resignation and he no doubt remembered the "illegal and unjust" dismissal of Lieutenant Washington A. Bartlett from the navy. However, the potential penalties Revere faced in his court-martial were much more severe.

On April 10, 1806, the United States Congress passed legislation creating the Articles of War. Six months after the passing of the law, every officer was obligated to subscribe to the 101 rules and regulations. The various acts covered not only officers, but non-commissioned officers, enlisted men, chaplains, and sutlers. Penalties ranged from fines as low as "one-sixth of a dollar" to "death."[2] The articles also identified situations in which courts-martial would be utilized and the makeup of such tribunals. Article No. 64 stated: "General courts-martial may consist of any number of commissioned officers, from five to thirteen, inclusively; but they shall not consist of less than thirteen where that number can be convened without manifest injury to the service."[3] Eight were appointed to judge Revere.

The officers who served on Revere's court-martial were a veteran group of soldiers including those who had fought in the Seminole Wars, the Mexican War, and a number of important Civil War battles prior to Chancellorsville. And all served as members in the Army of the Potomac during the fighting earlier in the month.

Major General Winfield Scott Hancock was appointed by General Hooker to serve as the President of the General Court-Martial. Hancock, thirty-nine years old, was a highly regarded officer who had been described as "superb" by General

George McClellan during the Peninsula Campaign of 1862. At Chancellorsville, Hancock commanded the Army of the Potomac's First Division, Second Corps and helped cover Hooker's retreat. Later, Hancock would play a crucial role in establishing Union defenses at Gettysburg and in 1880, he became the Democratic candidate for president.

Winfield Scott Hancock. Courtesy of the Robert Jones Collection.

The other officers who were asked to serve on Revere's court-martial included Major General John Newton and Brigadier Generals Jas. S. Wadsworth, William T. H. Brooks, Andrew A. Humpreys, John Gibbon, Francis C. Barlow, Romeyn B. Ayres, and Samuel K. Zook. Lieutenant Colonel E. R. Platt served as judge advocate.[4]

Newton, forty years old, who graduated second in his class at West Point in 1842, was a talented engineer who helped bolster the defenses around Washington, D.C., in early 1862. He served as a Sixth Corps brigade commander before being promoted to a major general in 1863.

Wadsworth, fifty-seven years old, had served as the military governor of Washington, D.C., and unsuccessfully sought the Republican nomination for governor of New York in 1862. At Chancellorsville, he commanded the Army of the Potomac's First Division, First Corps.

Brooks, forty-two years old, who had been twice wounded in 1862—first during the Seven Days Battles (at Allen's Farm) and later at Antietam—commanded the Army of the Potomac's First Division, Sixth Corps at Chancellorsville.

Humpreys, fifty-two years old, who had served as one of Major General George McClellan's staff officers, was an esteemed engineer who had served as a division commander during the Battles of Antietam and Fredericksburg. During the Chancellorsville campaign, he commanded the Army of the Potomac's Third Division, Fifth Corps.

Gibbon, thirty-six years old, author of the War Department's *Artillerist's Manual* in 1860, became Brigadier General Irwin McDowell's chief of artillery in 1861. He later became a brigade commander and provided new black felt hats to his Indiana and Wisconsin regiments. His Black Hat Brigade was later called the Iron Brigade due to the unit's bravery at South Mountain, Maryland, in 1862. Gibbon commanded the Army of the Potomac's Second Division, Second Corps at Chancellorsville.

Barlow, thirty years old, rose from the rank of private in the Twelfth New York, a 90-day regiment, in 1861 to brigadier general in the late summer of 1862. Wounded at Antietam, he commanded the Army of the Potomac's Second Brigade, Second Division, Eleventh Corps at Chancellorsville.

Ayres, thirty-seven years old, a captain of artillery at the First Bull Run, was promoted to brigadier general in late 1862 and commanded the Army of the Potomac's First Brigade, Second Division, V Corps at Chancellorsville.

Zook, forty-one years old, served as colonel of the Fifty-seventh New York in 1861. Despite a number of medical problems, Zook commanded a brigade at Fredericksburg and later served as brigadier general of the Army of the Potomac's Third Brigade, First Division, Second Corps at Chancellorsville.

Hooker ordered the chief quartermaster of the Third Corps to provide the General Court-Martial with the necessary accommodations. At 10:30 a.m. on May 13, the court-martial began at the Third Corps' headquarters. Following procedure, Revere "was asked if he objected to any member" of the court-martial, but he did not. Colonel Platt promptly swore in the appointed members of court and then Hancock swore in Platt.

Then the court immediately arraigned Revere of the charges:

"Charge 1st–Misbehavior before the enemy.

"Specifications–In this, that Brigadier-General J. W. Revere, U.S. Volunteers, commanding Excelsior (Second) Brigade, Second Division, Third Corps, while said division was engaged with the enemy at Chancellorsville, Virginia, did march his command an unnecessary distance to the rear to reform it, and then did march with his brigade, and such fragments of other regiments of the said division as he could assemble, to the United States Ford, about five miles from the scene of the action.

"All this without orders from his superior officers, about 8 o'clock on the morning of March 3rd, 1863.

"Charge 2nd–Neglect of duty, to the prejudice of good order and military discipline.

"Specifications–In this, that Brigadier-General J. W. Revere, U.S. Volunteers, commanding Excelsior (Second) Brigade, Second Division, Third Corps, did allow public property to the amount of 189 muskets, 178 sets of accoutrements, 259 bayonets, 28,440 rounds of small-arm ammunition, 1,779 knapsacks, 836 haversacks, 494 canteens, 2,000 shelter tents, and fifty-five pioneer tools, in the scribe of his command, to be abandoned, and to fall in the hands of the enemy."[5]

The charges were formally signed by Major H. Edward Tremain, the Area Defense Counsel who represented Revere. Before he pleaded to the charges, Revere asked permission to allow his division commander, Brigadier General David B. Birney, to join as his counsel and for Captain William H. Chester of Company G in the Fifth Excelsior Regiment "to assist in recording testimony." The court agreed to Revere's requests.

Revere promptly pleaded not guilty to all charges and specifications. He believed he was not guilty and his counsel would rely on the testimony of others to help him achieve an acquittal.

The prosecution called its first witness. Major General Sickles took the stand, swore the oath, and explained the positions of his units on May 3.[6] "General Birney's division was to the left of General Berry, and in front of the house which I mentioned as General Slocum's head-quarters," stated the Third Corps commander. "When we retired from that position, I took a second position in rear of Chancellorsville, where I established my head-quarters, formed on the road leading to United States Ford, and where, through staff officers, I directed commanding officers of brigades and divisions to report to me with their commands. General Berry was killed before this last movement."[7]

Sickles carefully explained the chain of command following Berry's death.

"The command of the Second Division devolved upon Brigadier-General Carr, to whom I communicated my orders," noted Sickles. "General Carr informed me, through a staff officer, that General Revere claimed the command as senior; I did not recognize the claim of General Revere."[8] Sickles continued his testimony and pointed out that the Second Brigade did not report because "Revere had taken his brigade, and he supposed a portion of the Third Brigade, to the rear." Sickles stated that after about ninety minutes had passed without hearing from Revere, he sent some staff officers to find him. They finally located Revere near the United States Ford. "I directed him to report to me in person for explanation, and he stated that he went down for ammunition," said Sickles. "I told him his explanation was not satisfactory, and relieved him from command."[9]

For the record, Judge Advocate Platt asked Sickles if he had given Revere "any orders to march his brigade from the field." Sickles replied that he had given no such orders.

However, Sickles provided the court with an explanation why Revere assumed command of the division. "I think he might have been under the impression that he was senior, because, although General Carr was originally his senior, General Revere's appointment was confirmed by the Senate, and General Carr's appointment was not acted on," said Sickles. "General Carr was subsequently appointed, and the letter of reappointment bore date in March '63. It was afterwards cancelled, and he was appointed from the original date, which re-established the relative rank, making Carr the senior. It was perhaps known to General Revere that General Carr's reappointment bore date in March, and perhaps known to him that General Carr's original date had been given to him."[10]

The question of seniority, however, seemed to be a moot point. Sickles stated that Revere had moved the brigade without orders and that charge remained the most serious. Since the Battle of Chancellorsville was a Union defeat, those in the highest positions of the Army of the Potomac—from Hooker to his corps, division, and brigade commanders—sought scapegoats. And Revere was an easy target.

The prosecution called Colonel J. Egbert Farnum, the commander of the First Excelsior Regiment (Seventieth New York) and Revere's second in command, to the stand. Farnum explained that after the rebels forced his regiment "to give way," he reformed them and joined Revere at the breastworks. "There General Revere assumed command of the division, or of the regimental fragments of the division that were there," remarked Farnum. "And marching by his orders, we struck a bee-line through the woods, striking the United States Ford road at a distance of about a mile and a quarter, I should suppose, from the White House."[11]

Farnum added that the unit marched another mile and a quarter. "We were then halted, and the men were allowed to rest," said Farnum. "Ammunition was sent for to supply the deficiencies of the troops, and distributed. The movements took place by order of General Revere."[12]

The judge advocate asked Farnum about the numerous weapons and accoutrements that were abandoned when Revere ordered the division to the rear. But Farnum noted "the property had been left the previous day." That statement gave Revere hope. He may have sensed that the prosecution's witness helped his case since the numerous items were not abandoned when his orders to leave the battlefield were issued.

Revere's counsel cross-examined Farnum:

"Question: Was or was not the distance marched by your brigade to the rear to reform, rendered necessary on account of the front being filled with troops waiting to into action?

"Farnum: It could not have been formed sooner, or in a more advantageous ground.

"Question: State the number of troops, with as much accuracy as possible, that were under General Revere's command when he commenced the march to the rear, and were they in fit condition to engage the enemy?

"Farnum: About 1,200 men; I should say they were not in fit condition to engage the enemy, having expended their ammunition to a considerable extent."[13]

Revere was, no doubt, feeling somewhat better about his defense. Although the charge against him for moving his unit without orders remained strong, for the first time, the court became aware of the primary reasons for his order: the condition of his men and the lack of ammunition. For some reason, the 28,440 rounds of ammunition were not brought up during the morning's questioning. Furthermore, Farnum's testimony suggested that Revere had to move his men a considerable distance to reform them because he had nowhere to organize them near the front.

Just after noon, the court called Brigadier General Joseph Carr to the stand. Carr pointed out that after General Berry "died about 7:26 a.m." on May 3, he was "notified by the chief of staff" that he was given command of the Second Division. Carr explained that he sent his assistant adjutant-general to Revere and informed him about the new command structure of the division.

At 12:40 p.m., the court took a recess, but reconvened at 1:30 p.m.

Next to testify was Lieutenant Colonel Cornelius D. Westbrook, commander of the One Hundred Twentieth New York. Like the previous witnesses who served in Sickles' Third Corps, Westbrook described the position of his regiment when Revere ordered it away from the front. Westbrook stated that when he and his men reached an area near the United States Ford, they "halted and were supplied with ammunition."

Revere's counsel asked Westbrook to assess the fitness of his regiment when it marched to the rear. "The men had some ammunition, but they needed rest and food, and the companies were much disorganized," said Westbrook, who pointed out that the 220 men he had at the first roll call of the day–actually about two-thirds of the regiment–had been reduced in a matter of hours to "a hundred to a hundred and fifty." Westbrook's remark reinforced Revere's contention that he attempted to reform the disjointed units within the Second Division.

In an effort to show the court that Revere's intention was to promptly return to the battlefield, the counsel for the accused asked Westbrook: "At the halt made by your regiment did you or did you not receive orders from General Revere to collect your stragglers, obtain ammunition, and get your command in readiness for action?"[14]

Westbrook replied that he "did receive such orders."

Major Michael W. Burns of the Seventy-third New York testified next. Burns acknowledged that he received orders from an aide to Sickles to "drive all the stragglers to the front." He also received an order from Revere to march "back through the woods" where his regiment received ammunition. "Before going into the field I left the knapsacks, the arms, tools and slings of the pioneers, and a majority of the haversacks, near the Chancellor House," added Burns. "I left nothing on the field except what was left by wounded men."[15]

After Burns was excused from the stand, the court adjourned at 2:45 p.m.

The first day of the court-martial had been a difficult one for Revere. The testimony–especially by Sickles–had been damaging, but comments made by other witnesses underscored the desperate condition Revere's men were in during the early morning hours of May 3. Revere maintained that since he believed he was the senior commander of his division–even Sickles stated that Revere believed it–he took the most appropriate action to ensure that his men could return to the battlefield rested, fed, and supplied with ammunition.

The court-martial resumed the next morning at 10:15 a.m. Judge Advocate Platt and the nine other officers were all in attendance. After the proceedings of the previous day were read and approved, Major Robert L. Bodine of the Twenty-sixth Pennsylvania was called to the stand.

Bodine recalled what happened when he met Revere on the battlefield. "General Revere rode up, asked me what regiment it was, told me that General Berry had been killed and General Mott wounded, and that he was senior officer and had command of the division; I signified my willingness to obey his orders," said Bodine. "He told me to follow him; that he was going to move the division."[16] When asked how far Revere had taken the division away from the battlefield, Bodine estimated the distance to be "a good four miles."

Bodine said that although his regimental numbers were down, he believed his men "could have given them a pretty good fight." But he added that "they were very hungry" since they hadn't eaten in nearly twenty-four hours.

Bodine also confirmed that his unit left "all their knapsacks, all their haversacks, and all their overcoats" on the battlefield. But he told the court that the order to leave the items was initially issued by General Carr and repeated by General Berry on Saturday, May 2.

Revere was more confident that he might be found not guilty of the second charge—neglect of duty, to the prejudice of good order and discipline—because Generals Carr and Berry had previously ordered the men to leave their equipment behind.

Colonel Napoleon B. McLaughlen of the First Massachusetts was called to testify and confirmed that General Carr had issued the order to leave the unit's equipment on the field. However, when McLaughlen was asked a theoretical question about the possibility of his unit's capability to recover the equipment under certain circumstances, he replied in the affirmative.

McLaughlen recalled that after his unit "ceased to engage the enemy," he noticed other portions of the Second Division emerging from the woods. "I attempted to rally, and General Carr moved us off the field."

For the moment, Revere must have been pleasantly surprised by the statement that General Carr also ordered troops off the field. McLaughlen's testimony seemed to undermine the first charge against Revere. The court was suddenly cleared. Revere may have had expectations that the proceedings were turning his way, but the court quickly reopened with McLaughlen returning to the stand. The questioning returned to the issue of the abandoned equipment. "We did recover them immediately upon retiring from the first line, and we had no difficulty in obtaining them," said McLaughlen. But under cross examination he admitted that only half his command was able to retrieve their knapsacks.[17] A newspaper later reported that the removal of equipment was widespread. "[L]eft in various places on the battlefields of Chancellorsville, overcoats, knapsacks, and blankets…were deposited, from time to time, by order of the brigade and regimental commanders, to relieve the men of their burdens while fighting. Of course the lines were constantly changing, and when the army was ordered by the general commanding to return, there was no time for the men to collect their goods, scattered over miles of ground."[18]

The court swore in Captain George Le Fort, the Fourth Excelsior Regiment's Acting Assistant Inspector-General, who confirmed the missing property listed in the second charge against Revere. When Le Fort confessed that he did not know how the property was lost, Revere's counsel asked him how he knew the equipment was missing. Le Fort replied that he "ascertained from the commandants of the companies and from personal inspection." But he added that he "had not inspected the brigade previously to the time mentioned."[19]

At 12:45 p.m., following Le Fort's testimony, the prosecution closed its case and the court took a recess. At 1:15, the court reassembled. The final afternoon hours of testimony would decide Revere's fate.

Major John P. Vinkelmeier, the Assistant Adjutant-General, Second Brigade, Second Division, Third Corps, was the next to testify.

"We stood under fire until seven a.m., and after the enemy ceased to fire we fell back, meeting on the way the troops ordered to the front; we came down to what they call White House, near General French's head-quarters. General Revere ordered me and the other staff officers to collect the fragments of the scattered regiments. After a great deal of effort, I succeeded in collecting about 600 or 800 men. General Revere reported with these men to General French, on the ground. General French ordered him to occupy the rifle-pits south of the plank-road. When marching up to the rifle-pits we found occupied by other troops already. General Revere ordered then the regimental commanders to him, and informed them that he intended to fall back in order to collect the stragglers, our men being very much exhausted, and almost without ammunition. We marched back through the woods to the first open space we could reach, where General Revere directed me to order details to pick up stragglers, and ordered the ammunition train up–in the mean time affording our men a little rest, and preparing them for marching to the front again. The detail was made by me, and the train ordered. We succeeded in collecting stragglers, and the train arrived about an hour afterwards, or so. Ammunition was distributed, when General Revere, anxious to get our troops back, ordered them to fall in, and march to the front. Our men had scarcely time to prepare what little provisions they had for eating. We came near the headquarters of General Sickles some time between two and three. When about half or three-quarters of a mile distant from those headquarters, we met Captain Chester, bringing an order from General Sickles for General Revere to return."[20]

Vinkelmeier was asked about the abandoned equipment. He noted that General Berry ordered the items set aside on Saturday. "It was impossible to recover them, the brigade being on the right, and the ground being too much occupied and intersected by other troops as well as the advancing enemy, as well as on account of the heavy cannon firing on the part of the enemy," he added.[21] Vinkelmeier remarked that he did not know where the ammunition came from, but he believed it was "from the front."

Lieutenant Charles Paul of the Fifteenth New Jersey, who served as an aide-de-camp to Revere, was the last witness called to testify. Paul reaffirmed Vinkelmeier's testimony and added that

Revere was eager to return to the front. "The general also sent to the river for provisions for the men," said Paul. "There being some delay in obtaining them, he decided not to wait, and marched his command to the front."[22]

Revere's counsel wanted Paul to remind the court that the accused did not unilaterally disengage from the fighting. "[General Berry's division] had ceased to engage the enemy," said Paul. "When reformed in [the] rear of French's division, we did not engage the enemy after we were repulsed from the woods."[23]

The court asked Paul if Revere received any orders from his superior officers during the time in question. "Not to my knowledge," replied Paul.

After Paul stepped down, the court asked Tremain if any additional witnesses needed to be called, but he declined to offer any. Surprisingly, the court did not raise the question about why Revere left the remainder of Berry's division on the field during the retreat. The court was cleared and the eight officers deliberated. After a while, Revere was called before the court shortly after 3 p.m. Revere stood silently as the verdict was read.

"Of the specification First Charge–Guilty, except 'while said division was engaged with the enemy at Chancellorsville, Virginia, did march his command an unnecessary distance to the rear to reform it, and 'then' and 'to United States Ford, about five miles from the scene of the action,' substituting for the latter clause, 'to about three miles from the scene of the action, towards the United States Ford.'

"Of the First Charge–*Not Guilty*, but *Guilty* of conduct to the prejudice and good order and military discipline.

"Of the Specification to Second Charge–Not Guilty.

"Of Second Charge–Not Guilty.

"And the court does therefore sentence him, Brigadier-General Joseph W. Revere, United States Volunteers, to be dismissed from the service of the United States.

> *W. S. Hancock,*
> *Major-General United States Volunteers,*
> *President of Court*
> *E. R. Platt, Lieutenant-Colonel and Judge Advocate*
> *Approved:*
> *Joseph Hooker, Major-General Commanding.* "[24]

The court adjourned at 3:30 p.m. The following day, the court reassembled to hear a reading of the previous day's proceedings. After the court approved the readings, it adjourned. Hooker officially approved of the proceedings and "under the Sixty-fifth Article of War, the record in the case [was] respectfully forwarded for the action of the President of the United States."

Revere was stunned at the verdict, but he remained composed. He later gave his sword to Brigadier General Birney, who provided counsel during the court-martial. On May 27, Birney wrote Revere: "I accept with great pleasure the sword."[25] Revere soon left for home, leaving behind uncollected mail in the Washington City Post Office.[26]

Although the court-martial was finished, Revere believed that the legal fight had only just concluded its initial phase; more was to be done.

NOTES

1. *New York Times*, May 10, 1863, 1. The correspondent, who wrote the article on May 8 at Falmouth, concluded his report with an abbreviated quote from William Shakespeare's *Othello*, Act II,

Scene 3: "Casio, I love you–but you're never again going to be one of my officers."

2. *Articles of War: An Act for Establishing Rules and Articles for the Government of the Armies of the United States* (1806). These articles, which also applied to the United States Navy, were in effect until 1951, when they were replaced by the Uniform Code of Military Justice.

3. Ibid., #64.

4. Joseph Warren Revere, *A Statement*, 23.

5. Ibid., 5-6

6. Article #73 included the oath: "You, swear, or affirm (as the case may be), the evidence you shall give in this cause now in hearing shall be the truth, the whole truth and nothing but the truth. So help you God."

7. Revere, *A Statement*, 26.

8. Ibid.

9. Ibid.

10. Ibid., 27.

11. Ibid.

12. Ibid.

13. Ibid., 28-29.

14. Ibid., 31.

15. Ibid., 32.

16. Ibid., 33. McLaughlen's named is spelled McLaughlin in Revere's *A Statement*.

17. Ibid., 35-36.

18. New Haven *Columbian Weekly Register*, 1.

19. Revere, *A Statement*, 36-37.

20. Ibid., 37-38.

21. Ibid., 38.

22. Ibid., 39.

23. Ibid.

24. Ibid., 40.

25. Birney to Revere, May 27, 1863. Revere Research Files.

26. Washington *Evening Star*, August 14, 1863, 1.

CHAPTER ELEVEN

THE FIGHT TO RESTORE HIS GOOD NAME

"How innocent I am of the offence."

While Revere's name was being tarnished due to the court-martial, the family's name was simultaneously elevated to popular heights due to the printing of Henry Wadsworth Longfellow's *Tales of a Wayside Inn*, a poetry collection that included "Paul Revere's Ride." The poem, which celebrated Revere's historic horseback journey of April 18, 1775, in which he warned his fellow colonists about the approach of British regulars, was first published in the January 1861 issue of

Atlantic Monthly. But the 1863 release of *Tales of a Wayside Inn* was more widespread. However, Joseph Warren Revere could not bask in his celebrated grandfather's glory.[1]

Ironically, Longfellow's grandfather, Brigadier General Peleg Wadsworth, brought charges against Paul Revere during the Revolutionary War's Penobscot Expedition in 1779. When Revere, an artillery officer, initially refused an order from Wadsworth, he was arrested and charges were brought against him. Hearings followed and Revere was asked to resign. Revere demanded a court-martial, which was granted in 1782. He was cleared of all charges.[2] Nevertheless, as historian David Hackett Fischer noted, it remained "the darkest episode in Revere's life." Revere's grandson would understand.

Colonel J. Egbert Farnum, the commander of the Seventieth New York, and other officers offered Revere support in the wake of the *New York Times*' reports about the general's actions at Chancellorsville. Writing from his headquarters at Falmouth on May 20, 1863, Farnum wrote:

"My attention having been called to certain articles in the New York City newspapers, which seem to reflect upon your courage, and which distort your actions at a certain point of the brigade's history, I beg to respectfully state, that so far as your personal courage and soldierly attributes are concerned, I have never heard officer or man question them. Of a certainty I know, that when the fire was warm, you were beside me calmly, and without any evidence of any other sentiment than that which actuated the whole command, awaiting some decisive movement. This much I know, as your next ranking officer in the field. As to the movements that were subsequently made, when the fighting was over, I do not feel called upon to express an opinion, as it has been made the business of a General Court-Martial; but for the careless and inconsiderate slanders that have been circulated, affecting you as a brave man, and an honorable soldier, I am with you responsible."

Farnum's letter was undersigned by the following Excelsior Brigade's field and staff officers:

Thomas Rafferty, Major Second Excelsior Regiment

John Leonard, Major Third Excelsior Regiment

[M.] William Burns, Major Fourth Excelsior Regiment

C. D. Westbrook, Lieutenant-Colonel One Hundred Twentieth New York Regiment

T. Evelyn Tyler, Captain Commanding Fifth Excelsior Regiment

J. P. Vinkelmeier, Major and Assistant Adjutant-General Excelsior Brigade

J. Elliott Crofts, Lieutenant and A.D.C.

Charles R. Paul, Lieutenant and A.D.C.[3]

The following month, Revere received a four-page letter from Captain William H. Chester, who assisted him in recording testimony during the court-martial. Written from "Headquarters Berry's Division" at Manassas Plains on June 17, Chester told Revere that Brigadier General Andrew A. Humphreys, a member of the court-martial, disapproved of the court's decision. "Gen. Humphreys now openly declares that your case is one of the most glaring outrages upon record in the military history of the war," wrote Chester. "[He] has openly stated that your case was settled without debate, without a dissenting voice, and you now [be] awarded 'an honorable acquittal.'"[4] An acquittal did not happen.

In July, Revere learned that his cousin, Colonel Paul Joseph Revere of the Twentieth Massachusetts, was mortally wounded at the Battle of Gettysburg. Paul died on July 4, ten months after his brother, Edward, was fatally shot at the Battle of Antietam. For a moment, perhaps, Joseph Warren Revere recalled the pleasant reunion he had with his cousins at Camp Lincoln a year earlier. Now both were dead as he awaited President Lincoln's action on the court's decision.

On August 10, 1863, Lincoln approved the sentence of the court-martial and the next day, the War Department issued General Orders No. 282, which confirmed the court-martial's sentence. On August 15, Revere was informed of the President's decision.

Still, encouraged by Chester's comments, Revere wrote to Humphreys asking for his support in an effort to overturn the court-martial's verdict. In a letter dated August 22, Humphreys bluntly informed Revere that Chester "had no grounds for writing you as he did, and that his statements are entirely unfounded." Although Humphreys acknowledged that Revere's case was discussed in his presence, he said he always "remained silent." "In no way directly or indirectly has any expression ever escaped me that gave any indication of the opinion or any act of myself or of any other member of the court or of anyone else of your case," wrote Humphreys. "I have maintained an absolute silence respecting you in connection with the charges upon which you were tried."

However, Humphreys offered a possible explanation for Chester's comments. Humphreys said that he reacted when informed that some "officer or officers" may have provided information to a New York newspaper about Revere's character. "I characterized such acts as outrageous, and probably expressed an opinion that officers guilty of them should be summarily dealt with," said Humphreys. "It occurred to me that perhaps Capt. Chester, at some subsequent time, in collecting this imperfectly may have referred my expressions to the charges against you."[5]

Humphreys realized that Revere's hopes would be dashed by his remarks, but he offered some reassuring comments. "I am not insensible, General, to the painful position in which you are placed," he wrote. "I am unable to express an opinion respecting your merits as a soldier founded upon my own experience, but I may repeat what I have heard said of you by General officers of this army of high standing, that your personal gallantry and professional acquirements were of a high order, and that added to these qualifications you had a long and varied experience in service."[6]

The *Boston Daily Advertiser* printed the results of the case on its front page on August 18 and the Trenton *State Gazette* followed on the next day. News of Revere's court-martial became more widespread when *Harper's Weekly* ran an article about it ten days later. The publication noted that Revere had "been found guilty of misbehavior before the enemy, and of conduct prejudicial to good order and military discipline [and] was sentenced to be dismissed from the military service of the United States."[7]

In September 1863, Revere attempted to gain public support by publishing his own interpretation of what happened at Chancellorsville and the subsequent court-martial. The publication, which he wrote from The Willows, was titled *A Statement of the Case of Brigadier-General Joseph W. Revere, United States Volunteers, Tried by Court-Martial, and Dismissed from the Service of the United States, August 10, 1863.* "I submit this statement in the belief that the public, more fully informed than the Court, will exonerate me from the censure cast upon me by its sentence," wrote Revere on the preface page. And he sent out as many copies as he could to those he thought would be able to help him.

Although Revere quickly created his *Statement,* he did not write it in haste. He carefully researched court-martial procedures in S. V. Benét's *A Treatise on Military Law and the Practice of Courts-Martials.*[8] Revere included five footnotes relating to Benét in *A Statement.*

Revere devoted most of the pamphlet's pages to the charges, the court-martial's proceedings, key documents, a map of the battlefield, and his defense. "If the reader will now compare the original charges with the evidence of the record, and will also compare the finding of the Court with the facts as above stated, he may see that as the charges were not supported by the case made for the prosecution, so the finding would have been justified if the matters just narrated had been offered by way of defence," stated Revere, who also questioned the operation of the court-martial. Revere believed that "a prisoner must be acquitted or convicted of every part of each of the several specifications and charges of which he stands accused."[9]

Revere explained what had happened on Sunday morning, May 3, 1863.

"It is clear then that, in a general sense, the 'scene of action' became the whole extent of this road, from Chancellorsville to the river, and that the peril and chance of conflict was no greater on our left than on our right, where the onset of Jackson might at any moment be expected. The distance from Chancellorsville to the White House is about three-quarters of a mile; from Chancellorsville to the ford is not less than four miles; and from the point to which my shattered brigade withdrew on Sunday morning, to the ford, is about three miles and a half. In the neighborhood of the White House the forest thins out to a small clearing of about ten acres; and around the brick house near the ford is a much larger open space, while between these two points the woods are dense. The open space around the White House was crowded on the morning of Sunday, after the action, with

198

troops moving in both directions, stragglers going to the rear, and artillery and infantry arriving constantly and debouching into it. It was occupied by the fresh troops of (I think) the Second Corps. Such was the crowd and want of space, that I was requested by several staff officers, one an A.D.C. of the general staff, to remove my troops in order to make room.

"Into this crowded spot, then, the only open one within some miles, we had been driven in disorder and complete disorganization after the engagement of Sunday morning, there being no second line of battle in our immediate rear, behind which we might rally."[10]

Revere detailed the seniority of the Second Division's brigade commanders and why he assumed command.

"The three brigades composing the Second Division of the Third Corps were commanded respectively by Brigadier-General Mott, in command of the Third Brigade; Brigadier-General Revere, in command of the Second; and Acting Brigadier-General Carr, in command of the First. The numbering of these brigades has no reference to the relative rank of their respective commanders. General Mott and myself were commissioned Brigadier-Generals, his commission bearing date in September, 1862, and mine in October, 1862. Brigadier-General Carr had been appointed to that rank by the President in September, 1862, but the senate had not confirmed his appointment. After the adjournment of Congress, and in March, 1863, he was reappointed by the President, and it was under that appointment only, dated in March, 1863, and giving him rank from that time, that he was an acting Brigadier-General at the battle of Chancellorsville. His original date had not been given to him. This appointment was afterwards cancelled, and a new one, antedated, given him. Some time after the return of the army, from the campaign of the early days of May, to the camp near Falmouth, he did there receive from the President an appointment, dated back to the original one of September, 1862; but he had not in May, nor has he now, a commission confirmed by the Senate. Thus neither by date of commission, nor by that of appointment, could he have outranked me. That he acquiesced, with others, in this view of his position, it is clear from the fact that at all reviews, marches, etc. of the Second Division, Third Corps, he was placed junior to both myself and General Mott; nor was either of us ever informed, by General Sickles or General Hooker, that any other claim as to rank for General Carr was made, either by them, until it was announced, just after the battle of Chancellorsville, that General Carr was in command of our division."[11]

In his *Statement,* Revere explained that once he rounded up the stragglers, rested his men, and provided them with ammunition, he initiated a return to the front.

"When within half a mile of General Sickles' bivouac, on this return march, I received orders (the first that were received by me from any one whatever during that day) by an aide from him, directing me to return, and shortly after a order to the same effect from General Carr was handed to me," remarked Revere, who added that he never sent an aide to Carr with orders for him to report back to him. "Major Burns testifies that he also met on this march an aide from General Sickles, with orders to do exactly what we were doing–bring the stragglers to the front. I reached the front at the head of about 2,000 men of the division, at half-past two in the afternoon, by my watch. I reported here to General Sickles, who relieved me of my command."[12]

Revere made a simple and effective plea before the court of public opinion. "To sum up in a few words–after the fight was ended, left without orders, and crowded off the field, I led away a handful of worn and disorganized men towards a point where, in my belief, an action might even then be going on, and brought them back within six hours, after retiring less than three miles, two thousand strong, refreshed and resupplied," he exclaimed. "Was this a breach of duty?"[13]

Revere also pointed out inconsistencies in how the court-martial arrived at its charges under the Articles of War and its subsequent verdicts.

"Accordingly, in my case, the first charge, that of misbehavior before the enemy was specifically brought under Article 52, which provides for that offence; and the second charge, that of neglect of duty, an offense not provided for in any specific article, was brought under the General Article (99)," argued Revere. "The Court acquitted me on both charges; but then proceeded to frame a new charge, to connect with it a part of the specification of the first charge under Article 52, and to pronounce a finding of 'guilty' under Article 99. This it was beyond their lawful power to do. A court-martial, after the prisoner is arraigned, cannot alter or amend the original charges, nor entertain additional ones."[14]

Revere also acknowledged the unspoken charge against him: cowardice. If he had been a coward under fire, as some claimed, why would he have assumed the larger command of a division? Wouldn't he have quickly fled the battlefield at the head of his brigade? "But cowardice, which is the essence of the charge of misbehavior before the enemy, is a crime that stands single, and admits no shades of shame," he remarked. "There is no other offence of which it is an aggravated form."[15]

Revere reminded readers of his many years of military service and his family's sacrifice. "The greater part of my life has been devoted, in the profession of arms, to the service of my country, following naturally the traditions of a family which gave one not undistinguished name to the Revolutionary War, and which has offered two other of its members to death for the State, in this one," he wrote.[16] He chronicled his years of service in Mexico, his appointment as commander of the Seventh New Jersey, his battlefield wounds, and his unblemished record–prior to the Battle of Chancellorsville. "Upon that record, and this Statement, asking only an impartial hearing, I invoke the judgment of that public opinion to which all are amenable, and which seldom fails, in the end, to do justice."[17]

Newspaper coverage continued. The articles concentrated on the charges and the verdict, but Revere fought back. He explained to the editor of the *New York Herald* that there was more to the case than the paper's brief report. "To correct the erroneous statement which has appeared in your paper of the finding of the sentence of a court martial in my case, I hereby enclose the general Order of the War Department," wrote Revere from his home on August 24, 1863. The newspaper published the detailed findings of the court, which included the "not guilty" verdicts on some of the charges.[18] Even the Southern newspapers provided press coverage. "Brigadier Gen. J. W. Revere has been dismissed from the Lincoln army for 'misbehavior before the enemy,'" reported Georgia's *Macon Telegraph*.[19]

One of the most damning newspaper reports came as a result of Philadelphia's *The Daily Age* when on October 16, 1863, it published a roster of forty Union generals who had been "killed or died from wounds in battle." At the bottom of the list were two entries: "Cashiered: Major General Fitz John Porter, Dismissed: Brigadier General J. W. Revere."[20] Revere did not respond to the newspaper.

Revere sought additional support and, fortunately, he received some. William Whiting, a solicitor of the War Department, wrote a letter on November 8, 1863, in which he promised to do "anything in my power to aid the General in getting justice done."[21] Ten days later, Washington's *The Daily Intelligencer* printed an article that was somewhat supportive of Revere. The article described the charges and listed Revere's major points that were included in his Statement. "The explanation is given with great clearness of statement, and deserves to be read and compared with the evidence by those who take an interest in our military history and in the good name of our military commanders," concluded the article.[22]

Maryland Senator Reverdy Johnson, who unsuccessfully defended Major General Fitz John Porter at his court-martial, wrote to Revere on November 19, 1863. Johnson was appalled that "such injustice could have been done a gallant officer at the expense of the best established principles of military law."[23] Johnson, who had served as President Zachary Taylor's Attorney General, would be elected to the U.S. Senate the next year and in 1865, he would defend Mary Surratt, a co-conspirator in the Lincoln assassination.

After he received a copy of Revere's *Statement*, General Philip Kearny's cousin, Edward, wrote Revere a letter on November 28, 1863. "My late cousin–General Philip Kearny–always looked on you and spoke of you as a brave and good officer, and I don't know the man who is better qualified to give an opinion." Kearny told Revere that the charges made against him "arose from jealousy" and that "an unjust verdict has been brought against you."[24]

Revere sent a copy of his *Statement* to Major General John Sedgwick. On December 16, 1863, Sedgwick wrote Revere from his headquarters near Warrenton, Virginia. "I cannot imagine how any Court Martial could have found such a verdict as they did, on evidence which would not have justified even a reprimand; and it has created great astonishment in the army here to all those to whom you were known," replied Sedgwick. "I cannot but think it will be set aside on application to the President."[25]

Revere considered various avenues of appeal, but they were impracticable since they would require support of General Sickles and Secretary of War Edwin Stanton.

But much had happened to Sickles since Chancellorsville. During the Battle of Gettysburg on July 2, 1863, Sickles was ordered by Major General George G. Meade, the new commander of the Army of the Potomac, to maintain a defensive position with his corps along a southern section of Cemetery Ridge. Sickles, however, ignored the order and instead advanced his corps nearly a mile forward into the Peach Orchard in order to secure higher ground. His move weakened Union defenses and exposed the Third Corps to Confederate fire from multiple sides–and units under Lieutenant General James Longstreet inflicted heavy casualties on Sickles' men. Sickles became one of the casualties when an artillery shell shattered the tibia and fibula of his left leg. It was later amputated.

Revere couldn't appeal to Stanton because he was a friend of Sickles; as a matter of fact, the secretary had once represented Sickles in a sensational murder case. On February 27, 1859, in Washington D.C., Sickles shot Philip Barton Key, the United States Attorney for the District of Columbia, because the son of the celebrated Francis Scott Key of "Star-Spangled Banner" fame was having an affair with his young wife. Although Key was unarmed, Stanton argued that his client was innocent because of temporary insanity. It was the first time that the temporary insanity defense was used successfully.

Revere had to bypass Sickles and Stanton and approach President Lincoln directly if he hoped to have the court-martial decision overturned and be reinstated. Revere wrote to Lincoln on February 4, 1864, and requested "to be reinstated in my rank as Brigadier General of Volunteers, in order to take part in the approaching spring operations."[26]

In the meantime, Revere submitted his resignation as a Brigadier General of Militia in New Jersey to Governor Joel Parker. But Parker, a Democrat who had once been a major general of militia in his home state, rejected Revere's offer. "I have read the proceedings of [the] court-martial and the review thereof," wrote Parker on January 18, 1864, from Trenton. "I am at a loss to perceive anything to justify the result reached in the case. I decline to accept your resignation as Brigadier General of Militia."[27]

Revere's friends, fellow soldiers, and politicians from New Jersey submitted letters and petitions to Lincoln in an attempt to persuade the president. Senator William Wright, a Democrat, and New Jersey's four Democratic congressmen—Andrew Rogers, Nehemiah Perry, George Middleton, and William G. Steele—petitioned the president on January 29, 1864: "We the subscribers…feeling that the judgment of the court martial in the case of Brig. Gen. Revere, has been rendered upon a mistaken state of facts and that the service of the government would be greatly advanced by his reinstatement into the service.…" New Jersey's other senator, John C. Ten Eyck, and Congressman John F. Starr, both Republicans, did not sign the petition.[28] However, fellow Republican Thomas D. Eliot, a member of Congress from Massachusetts, appealed to Lincoln on Revere's behalf for "clemency" in a letter dated February 1, 1864.[29]

Revere's plight reached a wider audience when *A Review of the Case of Brigadier-Gen. Joseph W. Revere, U.S. Volunteers, Tried by Court-Martial and Dismissed from the Service of the United States, August 10, 1863* was published in 1864. The pamphlet was a defense of Revere and a criticism of the court-martial. It reviewed the major elements of *A Statement* and included letters of support from Maryland Senator Reverdy Johnson and Miguel Azcarate, the former governor of the City of Mexico, who referred to Revere as a "Knight of the most illustrious Royal Order of Isabella the Catholic."[30]

But the publication was also critical of Revere's counsel: "We think it was a serious error in not making a defence before the Court, which at least could not then but have mitigated their severe sentence, or recommend the accused to the mercy of the revising power. The reason this was not done by the distinguished general (D. B. Birney) who conducted the defence, appears to have been that the charges on which the accused was tried were disproved by the evidence for the prosecution, in which the opinion of the court, by their verdict, show they fully concurred."[31]

While Revere was waging a fight to have his rank restored, a former officer in his command sought help from him to attain a rank. Lieutenant Colonel Cornelius D. Westbrook, commander of the One Hundred Twentieth New York, had received a serious hip wound at the Battle of Gettysburg. "The ball...remaining in my body, having penetrated the bone and lying within the pelvic cavity," remarked Westbrook in the March 26, 1864 correspondence. "I shall apply for entrance into the Invalid Corps and as you were my commanding officer at the battle of Chancellorsville I now request your recommendation for an appointment as Lieutenant Colonel in the Invalid Corps."[32] Westbrook also acknowledged that he read Revere's *Statement* and noted that he hoped that "at some future time [the] injustices [will] be corrected."

A. T. Goodman, an author who lived in Cleveland, Ohio, read Revere's *Statement*. "The country was greatly taken by surprise, in causing this indignation that so brave, loyal, zealous and able an officer as yourself had been even suspected as having failed to do

your whole duty–yea, all that could be expected from any man–
to your country," wrote Goodman on April 8, 1864. "I shall ever
preserve this able document, have it bound, and hand it to my
children–as a memorial received from as gallant an American
as ever fought under the American flag, for the defense of his
government."[33]

The communications in support of Revere had an effect on the
administration. The War Department offered to reinstate Revere,
but only if he resigned–and he would not be given an actual
command. Revere weighed the offer. Perhaps by waiting, Revere
would find more sympathy if George McClellan, the former
commander of the Army of the Potomac, won the presidential
election of 1864. McClellan ran as the standard bearer of the
Democratic Party with Congressman George H. Pendleton of
Ohio as his running mate.

As one Democratic newspaper reported during the campaign:
the "administration has now abandoned all the charges, the
finding and sentence of the Court Martial and acknowledges all
the proceedings to have been illegal, unjust and oppressive…but
McClellan will soon right all the wrongs amongst the gallant men
who surrounded him in the Army of the Potomac, at a time when
the nation stood in need of their service, and the administration
accepted only to betray them, to the jealousies of political generals
like the infamous Sickles."[34]

Revere, however, did not want to wait any longer to clear his
name. Even if McClellan defeated Lincoln, the new president
wouldn't be able to act on Revere's appeal until after the inauguration
in March 1865. Revere agreed to the War Department's offer and
tended his "resignation as Brigadier general of volunteers in the
service of the United States" from Morristown on September 2,
1864.[35] Eight days later, Assistant Adjutant General S. F. Chalfer

wrote Revere: "Your resignation has been accepted by the President of the United States, to take effect the 10th day of August, 1863."[36]

Two days later, Assistant Adjutant General E. D. Townsend of the War Department issued Special Order 302: "So much of General Orders, No. 282 from this office, dated Aug. 11th, 1863, as dismisses Brig.-Gen. Joseph W. Revere, U.S. Volunteers, from the service of the United States, is, by the direction of the President, hereby revoked, and his resignation is accepted, to take effect August 10th, 1863."[37] At least in part, the revocation was issued "in consideration of his otherwise excellent record."[38] However, politics played a role in Lincoln's decision. "He could not in justice have let it stand without ordering the trial of the other officers who had taken their commands to the rear without authority; and this he did on political grounds to be expedient."[39]

Since he had been reinstated, Revere qualified for a pension and began receiving $30 a month, "commencing on March 4, 1866."[40]

One of the first to congratulate Revere on his reinstatement was Lieutenant J. Elliott Crofts, who had co-signed Colonel J. Egbert Farnum's letter a year earlier in support for Revere. "Dear General," began Crofts on September 23, 1864, from his home in New York City. "Allow me to congratulate you on the success of your efforts to obtain a revocation of the most unjust sentence of the Court-Martial appointed to try your case."[41]

Francis Price, his good friend and an officer in the Seventh New Jersey, added his congratulations. "My dear General," Price wrote on September 28, 1864, from Fort Davis, Louisiana, during the Siege of Petersburg. "It gives me a great deal of pleasure to congratulate you upon your reinstatement and also to forward to you the enclosed letter of the officers of the Regiment."[42]

The *Boston Press and Post* was not satisfied with the outcome of the resignation and wanted Revere restored to active duty. "The Administration has now abandoned all charges, the finding and sentence of the Court Martial, and acknowledged all of the proceedings to have been illegal, unjust and oppressive, by their action, yet has not the magnanimity to return this officer to command because his place is needed for some political Brigadier, who endorses their policy; and only half repairs injuries that never could have been wholly repaired even by all the means in their power."[43] The newspaper associated Revere's court-martial with other Union officers who had "surrounded McClellan in the Army of the Potomac" and became victims of the "jealousies of political generals."

Brigadier General John Henry Hobart Ward, who commanded the Second Brigade in Brigadier General Birney's First Division, commiserated with Revere in a letter on October 5, 1864. Ward had been removed from command and arrested for being "grossly intoxicated" during the Battle of Spotsylvania Court House on May 12, 1864. He subsequently mustered out of service without the benefit of a legal hearing or a court-martial. "I did receive your pamphlet, and have exhibited it so often to officers and friends as illustration of the *wisdom, justice* and *impartiality* of the administration that it is full of finger marks and quite dilapidated," wrote Ward. "In reference to my case, I can only say that, so far as I can learn, I was arrested for drunkenness, although I have received no copy of any charges. I have exhausted all means in my power... to obtain a hearing."[44]

Despite his resignation and subsequent reinstatement, Revere was not satisfied. He wanted a new trial which would focus on the legality of the court-martial. He drafted a letter to President Lincoln on November 14, 1863, and then rewrote the letter the following day. "I have the honor, most respectfully to request that after a reversal of my case by your excellency, you should see proper…that a new trial may be ordered on such charges as I may be expected to answer to, and on the record of evidence for the prosecution already assembled," noted Revere. "I make this application in consequence of the principles of law that should a court martial act illegally, 'the person cannot be again be tried except on his own motion for a new trial.'"[45] At the time, Lincoln was preparing to travel to Gettysburg, Pennsylvania, where he would deliver his historic address about the famous battle. Upon his return to the White House, the president received another petition concerning Revere. Dated November 25, 1864, it included the signatures of such former Boston mayors as Josiah Quincy, Jr. and Frederick W. Lincoln, Jr.[46] Despite the numerous letters and petitions, Lincoln did not act upon Revere's request. The legal proceedings concerning the court-martial of Revere and the subsequent resignation agreement were over. Revere never commanded troops again, nor did he ever take the field of battle, but he referred to himself as "General" for the remainder of his life.

NOTES

1. In *Tales of a Wayside Inn*, Longfellow presented "Paul Revere's Ride" through the narration of a character called the Landlord. The best historical account of the legendary event is David Hackett Fischer's comprehensive *Paul Revere's Ride* (New York: Oxford University Press, 1994).

2. Charles Ferris Gettemy's *The True Story of Paul Revere* (Boston: Little Brown and Company, 1906) provides a chapter devoted to the disastrous expedition and the subsequent court-martial. According to Gettemy, six charges were filed against Revere, including one involving Wadsworth: "For Refusing Gen. Wadsworth, the Castle

Barge to fetch some men on shore [from] a Schooner, which was near the Enemy's ships on the Retreat up the River." Revere was subsequently arrested and sent to his home in Boston. After several days, the house arrest charge was dropped, but he was brought before a Committee of Inquiry. Gettemy explained that "Revere was also charged with being guilty of disobedience of orders upon several occasions, of unsoldierlike behavior in general, and in particular of having refused to assist General Wadsworth with a boat in a certain instance. To all of which he pleaded that the evidence showed him, if not innocent of every act charged, innocent at all events of guilty intent, saying: 'If to obey Orders, and to keep close to my duty is unsoldierlike, I was Guilty.'" The author added something that sounded similar to Joseph Warren Revere's predicament: "It is certain that Revere left the expedition and returned to Boston without specific orders from the commanding general to do so." The mixed results issued by the court led Revere to request a court-martial, which was granted. Delays pushed the court-martial to February 19, 1782, three months after Cornwallis surrendered to Washington at Yorktown. However, Revere was "acquitted with equal honor." In the August 26, 1976 edition of Baton Rouge, Louisiana's *Morning Advocate*, Dean Mayhew, an associate professor of history at Maine Maritime Academy, stated: "Wadsworth was clearly enraged with Revere. Had he known his own grandson would later make Revere a hero, he would have castrated himself on the spot."

3. Revere, *A Statement*, 48.

4. Chester to Revere, June 17, 1863. Revere Research Files. In the letter, Chester called Sickles "devious" and noted that he wanted "to be out of his reach."

5. Humphreys to Revere, August 22, 1863. Revere Research Files.

6. Ibid. Revere had also made an unspecified request to Assistant Adjutant General E. D. Townsend of the War Department on August 4, 1863, concerning the court-martial. Townsend replied

three days later and informed Revere "that the proceedings of the court in your case have been submitted to the proper authority, and until action is had upon them, you request cannot be granted."

7. *Harpers Weekly*, Vol. VII, No. 348, August 29, 1863, 547.

8. S. V. Benét, *A Treatise on Military and the Practice of Courts-Martials* (New York: D. Van Nostrand, 1862). Benét revised his book several times during the Civil War. A fourth edition was published in 1864 and a fifth edition was printed in 1866. Benét, an army ordnance officer and an assistant professor of ethics at the United States Military Academy, was the grandfather of Stephen Vincent Benét, the writer who won a Pulitzer Prize in 1929 for the narrative poem *John Brown's Body* (1928).

9. Revere, *A Statement*, 15-16.

10. Ibid., 11-12.

11. Ibid., 8-9.

12. Ibid., 15.

13. Ibid.

14. Ibid., 17. In his *Statement*, Revere cited several previous cases from 1843 and 1856, which he used to support his criticism of the court-martial.

15. Ibid., 18.

16. Ibid., 29. Revere is referring to the deaths of his cousins, Paul and Edward.

17. Ibid., 21.

18. *New York Herald*, September 3, 1863, 2.

19. *Macon Telegraph* (Macon, Georgia), September 23, 1863, 2.

20. *The Daily Age* (Philadelphia), October 16, 1863, 2.

21. Whiting to Thomas Lamb, November 8, 1863. Revere Research Files.

22. *Daily National Intelligencer*, November 18, 1863, 2.

23. Johnson to Revere, November 19, 1863. *A Review of the Case of Brigadier-Gen. Joseph W. Revere, U.S. Volunteers, Tried by Court-*

Martial and Dismissed from the Service of the United States, August 10, 1863 (Boston: J.H. Eastburn's Press, 1866), 6.

24. Kearny to Revere, November 28, 1863. Revere Research Files.

25. *True Democratic Banner*, September 22, 1864, 2.

26. Revere to Lincoln, February 4, 1864. The Abraham Lincoln Papers at the Library of Congress, Series 1, General Correspondence (1833-1916).

27. Parker to Revere, January 18, 1864. Revere Research Files.

28. Rogers, Perry, and Middleton to Lincoln, January 29, 164. Revere Research Files.

29. Eliot to Lincoln, February 1, 1864. Lincoln Papers at the Library of Congress.

30. *A Review of the Case of Brigadier-Gen. Joseph W. Revere.* Boston, 1864.

31. Ibid., 9.

32. Westbrook to Revere, March 20, 1864. Revere Research Files.

33. Goodman to Revere, April 8, 1864. Goodman had initially written Revere on January 11, 1864, in an effort to secure an autograph "for a volume of sketches of distinguished American Generals."

34. *True Democratic Banner*, September 22, 1864, 2. The newspaper championed the presidential campaign of candidate George B. McClellan, whom Revere admired, in a front page article titled "Who is Geo. B. McClellan?"

35. Revere Family Papers.

36. *True Democratic Banner*, September 22, 1864, 2; *Springfield Republican*, September 23, 1864, 2.

37. Ibid. Adjutant General's Office, War Department Revere, September 12, 1864, Revere Research Files.

38. Joseph G. Bilby and William C. Goble, *Remember You Are Jerseymen!: A Military History of New Jersey Troops in the Civil War* (Hightstown, New Jersey: Longstreet House, 1998), 117.

39. John Bigelow, Jr., *The Campaign of Chancellorsville: A Strategic and Tactical Study* (New Haven: Yale University Press, 1910), 355. One

thousand copies of this book were published in 1910. Princeton University's Firestone Library has an unnumbered copy in its Rare Books and Special Collections department.

40. James H. Baker, Commissioner, Department of the Interior, Pension Office, to Joseph W. Revere, October 12, 1872. Revere Research Files. Baker was a former Minnesota Secretary of State who commanded the Tenth Minnesota during the Civil War. In 1863, he became the Union Provost Marshal of St. Louis. In 1871, President Ulysses S. Grant appointed him as pension commissioner.

41. Crofts to Revere, September 23, 1864. Revere Research Files.

42. Price to Revere, September 28, 1864. Revere Research Files.

43. *Boston Press and Post*, September 29, 1864, 4.

44. Ward to Revere, October 5, 1864. Revere Research Files. Ward was seen by other officers sitting on a horse-drawn caisson and riding to the rear. Like Revere, Ward appealed to President Lincoln for "a hearing," but it was not granted. A month after his arrest, he was mustered out of the army.

45. Revere to Lincoln, November 15, 1863. Revere Family Papers. In his draft of the letter, Revere made page notation references to S. V. Benét's *A Treatise on Military Law and the Practice of Courts-Martials*.

46. Revere, et al. to Lincoln, February 4, 1864. Abraham Lincoln Papers at the Library of Congress.

CHAPTER TWELVE

FROM WHOM ALL BLESSINGS FLOW

"The President directs me to express to you his thanks for 'Keel and Saddle.'"

When Joseph Warren Revere returned home, he found sanctuary from the harsh realities of the war and the court-martial. He was pleased to be with his family and, despite lingering war wounds, content to work the fields. The mail received at The Willows varied from continuous letters of support to war-related correspondence. In September of 1864, Thomas Lamb, Rosanna's brother, wrote him about the impact of

215

the war on food and livestock prices. "The weather is very fine and I suppose you are busy gathering your harvest, which will be abundant for the price of all consumables is enormous."[1]

While Revere was tending to his crops in the autumn of 1864, Lincoln won re-election over Democratic candidate George B. McClellan and at the same time, his original unit, the Seventh New Jersey, was involved in the Siege of Petersburg. As the Union stranglehold tightened on Petersburg, the regiment directly engaged Confederate forces in Virginia at Jerusalem Plank Road and Deep Bottom, among other battle locations. It would take until early April of 1865 for Petersburg to finally fall, but when it did, the Confederates quickly abandoned Richmond. General Lee surrendered his army to General Grant on April 9 at Appomattox Court House in Virginia. Although some additional rebel forces were still in the field, the War Between the States had essentially ended and the era of Reconstruction had begun. However, an assassin's bullet prevented President Lincoln from leading the war-weary nation through its time of rebuilding and healing.

As a wounded veteran, Revere filed for a pension and received notice from Joseph Barret, the Commissioner of Pensions, on May 30, 1865, that his application had been approved. Revere was granted $20 a month.[2]

His wound from Manassas made it difficult for him to walk after an extended period of time and he was examined by Dr. Lewis Fisher, a surgeon, on August 3, 1866. The doctor stated that Revere was "totally incapacitated for obtaining his subsistence by manual labour." Fisher added that the wound he received at the Second Battle of Manassas "prevents [the] use of his right leg to any considerable extent, limb giving way if much used."[3] His pension amount was subsequently raised to $30.[4]

In early 1867, Revere was pleased to find out, albeit belatedly, that Jacob Zeilin, the U.S. Marine he had met in California during the Mexican War, had been appointed Colonel Commandant of the Marine Corps. Revere promptly sent him some gifts: a brigadier general's sash and sword belt. "I have been the recipient of many tokens of appreciation from my friends, but nothing has given me so much pleasure than the handsome manner in which you have paid your tribute to an old friend," wrote Zeilin, who added that he questioned how the court-martial "could make such a finding on the evidence placed before it."[5] Perhaps Revere's gift-giving gesture was based upon an astrological forecast he had conducted, because seven years later, Zeilin was promoted to brigadier general.

On October 12, 1868, Revere's namesake uncle died at age 91. The *Boston Journal* announced the elder Joseph Warren Revere as "the last of the children of Paul Revere." Revere's uncle and his legendary grandfather had founded the Revere Copper Company, a highly successful business enterprise in Canton, Massachusetts.

Whenever Rosanna felt that someone she knew was unaware of her husband's *Statement*, she sent them a copy. She was not content to allow the newspapers to shape public opinion about her husband even though the court-martial decision had been revoked several years earlier and her husband's rank had been "restored." Rosanna mailed a copy of *A Statement* to a Mrs. Austin, a friend in Boston, in early December 1868. She received a reply, dated December 11, in which the writer thanked her. "I am very glad to have seen an authentic statement of this affair–for I know nothing of the matter before except the statements in the newspapers," wrote Austin, who concluded that court's decision was "illegal and outrageous and the sentence unjust and abominable."[6]

On January 14, 1870, Revere wrote to New Jersey Governor Theodore Fitz Randolph, a fellow Democrat, for a position on the state's pilot commission. "I have served for more than twenty years in the U.S. Navy–viz.–from 1828 to 1850, when I resigned my commission as lieutenant," wrote Revere.[7] But he did not secure the position.

Revere enjoyed family gatherings, especially on such patriotic holidays as the Fourth of July. On one occasion, he had a large American flag hang from the second floor porch as a patriotic backdrop for a photograph of his family and other guests. Like the times many years earlier when he overheard sailors' stories, perhaps Revere shared his Gothic adventures with those guests willing to listen. Certainly, he had tales to tell–but some would remain untold.

The Revere Family and guests at The Willows, c. 1870.
From the Collection of the Morris County Park Commission.

The 1870 census acknowledged Revere as a farmer, although he almost became a New Jersey Pilot Commissioner. He heralded his many years of service in the navy in his application, but his offer to serve was rejected. The fifty-eight-year-old veteran of the Mexican and Civil Wars, the naval officer who had circumnavigated the globe, the man who earned medals from foreign nations, the author, the daring entrepreneur who had once driven herds of cattle during the Gold Rush was now content to supervise the handful of workers who toiled in his fields of wheat, corn, potatoes, and grapes. According to the 1870 census, Revere's property of "77 improved acres and 10 acres of woodlot" included four horses, seven cows, and three pigs. His land generated 711 bushels of wheat, 350 bushels of corn, 200 bushels of oats, 150 bushels of Irish Potatoes, 400 pounds of butter, and 20 loads of hay.[8]

On July 4, 1871, a Civil War memorial monument was dedicated on the Morristown Green. A huge crowd viewed a "procession, numbering probably 1,000 persons" and heard speeches by various dignitaries, including Morris County freeholder E. E. Lewis and New Jersey Governor Randolph, who in his speech praised the late Major General Phil Kearny and the "brave and gallant townsman, [Major General] Fitz-John Porter."[10] However, Randolph never mentioned Revere in his remarks, which was somewhat surprising. Revere's dismissal from the service had been revoked eight years earlier, while Porter was still in the process of fighting to have his dismissal overturned. Yet, in Randolph's eyes, Porter was seemingly Morristown's only "gallant townsman." Perhaps Randolph's decision not to mention Revere was based upon something related to the state pilot's commission which Revere had unsuccessfully applied for a year earlier. For Revere, though, Randolph's selective ceremonial comments were awkward and unfortunate, to say the least.

Age and health problems made farming more difficult for Revere. In November of 1871, he offered his Concord grape acreage for sale and later leased all of his farmland.[9] Still, he remained active in community affairs, including new projects. He became a patron of the new "Select Classical School for Boys," which had opened in Morristown a few months earlier.[11]

In 1872, Revere and his family moved to Morristown's historic Sansay House, a place where the celebrated Marquis de Lafayette had visited in the summer of 1825 during his celebratory tour of the United States.[12] That same year, Revere's only surviving male sibling, Frederick Ballestier Revere, died on October 6 in Tours, France.

Revere's pension certificate had "been worn out." He "applied for and received a new one dated Department of the Interior, October 12, 1872, 'disability total.'"[13] Despite his physical condition, he managed to travel to New York City, where he visited friends.

While residing at the Sansay House, Revere finished his second book, *Keel and Saddle: A Retrospect of Forty Years of Military and Naval Service*. He dedicated the book to his cousins, Paul and Edward–"both dying on the field of honor in the moment of victory."

Revere was selective in his writings. He did not mention the infamous court of inquiry or the disgraceful Court-Martial and he failed to provide details about other times in his life; as a matter of fact, the book appeared to have been written by a cavalier bachelor. There are no important references about his wife or children, no mention of letters from his family, no phrases which suggest a longing for home. Furthermore, *Keel and Saddle* was an uneven volume. He frequently punctuated his thirty-five chapters with awkward stories of others: a Pole who had escaped from Russia, the Portuguese Count of Miranda, Spanish Mexico's Don Alvaro Lopez, and more. Revere's Boston-based publisher, James R. Osgood and Company, added an eighty-page section of non-related material titled "Puffs From Picket-Pipes" and printed it in 1872.[14]

The press heralded his autobiography with appropriate fanfare. "[Revere], an army officer of considerable distinction, and an inheritor of a historical name, sits down in his old age to tell the story of his life," reported the *San Francisco Bulletin*.[15] *The North American Review* proclaimed that the book "has not a dull page in the whole account of the writer's adventures."[16] New Haven, Connecticut's *Weekly Register* printed an excerpt from the book titled, "The Death of Stonewall Jackson–A Strange Story of 1852 and 1863."[17] Confederate general Jubal Early was one of the first to criticize "Revere's chimerical nonsense" about the alleged Jackson encounters in an 1873 issue of *Southern Magazine*.[18]

No matter, though. Revere was proud of *Keel and Saddle*. He sent a copy to President Ulysses S. Grant, who replied with a thank you letter written by Orville E. Babcock, the chief executive's personal secretary. "The President directs me to acknowledge the receipt of and to express to you his thanks for the copy of 'Keel and Saddle,' you were kind enough to send him."[19] Another copy of the book was sent by Josiah C. Hammond, a Revere family friend, to George Brigham Revere, the author's first cousin.[20]

Revere leased The Willows to a few tenants over the next several years. "Its most noted tenant, however, was Bret Harte, who, with his family, lived there sometime around 1874, and gathered material for his novel *Thankful Blossom* while in the area."[21]

At the age of sixty-three, Revere took one more adventurous journey. Despite his walking difficulty, he sailed for France in the spring of 1875, where he sojourned to Vienne, a city on the Rhone

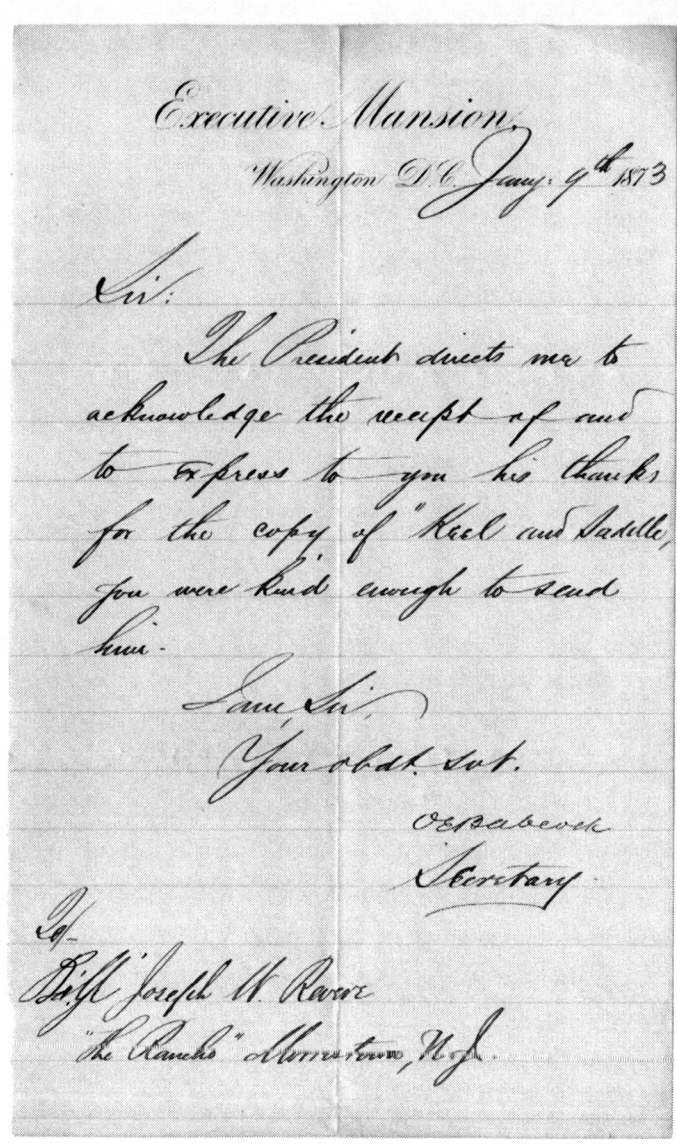

President Ulysses S. Grant's thank you note
to Revere for 'Keel and Saddle.'
From the Collection of the Morris County Park Commission.

in the southeastern part of the country. Revere composed a small travel diary which seemed similar to the detailed cultural and geographic notes that appeared in *Keel and Saddle*. "I arrived at the small city of Vienne," wrote Revere on the first page of the text, which suggested that Rosanna did not accompany him.[22] Once again, she remained home without her husband.

In the diary, Revere commented on Vienne as the one-time "cradle of western Christianity," the place where Hannibal conducted part of his "victorious march" in 218 B.C., and where the De Rivoire Family lived–"from which the American Reveres are descended."[23] Revere also researched the evolution of the Revere family crest, which featured three fleur-de-lis in an angled line (from upper left to lower right) backed by three stripes. He must have been somewhat surprised to learn that he depicted the crest in The Willows' large dining room mural incorrectly with a reversed line of fleur-de-lis.

In 1876, during the nation's centennial, *Records of Officers and Men of New Jersey in the Civil War, 1861-1865*, was published. In it, William S. Stryker, New Jersey's Adjutant General, wrote: "The reputation of New Jersey troops was fully sustained during the entire war, being represented on all the principal battlefields."[24] Since the publication concentrated on statistical data rather than subjective commentary, Revere was more than happy to merely be mentioned as receiving his promotion to brigadier general, but other publications which included more uncomfortable entries would be forthcoming.

Another business venture soon manifested itself. On December 31, 1877, Revere granted Dr. Thomas Flagler, the family physician, permission to search and mine for iron ore in the fields located a few hundred feet behind The Willows. Revere agreed to supply the necessary timber and Flagler agreed to "fill up and level off said shafts and excavations and leave said land horizontally in its present natural conditions as near as may be reasonably possible."[25]

Revere didn't consider his contractual arrangement particularly risky since Morris County was known for its rich iron deposits. George Washington's Continental Army had relied on the county's ore during the Revolutionary War and in the early nineteenth century, iron production was booming in such appropriately named places as Mine Hill and Ironia. In Morristown, not far from The Willows, the Speedwell Iron Works was one of the county's most successful enterprises. By 1880, Morris was the nation's third-ranked county in the amount of iron ore mined, with 568,420 tons.[26]

According to the contract, Revere was to receive "50 cents per ton for all ore mined and taken away from said premises." Flagler's Morristown Mining Company began digging on January 2, 1878, and the workers reached a vein of iron ore only ten feet below the surface. On January 11, *The Jerseyman* reported: "Within six days thirty tons of excellent ore was taken out without the trouble of blasting, and the vein is growing wider as the work progresses."[27] A month later, the newspaper stated: "They are raising about 20 tons of ore a day, and have 600 to 800 tons raised."[28]

Although the Morristown Mining Company continued work in the fields, Revere signed a one-year lease with Charles Grant Foster, who agreed to pay $600 for The Willows and the farmland on March 28, 1878. Like Revere, Foster had served in the Civil War. He joined the Twenty-second Connecticut Volunteer Infantry in 1862 at the age of nineteen and rose to the rank of lieutenant.[29] Despite the nearby mining activities which carried into the early 1880s, Foster enjoyed The Willows so much that he twice renewed his lease.[30]

Revere was given a membership in the Associated Pioneers of the Territorial Days of California, a New York-based organization founded on February 11, 1875, which recognized those Americans who had arrived in California prior to 1850. Revere was granted membership number eighty on January 20, 1878.[31] His association with the organization no doubt brought back fond memories of the pleasant and adventurous times he had experienced thirty years earlier on the West Coast. But one California event, Revere's encounter with the naval court of inquiry, was a matter better forgotten.

In the years following the Civil War, Revere would receive letters from men who had served under his command. Some were congratulatory; others made requests for letters of recommendation, especially concerning pensions. But one was particularly melancholy. Ellen Lammond, who had married Captain Daniel Hart of the Seventh New Jersey in a joyous outdoor ceremony in camp on March 12, 1863, wrote Revere on November 12, 1878. "I had the misfortune to lose my husband, past April [11], while serving with his regt. (25 U.S. Infantry) at Fort Stockton, Texas," she wrote. "He was compelled to use all his pay to support his family and help keep clear of debt, which I am proud to say he did." But with her husband's death, Hart's widow had no source of income. She informed Revere that she was seeking a "position under the government," but had no political connections to secure the unidentified job. She asked Revere to contact his "neighbor and friend," Senator Theodore Fitz Randolph, the former New Jersey governor, on her behalf.[32] However, there is no document which states that Revere was able to assist Hart's widow.

By 1880, Morris County's population topped 50,000. Morristown, the small colonial hamlet which served as George Washington's headquarters during the Revolutionary War, had become a vibrant community and a place where the wealthy of the Gilded Age spent their leisure.

Revere had come to possess a number of items that had belonged to his famous grandfather and he donated them to the Ford Mansion, the site of Washington's Headquarters. Munsell's *History of Morris County* noted: "On the walls are revolutionary portraits and engravings, among others a portrait of Paul Revere, and with it his commission in the British army, the property of General Joseph W. Revere of Morristown."[33]

Revere, however, could not fully enjoy his leisure hours; his war wound made walking more difficult and he became weaker. His heart, which may have been affected by rheumatic fever, no longer served him well. Revere's neuralgia became more severe and he suffered from periodic bouts of pain. But he carried on.

On April 14, 1880, Revere was bound for Manhattan to visit some friends. He boarded the Morris and Essex Railroad in Morristown and traveled to Hoboken. At the Hoboken Terminal, he boarded the steam ferry, which took him to the Barclay Street pier in Manhattan where his friends awaited. But as the ferry crossed the Hudson River, he became severely ill. Revere was brought back to Hoboken, where he was placed in Burch's Hotel. He remained at the hotel for several days, but did not improve. On April 19, one day after the one hundred and fifth anniversary of his grandfather's legendary ride, Revere's condition worsened and he died the following morning at 2:30 a.m.[34] Dr. Flagler performed the autopsy and described the "official causes of death: heart disease, rheumatism, and neuralgia."[35]

On April 23, *The Jerseyman* printed his obituary. It included a biographical excerpt from the *New York Herald*, which stated that the general's life was "full of adventure." The ninety-eight line, single-column obituary concentrated on his years of military service and included thirty-one lines devoted to his actions at the Battle of Chancellorsville, his court-martial, and the subsequent efforts to clear his name.[36]

At the funeral, Dr. Flagler served as one of Revere's pallbearers. The others were General Fitz John Porter, who had also suffered the disgrace of a court-martial during the war; Richard Clarke; Alfred Mills; Gustavis Tuckerman; Judge VanCleve Dalrymple; Statts S. Morris; and Henry William Miller, a retired U.S. Navy officer who later became the mayor of Morristown.[37]

According to his written wishes, Revere's body was "dressed in the uniform of [the] rank to which [he was] legally entitled–that of a brigadier general of the U.S. Army–in [placed] in a plain casket or coffin...."[38] Revere had also provided instructions about the style and size of his headstone and the inscriptions–"to be in plain Roman characters"–that would grace it.[39] He was buried in Morris Township's Holy Rood Cemetery, which is owned and maintained by the Church of the Assumption of the Blessed Virgin Mary. Later, another simple gravestone with his name, "Brig. Gen. U.S. Army Civil War," and his birth and death dates was placed at Revere's burial site.

NOTES

1. "Joseph Warren Revere, Farmer" in Revere Research Files.
2. Barrett to Revere, May 30, 1865. Revere Family Papers. Revere had to take an oath following his pension approval. On September 14, 1865, before Alexander Dickinson, a Morris County Justice of the Peace, Revere swore: "I Brigadier General and Colonel Joseph W. Revere, a pensioner of the United States, do solemnly swear that I will support, protect and defend the Constitution of the United States against all enemies whether domestic or foreign and that

I will bear true faith and allegiance and loyalty to the same, any ordinance, resolution or law of any State, Convention or Legislature to the contrary notwithstanding, and further that I do this with a full determination, pledge and purpose, without any mental reservation or evasion whatsoever, and further, that I will well and faithfully perform all the duties which may be required by law. So help me God."

3. Examining Surgeon Certificate, August 3, 1866. Revere Research Files.

4. Certificate of W. T. Otto, Acting Secretary of the Interior, August 15, 1866. Revere Research Files.

5. Zeilin to Revere, March 18, 1867. Revere Research Files.

6. Austin to Rosanna Revere, December 11, 1868. Revere Research Files.

7. Revere to Randolph, January 14, 1870. Revere Family Files.

8. 1870 Census Report in "Biographical History" in Revere Research Files. Besides farming, Revere offered a prized horse named Jupiter for stud in an advertisement which appeared in the April 18, 1868 edition of *The Jerseyman*.

9. *The Jerseyman*, Nov. 1, 1871. A typed composite of the publication's ad can be found in the Revere Research Files. According to "Joseph Warren Revere, Farmer," a typed document in the Revere Research Files: "A calculation for the area needed for Revere's 500 plants is a little less than 20 acres, less if some were planted along a stone wall. They would have produced, minimally, an annual harvest of some 40 tons of grapes."

10. Ibid., July 8, 1871, in Mitros, *Gone to Wear the Victor's Crown*, 185-190.

11. New York *Evening Post*, August 28, 1871, 3. The school opened on September 6, 1871.

12. W. Jay Mills, *Historic Houses of New Jersey* (J.P. Lippincott Company, Philadelphia, 1902), 225-226. The house was built on De Hart Street

by Monsieur Louis Sansay, a French dancing master, in 1807. On July 14, 1825, Sansay hosted a banquet for the Marquis de Lafayette at the house. Sansay's dance studio supposedly went out of business after Rev. Albert Barnes of Morristown's Presbyterian Church on the Green condemned dancing as sinful behavior. According to Mills, Sansay's home "was purchased by Jacob King, a member of the well-known King family...and afterwards was sold to General Joseph Revere."

13. Copy of Oath, Revere Family Files.

14. *Keel and Saddle* carried an 1873 date on its title page, but on the following page the publisher stated: "Entered according to Act of Congress, in the 1872." Reviews and excerpts appeared in various newspapers in the late autumn of 1872.

15. *San Francisco Bulletin*, December 14, 1872.

16. *The North American Review*, Vol. 116, Issue 238, January 1873, 184. The periodical was critical, however, with the book's non-related stories: "Of less interest are the four stories added at the end of the volume, which smack of the magazine."

17. *Weekly Register* (New Haven, Connecticut), November 23, 1872, 2. The San Francisco *Elevator's* March 1, 1873 version began by stating that Revere met Jackson in New Orleans in 1862–a typographical error that set the meeting during the Civil War.

18. Gary W. Gallagher, ed., *Chancellorsville: The Battle and its Aftermath* (Chapel Hill, North Carolina: University of North Carolina Press, 1996), 126. Early's comments were reprinted in the *Southern Historical Society Papers* in 1878. See Sears, *Chancellorsville*, 563. Gallagher calls Revere's story "the most ludicrous" of all which were offered following Jackson's death. Gallagher described Jackson as a "major" in *Keel and Saddle*; Revere identified him as a lieutenant in the text.

19. O. E. Babcock to Revere, January 9, 1873; Revere Research Files. The letter was addressed to "The Rancho" in Morristown, New

Jersey. Based upon the date of Babcock's letter, *Keel and Saddle* was indeed printed in 1872.

20. George Brigham Revere (1823-1882) was the son of Joseph Warren Revere (1777-1868). The inscription in the book reads: "Geo. B. Revere from Josiah C. Hammond, May 7, 1873." William R. Chemerka Collection.

21. "Biographical History," Revere Research Files. This incomplete seven-page document notes that in a letter from Mrs. Frances Bret Harte to Julia Keese Colles in 1890, "the story of 'Thankful Blossom' although inspired and suggested by my residence at Morristown at different periods was not written at that place." As a young man, Harte moved to California in 1853. *Thankful Blossom: A Romance of the Jerseys, 1779* was a four-part serialization that was published in the New York *Sun* in December 1876.

22. *Joseph Warren Revere journal the Rivoire family*, 1875, Revere Family Papers, microfilm edition, 15 reels (Boston: Massachusetts Historical Society, 1979), reel 4. The account was recopied by hand in 1884 by John Revere, Joseph Warren Revere's cousin, and is also part of the Revere Family Papers.

23. Ibid. According to *The New England Historical and Genealogical Register* (October 1991): "The Rivoire family originated in the area of Sainte-Foy-la Grande (Gironde), formerly Sainte-Foy-en-Agenias, on the Dordogne River sixty kilometers east of Bordeaux and twenty kilometers west of Bergerec."

24. *Records of Officers and Men of New Jersey in the Civil War, 1861-1865,* Vol. I (Trenton, New Jersey, John L. Murphy, Steam Books and Job Printer, 1876), 8. The publication identifies a Private Joseph Revere–no relation to Joseph Warren Revere–of the Thirty-fourth New Jersey's Company C, who joined the regiment on March 31, 1865, and deserted on August 2, 1865, while stationed in Alabama.

25. "Iron Mining at Fosterfields." Revere Research Files.

26. http://www.co.morris.nj.us/history/history.asp

27. *The Jerseyman*, January 11, 1878.

28. *The Jerseyman*, February 22, 1878. According to an "Iron Mining at Fosterfields" note, Revere was earning approximately $200 a month.

29. Mary De Rose, "Joseph Warren Revere: His Civil War Years," The Farm & Mill Gazette, Vol. 9, No. 4 (Morristown, NJ: Friends of Fosterfields, Fall 1994), 1.

30. "Biographical History," 10. Foster's 1879 lease was for $650; the 1880 lease was for $850.

31. Revere's membership certificate was sold at auction in 2009.

32. Hart to Revere, November 12, 1878. Revere Family Papers. The Harts had one child–a son, Harry–who born at Fort Stockton in 1876. Hart's death in 1878 was due to complications associated with malaria. Ellen Lammond Hart died on September 4, 1894.

33. *History of Morris County, New Jersey, with Illustrations and Biographical Sketches of Prominent Citizens and Pioneers* (New York: W. W. Munsell & Co., 1882), 167. Paul Revere had served as a second lieutenant of artillery in the provincial forces of the British Army during the French and Indian War. In 1933, Washington's Headquarters became part of Morristown National Historical Park, the nation's first historical park. The park includes the Ford Mansion (Washington's Headquarters), Fort Nonsense, the Jockey Hollow Encampment Area, the Wick House: St. Clair's Headquarters, and other military unit encampment sites. The Washington Headquarters Museum is located near the Ford Mansion. A recent search for the commission document at the museum proved unsuccessful. According to a staff member of the National Park Service, no record of the document exists.

34. *Cincinnati Daily Gazette*, April 23, 1880, 5.

35. Joseph Warren Revere obituary, Revere Research Files.

36. *The Jerseyman*, April 23, 1880, 2.

37. Ibid.; Langstaff, *New Jersey Generations*, 81. Miller was also a member of the Washington Association. He purchased stock (ownership

certificate #53) in the organization sometime between 1874 and
1883.

38. Joseph Warren Revere Codicil, June 20, 1866, 6. Revere Research
Files.

39. Ibid. Revere provided additional instructions about his grave marker
in the codicil. He even drew the family crest in the document,
but he drew the fleur-de-lis line incorrectly. Fortunately, though,
the fleur-de-lis line on the family crest was depicted correctly on
his headstone. However, the other small grave marker incorrectly
identified his birth date as May 18, 1812.

CHAPTER THIRTEEN

LEGACY

**"Besides being a good disciplinarian,
[he] was not much of a soldier."**

Rosanna was alone. Although Paul and Augustus were with her, her husband of nearly thirty-eight years was gone. Yet there was something about her loneliness that she found familiar since for most of her married life her husband had not been home. She recalled his many years in the navy, his time in California, and his service in the Civil War. In fact, it was only since he returned from the great rebellion that he had remained at The Willows for an extended period of time.

Joseph Warren Revere was dead, but his legacy remained–and it would be shaped by Civil War veterans who wrote memoirs and penned regimental histories and newspapers which published anniversary articles about key battles and events. Although not a major battlefield commander, Revere was destined to appear in some of the assorted publications and, as expected, the comments weren't particularly complimentary.

Ezra Carman, who had served as Revere's second-in-command in the Seventh New Jersey, wrote *Seventh New Jersey Infantry to Battle of Williamsburg*, a personal account of his Civil War experiences. Although the volume included some diary passages that he had written during the war, it was mostly a reflective work which included maps and images of soldiers and political figures. Of Revere, Carman said: "He was a fine scholar, a gentleman of wealth, but besides being a good disciplinarian, was not much of a soldier."[1] In 1881, Theodore A. Dodge wrote in *The Campaign of Chancellorsville:* "Revere certainly gives no satisfactory explanation of his conduct" at the battle.[2] The Comte De Paris, the grandson of French King Louis Philippe I (1830-1848) who served in the Union Army, wrote a multi-volume history of the war in which he described the aftermath of Revere's battlefield actions as "evil consequences."[3] Revere's sons would work diligently to repair their father's reputation as a soldier.

A year after Revere's death, Rosanna sold The Willows, the farmland, and all the other buildings and property to Charles Foster, a New York commodities broker who had leased the property since 1878. A seven-page inventory and appraisal of Revere's property was conducted by James P. Sullivan and Theodore Ayers, Jr.[4] The most expensive single piece of personal property was a "gold watch and chain" ($200). But the inventory included such diverse items as a "deer head" ($5), two "bronze dogs" ($5), a "billiard table" ($5), a "bust of 'Henry 4th'" ($1), and two "pair of Chinese shoes" (.50). Revere's library of 400 books was appraised at $200 and his precious medals were valued at $50. Foster purchased $1,500 worth of the inventoried items, primarily furniture and farm equipment.

Rosanna Revere returned to The Willows and it wasn't a social call. "When Pa bought the house he bought everything in it, furniture and everything," recalled Caroline Foster, the daughter of Charles Foster. "Then Mrs. Revere would come up and say, 'Oh, that chair belonged to Joe and couldn't I have it back?' And by the time she got through she had gotten everything out of it but two bureaus upstairs and the dining room furniture."[5] However, Revere's widow did return "often to look over the house again."[6] Revere's land became Fosterfields, but the name of his Gothic Revival home remained unchanged.

A survey of San Geronimo that was originally conducted by R. C. Matthewson in 1858 in order to confirm its boundaries was filed with the secretary of the interior to help settle any potential claims against the property.[7]

As a widow of a pensioner, Rosanna was entitled to a pension. The Pension Act of July 14, 1862, granted pensions to "widows of officers, soldiers, or seamen dying of wounds received or of disease contracted in the military or naval service."[8] After securing a copy of her marriage certificate from the Boston City Registrar on March 7, 1881, she made her claim to the Pension Office at the Department of the Interior, but was rejected. In a letter dated February 28, 1882, William Wade Dudley, the Commissioner of Pensions, noted: "You are informed that your claim… as a widow of Joseph W. Revere, late colonel of the 7th N.J. Vols was rejected Feb. 23, 1882, for the reason that the immediate cause of the officer's death (heart disease, rheumatism, and neuralgia) is not shown to have been the result of any injury received or disease contracted while in the service of the United States and line of duty."[9]

Rosanna refused to accept the rejection and quickly solicited assistance to secure her pension claim. In 1887, Francis Price came to her rescue when he completed a four-page document which chronicled her husband's struggle with rheumatism, a developing condition that he first acquired in the autumn of 1861 during the cold and rainy march from Washington D.C. to Chaptico, Maryland.[10]

The Washington bureaucracy moved slowly and cautiously. A letter from the Pension Office on April 19, 1887, requested that she provide proof if she had "remarried since 1880."[11] However, it cannot be confirmed whether Rosanna received a full pension.

Joseph Warren Revere's only surviving sibling, his unmarried sister Helena Louisa Revere, died on August 15, 1885. She was seventy-six years old.

Rosanna, always cognizant of the Revere family legacy, hosted a meeting at her home on April 15, 1891.[12] The group of "representative women of the founders of New Jersey" helped establish the New Jersey chapter of the Daughters of the American Revolution (DAR), the national volunteer organization which had been founded only a year earlier. Rosanna was appointed Honorary Regent of the state DAR. In November 1895, Rosanna invited a dozen local women to her home, where they formed a local DAR chapter. Rosanna was elected First Regent in what was to become the Morristown chapter of the Daughters of the American Revolution.[13]

Paul Revere promoted the positive aspects of his father's legacy whenever he could. Revere was invited to a reunion of the Seventh New Jersey, where he praised the regiment. One newspaper reported that "Paul Revere, son of Gen. Revere, the first colonel of the 7th, responded to call and made a most excellent speech, among other things referring to the torn and stained battle flags as the silent evidence of the trying and glorious scenes passed through by their defenders."[14] There was no mention in the newspaper of his father's actions at Chancellorsville or the subsequent court-martial.

Paul Revere was upset when he read General Francis Amasa Walker's *History of the Second Army Corps in the Army of the Potomac*, which was published in 1886. Walker, the President of the Massachusetts Institute of Technology and a former brevetted brigadier general, was simple and direct in his description of Revere at Chancellorsville. "General Joseph Warren Revere, of New Jersey, assumes command of the division and orders a retreat," wrote Walker, who added a short footnote to this "fatal error" on page 243: "For this act General Revere was tried and dismissed [from] service."[15]

Although Walker was correct, Paul wrote to him on February 14, 1887, and pointed out the "unintentional injustice" done to his father in the book. He also sent a copy of his father's *Statement* in the mailing. "Clearly then it is not in accordance with the facts to charge General Revere with assuming command of Berry's division and ordering its retreat in face of the enemy with the result of a break in the federal lines and the loss of the plateau at Chancellorsville," wrote Revere's son. He added that the "patent illegality of the findings and the injustice of the sentence have been condemned by the best military and legal authorities of the country" and urged Walker to make the necessary correction in the next edition of his work.[16] Walker, however, did not publish a second edition.

Revere's son kept a watchful eye for other books that might include a description of his father's actions at the Battle of Chancellorsville. On June 27, 1887, Paul Revere wrote to the Adjutant General's Office and asked that the entry for his father in the massive *War of the Rebellion* volumes include testimony from others which countered the findings of the court-martial. However, he was rebuked by Brigadier General Richard C. Drum, the adjutant general, in a terse letter dated July 18, 1877. "I am directed by the Secretary of War to inform you that, as the present series of the War records embraces only the formal official reports, Union and Confederate, of seizures of United States property in the Southern States, and of all military operations in the field, with the correspondence, orders and returns relating specially thereto, it seems plain that neither the statement, or review, or supplement to the Statement of the accusal, can have any place in the present volumes," wrote Drum. "They were all written by gentlemen who at the time were under no official responsibility, and in no sense are the statements and other papers official." Drum provided the volume's reference to Revere in the letter: "Brigadier General Revere was convicted by Court-martial, and dismissed, for marching his command, without orders from his superior officer, to about three miles from the scene of action and towards the United States Ford; but by direction of the President this dismissal was revoked, and General Revere's resignation was accepted. (G.O., No. 282, A.G.O., 1863, and S.O., No. 302, A.G.O. 1864)"[17]

The Seventh New Jersey held a reunion in Morristown on September 19, 1887. The *Trenton Evening Times* noted that "Gen. J. W. Revere, the first Colonel of the Seventh, was from Morristown, and his son is now a resident and a prominent citizen of that place." The newspaper added that Gen. Sickles was "expected to be present."[18] A Sickles appearance at a Revere-related event could have been problematic, but no controversy was reported at the reunion.

A claim for naval "mileage" was sent to the U.S. Senate's Appropriations Committee in the name of "J. W. Revere" and approved on July 7, 1898.[19] This claim may have been filed by his sons.

In 1899, Revere was treated very kindly in the *Biographical and Genealogy History of Morris County New Jersey*. His entry stated that at Chancellorsville, he was "censured by General Sickles and was for a time deprived of his rank, but the opinion of the men he had commanded, and that of Generals Meade and Sedgwick and other high officers, held him innocent of any offense. President Lincoln declared that he had been unjustly treated, restored him to his rank and he was subsequently named brevet major-general."[20] The volume also stated that General Hooker regarded Revere as "the best disciplinarian in the service."

Joseph Warren Revere's name was brought up on the floor of Congress in 1893 when John York, seventy-three years old, an original member of the "Bear Flag" party who remained in service under Lieut. Revere until October 5, 1846, sought a pension.[21] Although York received an honorable discharge for his service, his name was not listed on any muster role and, as a result, was refused a pension "under the act of January 29, 1887." Missouri Congressman Robert Patterson Clark Wilson, who served on the House of Representatives' Committee on Pensions, championed York's effort. "Several persons testified that they served with York at Sonoma under Revere for several months," stated Wilson.[22]

Unlike his father, Paul Revere never married. He resided with his mother and brother, Augustus. After earning a law degree at Harvard, Paul Revere worked as a lawyer in the early 1880s and later served on the boards of several banks and real estate firms. He was elected as a Democrat to two terms—1883-1885 and 1888-1890—on the Morristown Town Council and later served as president of the Morristown Democratic Club. Revere was a member of the Aztec Club, the Sons of the American Revolution, and the Washington Association.[23] He was also a co-founder of Morristown's All Souls Hospital.

Paul Revere died at age forty-five on November 10, 1901, and his funeral was held two days later at the Church of the Assumption in Morristown. He was buried next to his father in Holy Rood Cemetery in Morris Township. His biographical sketch in the *Biographical and Genealogy History of Morris County New Jersey* concluded with: "He comes of a notable family, but is honored for his own sterling virtues and upright life, rather than for the heroic deeds of ancestors."[24]

Although Revere died in 1880, apparently it later was discovered that he still had title to property in California. The means with which to deal with that fact involved a legal reality: when property in California was owned by a decedent who died elsewhere, a "probate" nonetheless would be needed in California (where the property was located) in order to pass it to heirs or devisees under the Will. Thus, an administrator of the Will of the decedent would have had to "open" that probate–twenty-four years later–and give formal published notice to creditors in California that–if they had a "claim" against the estate–they had a certain amount of time to file.[25]

During the summer of 1904, P. J. Layne, the administrator of Joseph Warren Revere's estate, placed numerous "notice to creditors" ads in the San Diego *Evening Tribune*. Creditors were given "four months after the first publication" of the notice to provide documentation to Layne at his office in the First National Bank of San Diego. If no claims were filed, Revere's property in California would be distributed to others free of the claim. It appears the property included five acres of land and $500. Months later, it was distributed. Thus, title to the property passed to others free of any claims in accordance with the Will. A year later, a similar notice was placed in the *Evening Tribune* on behalf of Paul Revere's estate, which was, according to the newspaper ad, "of small value."[26]

Upon Paul Revere's death, Augustus Revere became the last surviving child of Joseph Warren Revere. He served as the manager of the New York-based Post and Flagg banking house's Morristown office and remained at his position when the firm was later purchased by Taylor, Auchincloss, and Joost. He was an elected vestryman at Morristown's Church of the Redeemer and was active in the Morristown Club, a social organization of prominent area residents that was created in 1884.[27]

Like his brother, Augustus kept the memory of his father alive. After a trip to Richmond, Virginia, in the spring of 1905, he donated two flags that his father possessed to the city's Confederate Museum. One was the regimental banner of the Thirty-seventh North Carolina, which was captured at the Battle of Malvern Hill on June 1, 1862, by the Seventh New Jersey. The other flag belonged to the Fifty-third Virginia and was reportedly captured at Chancellorsville.[28] Ironically, Revere was on sick leave when the first flag was captured and, of course, he had been removed from command when the second flag was taken. Augustus'"highly prized" gesture was well received by the museum. "[General Revere's] son says they have been in family ever since, and he now desires that they shall be returned and placed... in the Virginia and North Carolina rooms," reported the *Richmond Times Dispatch*.[29]

Augustus also "sent a flag carried by the Excelsior Brigade, New York State Volunteers, to Adjutant-General Nelson B. Henry, of New York, which has been deposited in the office of the War Bureau of the State capitol at Albany."[30] Augustus presented the American flag that his father raised in Sonoma to the Eschscholtzia chapter of the DAR in California.[31]

California never forgot Revere and the other soldiers who raised American flags for the first time during the Mexican War. The sixtieth anniversary of the multiple flag raisings was celebrated in grand style in San Jose, where approximately 200 people gathered on July 13, 1906. Major E. A. Sherman, the featured speaker at the event, read the names of all the flag raisers and the dates and locations of the raisings. Speaker J. W. Hines noted: "To simply mention names like Sloat, Montgomery, Revere, Sutter, Fallon, Fremont, Dupont and Stockton is but to immortalize any scene or any work of which they might form a part."[32]

The next year, Augustus was elected as Democratic alderman in Morristown's fourth ward. Augustus, who, like his brother, never married, died at home at the Sansay House on May 20, 1910. A successful financier, he left a sizeable estate of $150,000. He provided for the care of his mother until her death. His estate distributed a $50,000 endowment to the Church of the Redeemer for its general fund and a new building. The sum of $20,000 went to the Morris Trust Company, which would provide the income to his cousin Maria Amelia Revere of Canton, Massachusetts, and $20,000 went to Harvard University for the creation of a Revere Family Memorial Fund, which would be "used for the purchase of books and plaster casts or other art objects for the use of the School of Architecture or for the assistance of needy students." The will also distributed $10,000 to "All Souls hospital, Morristown [for] the Paul Revere Memorial Fund and...for the erection of a new building." Fifty thousand dollars was allocated for a public library; additional amounts went to the Church of the Assumption, the Market Street Mission, and others.[33]

Augustus' obituary in *The Jerseyman* noted that the "residue of the estate, which is said to aggregate close to a quarter of a million dollars, is left to the Church of the Redeemer."[34]

However, one part of Augustus' will was never carried out. The sum of $6,000 was to be used for the "erection of a granite and bronze base for the flag pole in the park and to bear the inscription 'Erected in memory of General Joseph Warren Revere,' and $1,000 to be used for the securing of an oil portrait of Gen. Revere to be placed in the state house at Trenton."[35] The painting, which was hung on June 18, 1912, was the work of Charles Noel Flagg, the son of Jared B. Flagg, who painted Revere's first portrait in 1837. The *Trenton Evening Times* reported that "in the picture, General Revere is presented as a Colonel of the Seventh New Jersey Volunteers before he was made a Brigadier General."[36]

When no work was done on the flagpole monument in Morristown, the executor of the estate, the Morristown Trust Company, initiated legal proceedings "against the Mayor and Aldermen of Morristown and others" as to why Augustus' wishes for the monument were not carried out. "The Court of Chancery has been asked to settle litigated questions concerning the will," noted the *Trenton Evening News* on September 10, 1913.[37] Three days later, the *New York Times* reported that "the town has never given consent to the erection of the flagstaff base, and the bill is filed to have the court what use should be made of the money."[38]

The flagpole monument was never constructed.[39] However, in 1914, a monument to Revere was erected in Sonoma by the Native Sons of the Golden West and the State of California to commemorate the raising of the Bear Flag in 1846. The inscription on the plaque read: "On July 9, 1846 the Bear Flag was hauled down and the American Flag here raised in its place by Lieutenant Joseph W. Revere, U.S.A., who was sent to Sonoma from San

Francisco by Commander John D. Montgomery of the U.S. Sloop of War 'Portsmouth.' following the raising of the American Flag at Monterey July 7, 1846 by Commodore John Drake Sloat."[40]

Rosanna Duncan Lamb Revere.
From the Collection of the Morris County Park Commission.

Only two months after Augustus' death, Rosanna died on July 26, 1910. She was buried next to her husband in Holy Rood Cemetery. At the age of ninety-one, she was the oldest member of the Daughters of the American Revolution. But Rosanna had no will and her estate of $53,230.27 was claimed by Eliot Tuckerman, a first cousin once removed who lived in Manhattan. His claim as "Administrator of Rosanna D. Revere" to the surrogate of Morris County on September 22, 1910, contained a detailed inventory of her property, some of which that had been "sold at private and public sales," and a list of ten other "first cousins once removed and first cousins, Rosanna Lamb and Horatio A. Lamb."[41] The estate was distributed among the twelve.[42]

Her obituary in the *Boston Globe* included a generous reference to her husband's "notable career, first in the naval and then in the military service, participating in both the Mexican and the Civil wars."[43]

With every passing decade, Joseph Warren Revere's legacy was occasionally strengthened by sympathetic writers who focused on his accomplishments and adventures, occasionally embellishing his biography with benevolent exaggerations. Typical was writer Grace Vogt, who penned an article forty years after Revere's death. In "A Hero of Many Wars," Vogt avoided the court-martial and described Revere as a "picturesque character" who "had keen interest in the occult" and "a brilliant career in the War of the Rebellion."[44]

On September 9, 1926, the La Mesa Battlefield monument was unveiled in Vernon, California. "The monument, consisting of four granite boulders, perpetuates the memory of Com. Robert Field Stockton and Lieut. Joseph Warren Revere, who commanded the small band of Americans who drove off the Mexican soldiers," reported the *San Diego Union*.[45]

In 1935, in the *Dictionary of American Biography*, Revere was described as "naval officer, adventurer, and general in the Civil War." The sanitized entry, which noted that he "resigned from the navy in 1850 because of slow promotion," did include his actions at the Battle of Chancellorsville: "He was court-martialed and dismissed, but the sentence–severe in view of his previous record for ability and gallantry–was revoked on Sept. 10, 1864, by President Lincoln, and his resignation accepted."[46] The general's legacy continued to undergo a positive transformation–at least for a while.

Two years later, the California's *Riverside Daily Press* heralded Revere in an article about the Bear Flag Revolt and the fate of the banner. "Some years later he gave it to the Society of California Pioneers where it remained until 1906 [when it] was lost in the fire that devastated a large portion of San Francisco."[47]

During the Civil War centennial, Revere received his most favorable press when Carl B. Scherzer wrote 41 articles about "Morris County's Role in the Civil War" in the *Morristown Daily Record*. Scherzer credited the Seventh New Jersey's "brilliant record…to the training and discipline it received under Colonel Revere." The journalist noted that at the Battle of Chancellorsville, "Revere ordered his shattered brigade, which had been badly mauled and disorganized, to the rear in order to reform it and replenish its ammunition, [and later] arrived at the front with approximately 2,000 men. Sickles…was displeased by Revere's withdrawal."[48]

Over the years, Charles Noel Flagg's 1912 portrait of Revere was crowded off the walls of the New Jersey state house by canvases of prominent politicians. Unceremoniously, it eventually found its way to the boiler room of the Trenton National Guard Armory, where it remained for years; it was not discovered until October 1962. Along with ten other paintings, Revere's image was rescued and restored by Major Cajetan A. Tocco, the National Guard's public information officer and a self-proclaimed amateur painter.[49] However, a fire destroyed the armory and its contents in 1975.

The Willows survived, thanks to Caroline Foster, who inherited the property from her father in 1927. She maintained the house's nineteenth-century Gothic Revival appearance and bequeathed it to the Morris County Park Commission in 1979. The Willows underwent a major restoration from 1986 to 1989 and "was restored to its 1880-1910 appearance." Numerous studies were conducted prior to the restoration and one found that gas lighting, though readily available at the time, was never used. Instead, Revere and his family used kerosene lamps and candles for interior illumination.[50]Although the house "survived in very good condition," a number of repairs were made. "The restoration program included the structural repair to the roof, framing, porches, siding, flooring and chimneys."[51] When the restoration was completed, a number of the rooms reflected the style of the Fosters. Others, like the dining room, appeared as if Joseph Warren Revere and his family had merely left for the day. In fact, the structure seems to have a unique and almost mysterious lived-in quality about it.

The Willows became a historic house museum that is open for tours. Over the years, special programs have been conducted at the house and the grounds, including recreated Civil War encampments. An episode in Revere's life was dramatized at The Willows in 1997 when Joan Schaible's *A Civil War Trilogy* was performed.[52] The three-act play depicted a fictitious July 1861 meeting between Revere, Rodman Price, and John C. Frémont. Scenes, which featured actors and actresses portraying other members of the household's nineteenth-century staff, were performed in three of the house's rooms. Six years later, another dramatic event was staged at The Willows. *Meet the Revere Household* debuted on May 17, 2003, the 191st anniversary of Revere's birth. The production traced the lives of those who resided and worked in the house from 1855 to 1872.[53] Since that performance, guests visiting The Willows have occasionally been greeted by historical interpreters who portrayed Joseph Warren Revere and his wife.

Despite several favorable depictions of Revere in various early and mid-twentieth century publications, later accounts by historians have been universally critical of Revere's "less than courageous" actions at the Battle of Chancellorsville and none have embraced any of the explanations which were printed in his *Statement*. In 2000, one author summed up Revere's Civil War exploits in a chapter section titled "To the Rear, March."[54] As recently as 2010, Revere was described in *New Jersey Goes to War*, a collection of 150 one-page biographies, as the officer who "left a hole in the Union line" at Chancellorsville.[55] Clearly, Revere's legacy remains tainted by his actions on May 3, 1863. It appears that Joseph Warren Revere was simply not prepared to command a large military unit during the heat of battle. He was quite capable of leading a regiment–although he wasn't a drill master–and he was a satisfactory brigade commander, but the demands which faced him as a division commander at Chancellorsville were seemingly beyond his abilities. He was not the first soldier to fail under such circumstances and he certainly will not be the last.

As a man of business, he was imaginative and hardworking–an adventurous risk-taking entrepreneur, to be sure. As a husband, Revere was unfaithful early in his marriage; as a father, he was devoted and caring, although he was absent during most of his children's formative years. In a way, he was like so many other Victorian Era men of his class: a patriotic, church-going, industrious, head-of-household provider–but not a loving husband. Only his Gothic adventures separated him from other men.

Revere Family gravesite. Photo by William R. Chemerka.

Joseph Warren Revere, Rosanna, Paul, Augustus, and Frances are buried together in Morris Township's Holy Rood Cemetery, which is located several miles away from The Willows. But their final resting places have not been forgotten. Over the years, on Veterans Day or other patriotic holidays, small American flags have been placed on Revere's grave by admirers, veterans, and Civil War historical interpreters. On October 7, 1978, the Morristown chapter of the Daughters of the American Revolution dedicated a grave marker to Rosanna.

Revere's gravestone features the Revere family crest and Latin inscriptions about *Josephus Warren Revere*. The bottom of the stone reads: *implora pacem eternam ora pro anima sua*, which translates to "You may ask eternal peace for his soul."[56]

Joseph Warren Revere headstone.
Photo by William R. Chemerka.

250

NOTES

1. Ezra A. Carman, *Seventh New Jersey Infantry to Battle of Williamsburg*, 1873, 7. New Jersey Historical Society, Newark, New Jersey.

2. Theodore A. Dodge, *The Campaign of Chancellorsville* (Boston: Ticknor, 1881), 137.

3. Comte De Paris, *History of the Civil War in America*, Vol. III (Philadelphia: Porter and Coates, 1883), 90.

4. Schedule A. Joseph Warren Revere inventory, February 28, 1882. Revere Family Files. According to the *Biographical and Genealogical History of Morris County, New Jersey,* Revere's collection at one time included "a rhinoceros-hide shield from the Malay islands; an old helmet supposed to have belonged to a follower of Cortez; a dagger used by the French actress, Rachel; [and] the sword received from the governor-general of India," among other items.

5. Caroline Foster, interview with Clayton Smith, "Caroline Foster discusses Morristown Green, Fosterfields and Washington Valley," 1967. Transcript, p. 33. FF archives, Oral History (OH-2), Collection of the Morris County Park Commission.

6. Caroline Foster. Interview. Morristown and Morris Township Library. Oral History, Tape 1. Transcript, p. 2. FF archives, Oral History (OH-22), Collection of the Morris County Park Commission.

7. *Message from the President of the United States to the two Houses of Congress at the commencement of the first session of the Thirty-Sixth Congress* (Washington: Government printing Office, 1860), 332; *Report of the Secretary of the Interior being part of the Message and Documents communicated to the two Houses of Congress at the beginning of the second session of the Forty-Seventh Congress, Vol. 1* (Washington: Government Printing Office, 1882), 290.

8. *Instructions and Forms to be Observed in Applying For Army Pensions Under the Act of July 14, 1862* (Washington: Government Printing Office, 1862), 3. Revere Family Files.

9. Letter from William W. Dudley, Pension Office, Department of the Interior, Washington, D.C., to Rosa. D. Revere, Morristown, Morris Co., NJ, Feb. 28, 1882. Revere Research Files.

10. Statement of Francis Price of Bergen County, New Jersey, 1877. Revere Research Files.

11. Pension Office, Department of the Interior to Mrs. Rosa D. Revere, April 19, 1877. Revere Family Files.

12. *A History of the New Jersey State Society of the National Society of the Daughters of the American Revolution, 1891-1995*, [1995], 9. See also *A History of the New Jersey State Society of the National Society of the Daughters of the American Revolution*, 1891-1974 (Neshanic, NJ: Neshanic Printing Co., Inc., 1972), 13. However, according to the June 27, 1891 edition of the New York *Herald*, Rosanna attended a meeting "at the residence of Mrs. De Witt Clinton Mather, in Somerset county, and formed a State organization" in the spring of 1891.

13. *Morris County's Daily Record*, Morristown, New Jersey, November 3, 1960.

14. Undated newspaper article in the Revere Research Files.

15. Francis Amasa Walker, *History of the Second Army Corps in the Army of the Potomac* (New York: Charles Scribner's Sons, 1886), 243.

16. Paul Revere to Walker, February 14, 1887, Revere Family Files.

17. Letter from Adjutant General, Washington, D.C., to Paul Revere, Morristown, July 18, 1887. Revere Family Files.

18. *Trenton Evening Times*, August 11, 1887, 2.

19. *Alphabetical List of Private Claims which were brought before the Senate of the United States with the Action of the Senate thereon, from March 4, 1891 to March 4, 1899, Vol. 2–L to Z* (Washington: Government Printing Office, 1900), 1088. The dollar amount of the claim was not identified.

20. *Biographical and Genealogical History of Morris County, New Jersey*, 98. This description was supposedly authorized by Congress in 1866.

However, one wonders why the Republicans controlling the Thirty-ninth Congress of the United States gave the discredited Revere a promotion. Lincoln, of course, never "declared that he had been unjustly treated." Furthermore, the president only "restored him to rank" as a condition of his resignation.

21. Wilson to House of Representatives, Fifty-second Congress, Second Session, Report No. 2424 [to accompany H.R. 9859], February 4, 1893. Revere is mentioned four times in the report about York. On May 10, 1902, the Committee on Pensions recommended a $12 per month pension for York, who was described as 81 years old, totally disabled, and dependent on a son for support.

22. Ibid.

23. The Washington Association was founded on June 28, 1873, and charted by a special act of the Legislature of New Jersey on March 20, 1874, "to acquire and preserve the Ford Mansion, Washington's Revolutionary War Headquarters during the bitter winter of 1779-1780" and "memorializing George Washington, commemorating the heroism and fortitude of the Continental Army" and "collecting and preserving Revolutionary War documents, relics, and other objects of interest." Members of the organization are shareholders, each owning a numbered share of stock. Paul (stock #297) and Augustus (#290) both joined in 1891. Upon their deaths, the stock was reverted back to the State of New Jersey. Alfred Mills, one of Joseph Warren Revere's pallbearers, was also a member of the organization. In 1933, the organization transferred the Ford Mansion to the Department of the Interior. As a result, the first National Historical Park was created. The Washington Association serves as an advisory body to the park. Sections of a museum were constructed between 1935 and 1937, but the economic impact of the Great Depression limited its completion. The museum, which was originally constructed between 1935 and 1937, was renovated and expanded in the first decade of the twenty-first century and continues to be refurbished.

24. *Biographical and Genealogical History of Morris County, New Jersey,* 98.

25. Charles S. Bargiel to author, May 22, 2012.

26. San Diego *Evening Tribune,* January 12, 1905, 4.

27. *New York Herald-Tribune,* October 21, 1895, 4. Augustus Revere served as the treasurer of the Morristown Club, which remains a viable organization to this day.

28. Undated publication page. Revere Research Files.

29. *Richmond Times Dispatch,* May 21, 1905, 9. New Jersey's *Woodbury Daily Times* carried a similar story in its May 22, 1905 issue.

30. Ibid. The article described the captured banner as "a silk flag, 5x7 feet, bordered with yellow fringe and having bullion tassels."

31. *Ninth Report of the National Society of the Daughters of the American Revolution, October 11, 1905, to October 11, 1906* (Washington: Government Printing Office, February 25, 1907), 52. The report described the flag as "pretty ragged and dilapidated."

32. *San Jose Mercury News,* July 14, 1906, 5.

33. Undated newspaper clipping, "Mr. Revere's Bequests." Revere Research Files.

34. *The Jerseyman,* July 29, 1910, 1.

35. Undated newspaper clipping, "Mr. Revere's Bequests." Revere Research Files.

36. *Trenton Evening News,* June 19, 1912, 2.

37. Ibid., September 10, 1913, 2.

38. *The New York Times,* September 9, 1913, 9.

39. Documentation could not be located which explained the findings of the court.

40. The monument was erected on June 14, 1914.

41. Petition of Eliot Tuckerman to the Surrogate of Morris County in Revere Research Files. Listed on the surrogate's document were Rosanna Lamb and Horatio A. Lamb, Eliot Tuckerman and his family, six members of the Comstock family, and Margaret Allen.

42. Revere Research Files. This typed note added: "Nothing was left to charity or the Revere family."

43. *Boston Globe*, July 29, 1910, 7.

44. Grace J. Vogt, "A Hero of Many Wars," August 20, 1920. Revere Research Files.

45. *San Diego Union*, September 10, 1926, 5.

46. *Dictionary of American Biography*, Vol. XV (New York: Charles Scribner's Sons, 1935), 513-514.

47. *Riverside Daily Press*, September 9, 1937, 6.

48. Carl B. Scherzer, "Morris County's Role in the Civil War," *Morristown Daily Record*, May 11, 1961.

49. *Trenton Evening Times*, January 7, 1963, 24. Tocco volunteered to restore the painting when the National Guard stated that it could not afford the estimated $7,000 restoration costs.

50. Paula Sagerman, *The Willows: Restoration Manual*, 15.

51. Ibid. Other items were addressed. "Pest control measures and maintenance inspections began. The weather coverings such as the roofing and water drainage system were repaired and replaced, and the grading was improved. Unstable building elements were removed and stored for future work. The foundations and interior and exterior carpentry were repaired. The heating, humidification, dehumidification, plumbing, electric, security and fire detection and suppression systems were renovated."

52. *A Civil War Trilogy* by Joan Schaible was performed on June 13, 14, and 15 in 1997. Directed by Kathie Cirelli, the short three-act play was performed four times a night and featured Nick DeRose as Frémont, Bruce Hunter as Price, and Bill Chemerka as Revere.

53. "Meet the Revere Household" (aka "The Reveres at the Willows: 1855-1872") featured Dorothy Swid as the pre-1855 narrator, Terry Kenneweg as the 1855 foyer maid, Sharon Reider as Rosanna Revere in 1863, Bill Chemerka as Joseph Warren Revere in 1863, Christine

Glazer as the 1872 cook, and Jennifer Friedland as the post-1872 narrator.

54. C. Brian Kelly, *Best Little Ironies, Oddities and Mysteries of the Civil War* (Nashville, TN: Cumberland House Publishing, 2000), 171-174.

55. Joseph G. Bilby, ed., *New Jersey Goes to War: Biographies of 150 New Jerseyans Caught Up in the Struggle of the Civil War, including Soldiers, Civilians, Men, Women, Heroes, Scoundrels–and a Heroic Horse* (Wood-Ridge, NJ: New Jersey Civil War Heritage Association, 2010), 106. Revere's one-page biographical sketch features a few errors. His birthday is incorrectly identified as May 18, 1812 (it was the previous day). Also, Revere is incorrectly identified as writing *A Tour of Duty* after he served in the Civil War (the book was published in 1849). Furthermore, he was not "cited for bravery in pulling down the California Republic 'Bear Flag.'" In addition, Revere did not own a "200 acre farm" in 1854 (his land totaled 88 acres). Also, Revere is not buried in Morristown (he is buried in Morris Township).

56. Translation courtesy of Diana Loughman, Cemetery Director of the Holy Rood Cemetery, Morris Township, New Jersey. The headstone features another Latin phrase: *Pulvis est ossa*, which Loughman translated as "the earth is bones."

Joseph Warren Revere.

APPENDIX A

Joseph Warren Revere and Family

Joseph Warren Revere
May 17, 1812–April 20, 1880

Rosanna Duncan Lamb Revere
April 16, 1819–July 26, 1910

Augustus Lefebvre Revere
August 8, 1861–May 20, 1910

Paul Revere
September 28, 1856–November 10, 1901

Frances Jane Revere
March 26, 1849 September 25, 1859

Thomas Duncan Revere
November 22, 1853–September 18, 1856

John Revere
November 26, 1844–April 22, 1849

APPENDIX B

**Brigadier General Joseph Warren Revere's Brigade
within the Army of the Potomac's Order of Battle
at the Battle of Chancellorsville, 1863**

Army of the Potomac

Major General Joseph Hooker

I Corps: Major General John F. Reynolds

II Corps: Major General Darius Couch

III Corps: Major General Daniel E. Sickles

    First Division: Brigadier General David B. Birney

    Second Division: Major General Hiram G. Berry

        First Brigade: Brigadier General Joseph Carr

        Second Brigade: Brigadier General Joseph
            Warren Revere

            70th New York: Colonel J. Egbert Farnum

            71st New York: Colonel Henry L. Potter

            72nd New York: Colonel William O. Stevens

            73rd New York: Major Michael W. Burns

            74th New York: Lieutenant Colonel William
               H. Lounsbury

           120th New York: Lieutenant Colonel
               Cornelius D. Westbrook

        Third Brigade: Brigadier General Gershom Mott

Third Division: Brigadier General Amiel W. Whipple

V Corps: Major General George G. Meade

VI Corps: Major General John Sedgwick

XI Corps: Major General Oliver O. Howard

XII Corps: Major General Henry W. Slocum

Cavalry Corps: Brigadier General George Stoneman

APPENDIX C

Recapitulations of Casualties in the Second Brigade,
Second Division, Third Army Corps in the Operations
near Chancellorsville, Virginia

Source: Revere Family Papers, Collection of the Morris
County Park Commission

O= Commissioned officers   E= Enlisted Men

	Killed		Severely Wounded		Slightly Wounded		Missing		Totals		Aggregate
	O	EM	O	EM	O	EM	O	EM	O	EM	O + EM
Brigade Staff					1				1		1
70th NY		4		5		6		17		32	32
71st NY		1		5	2	8		23	2	37	39
72nd NY	3	7	6	17	2	7	1	58	12	89	101
73rd NY	1	2	2	9		20		4	3	35	38
74th NY		3	1	9	2	10		15	3	37	40
120th NY		4	1	20		28		13	1	65	66
Totals	4	21	10	65	7	79	1	130	22	295	317

BIBLIOGRAPHY

Manuscript, Thesis, and Interview Sources

Madison (New Jersey) Historical Society
Heyward Emmell Journal

Massachusetts Historical Society
Joseph Warren Revere: Account of the Rivoire Family

Morris County (New Jersey) Park Commission
    Revere Family Files
    Revere Research Files
    Caroline Foster interview (transcript)

Morristown and Morris Township Library
 Local History and Genealogical Department

New Jersey Historical Society
 Ezra A. Carman Papers: *Seventh New Jersey Infantry to Battle of Williamsburg*

New Jersey State Archives
Regimental documents and records of the 7th New Jersey
 Regiment of Volunteers

University of Pennsylvania
 Tribert, Renee Elizabeth. "Gervase Wheeler: Mid-Nineteenth Century British Architect in America." Master of Science thesis, University of Pennsylvania, 1988.

Newspapers
[Egg Harbor City, NJ] *Atlantic Democrat*
[Baltimore, MD] *The Sun*
[Baton Rouge, LA] *Morning Advocate*
Boston Daily Atlas
Boston Evening Transcript
Boston Globe
Boston Journal
Boston Press and Post
[Charleston, SC] *City Gazette and Commercial Daily Advertiser*
Charleston Courier
[Charleston, SC] *Southern Patriot*
Cincinnati Daily Gazette
[Harford, CT] *Daily Courant*

[Morristown, NJ] *The Jerseyman*

[Morristown, NJ] *Morris County's Daily Record*

[Morristown, NJ] *Morristown Daily Record*

[Morristown, NJ] *True Democratic Banner*

Newark Advertiser

New-Bedford Mercury

[New Haven, CT] *Columbian Weekly Register*

[New Orleans, LA] *The Daily Picayune*

[Watertown, NY] *New-York Daily Reformer*

[New York, NY] *The Evening Post*

New York Herald

New York Herald-Tribune

New-York Spectator

The New York Times

[Philadelphia, PA] *The Daily Age*

[Philadelphia, PA] *National Gazette*

Richmond Enquirer

Richmond Times Dispatch

Richmond Whig

Riverside [CA] *Daily Press*

[Saint Johnsbury, VT] *The Caledonian*

[San Diego, CA] *Evening Bulletin*

San Francisco Bulletin

[San Francisco, CA] *The Elevator*

Savannah Georgian

[Springfield, MA] *Springfield Republican*

Trenton Evening News

Trenton Evening Times

[Trenton] *State Gazette*

[Washington, D.C.] *Daily National Intelligencer*

[Washington, D.C.] *Evening Star*

West Jersey Press
Woodbury [NJ] *Daily Times*

Books and Manuals

Benét, Stephen Vincent. *A Treatise on Military Law and the Practice of Courts-Martials.* New York: D. Van Nostrand, 4th edition, 1864.

Bilby, Joseph G., ed. *New Jersey Goes to War: Biographies of 150 New Jerseyans Caught Up in the Struggle of the Civil War, including Soldiers, Civilians, Men, Women, Heroes, Scoundrels— and a Heroic Horse.* Wood-Ridge, NJ: New Jersey Civil War Heritage Association, 2010.

Bilby, Joseph G. and William C. Goble. *Remember You Are Jerseymen!: A Military History of New Jersey Troops in the Civil War.* Hightstown, NJ: Longstreet House, 1998.

Biographical and Genealogical History of Morris County, New Jersey. New York: The Lewis Publishing Co., 1899.

Casey, Silas. *Infantry Tactics for the Instruction, Exercise, and Manœuvres of the Soldier, a Company, Line of Skirmishers, Battalion, Brigade, or Corps D'Armée Vol. I.* New York: D. Van Nostrand, 1862.

Comte De Paris. *History of the Civil War in America, Vol. III.* Philadelphia: Porter and Coates, 1883.

Dictionary of American Biography, Vol. XV. New York: Charles

Scribner's Sons, 1935.

Dodge, Theodore A. *The Campaign of Chancellorsville*. Boston: Ticknor, 1881.

Esposito, Vincent J., ed. *The West Point Atlas of American Wars, Vol. 1, 1689-1900*. New York: Frederick A. Praeger, 1959.

Fischer, David Hackett. *Paul Revere's Ride*. New York: Oxford University Press, 1994.

Furguson, Ernest B. *Chancellorsville 1863: The Souls of the Brave*. New York: Knopf, 1992.

Fowler, Will. *Santa Anna of Mexico*. Lincoln, NE: University of Nebraska Press, 2007.

Gettemy, Charles Ferris. *The True Story of Paul Revere: His Midnight Ride; His Arrest and Court-Martial; His Useful Public Services*. Boston: Little Brown and Company, 1906.

Hardee [William J.]. *Rifle and Light Infantry Tactics*. Memphis, TN: E.C. Kirk and Co., 1861

Hayward, John. *Give it to Them, Jersey Blues! A History of the 7ᵗʰ Regiment, New Jersey Veteran Volunteers in the Civil War*. Hightstown, NJ: Longstreet House Press, 1998.

Heitman, Francis B. *Historical Register and Dictionary of the United States Army, from its Organization, September 29, 1789, to*

March 2, 1903. Washington, D.C.: Published under Act of Congress, 1903.

A History of the New Jersey State Society of the National Society of the Daughters of the American Revolution, 1891-1995 [1995].

Jackson, William J. *New Jerseyans in the Civil War: For Union and Liberty.* New Brunswick, NJ: Rutgers University Press, 2000.

Krick, Robert C. *Chancellorsville: Lee's Greatest Victory.* Washington, D.C.: Civil War Preservation Trust, 2010).

Langstaff, John Brett. *New Jersey Generations: Macculloch Hall, Morristown.* New York: Vantage Press, 1964.

Longacre, Edward G. *The Commanders of Chancellorsville.* Nashville, TN: Rutledge Hill Press, 2005.

Louis Raymond Francine Brevet Brigadier-General U.S. Volunteers. 1910. Hightstown, NJ: Longstreet House Press, Reprint, 2000.

Malcolm, Jim, ed. *The Civil War Journal of Private Heyward Emmell, Ambulance and Infantry Corps: A Very Disagreeable War.* Madison, NJ: Fairleigh Dickinson University Press, 2011.

Mason, Jack and Helen Van Cleave Park. *Early Marin.*, Inverness, CA: North Shore Books, 1971.

"Memoirs of Andrew S. Church." *Quarterly of the Society of California Pioneers*, Vol. III, No. 4, December 31, 1926.

Mills, W. Jay. *Historic Houses of New Jersey*. Philadelphia: J.P. Lippincott Company, 1902.

Mitros, David, ed. *Gone to Wear the Victor's Crown: Morris County, New Jersey and the Civil War–A Documentary Account*. Morris County, NJ: Morris County Heritage Commission, 1998.

Morristown–History–Civil War. Program of meeting held in the First Presbyterian Church, Morristown, N.J. to bid farewell to Company K, 7th N.J. Vol., October 1, 1861. Morristown and Morris Township Library, Misc. Mss., Local History and Genealogy Department.

Mott, Dr. Valentine. *Biographical Memoir of the Late John Revere, M.D., Professor of the Theory and Practice of Medicine in the University of New York*. New York: Joseph H. Jennings, 1847.

W.W. Munsell. *History of Morris County, New Jersey with Illustrations and Biographical Sketches of Prominent Citizens and Pioneers*. New York: W.W. Munsell and Co., 1882.

New England Historical and Genealogical Register, Boston, 1991.

Rae, John W. and John W. Rae, Jr. *Morristown's Forgotten Past–The Gilded Age: The Story of a New Jersey Town, Once a Society Center for the Nation's Wealthy*. Morristown, NJ: John W. Rae, 1979.

Proceedings and report of the board of Army officers, convened by special orders No. 78, headquarters of the Army, Adjutant General's Office, Washington, April 12, 1878, in the case of Fitz-John Porter. Washington: Government printing Office, 1879.

Records of Officers and Men of New Jersey in the Civil War, 1861-1865, Vol. I. Trenton, NJ: John L. Murphy, Steam Books and Job Printer, 1876.

Revere, Joseph Warren. *Keel and Saddle: A Retrospect of Forty Years of Military and Naval Service.* Boston: James R. Osgood and Company, 1873.

_____. *A Statement of the Case of Brigadier-General Joseph W. Revere, United States Volunteers.* New York: C.A. Alvord, 1863.

_____. *A Tour Of Duty in California; Including a Description of the Gold Region: and an Account of the Voyage Around Cape Horn; with Notices of Lower California, the Gulf and Pacific Coasts, and the Principal Events Attending the Conquest of California.* New York: C.S. Francis and Co., 1849.

A Review of the Case of Brigadier-Gen. Joseph W. Revere, U.S. Volunteers, Tried by Court-Martial and Dismissed from the Service of the United States, August 10, 1863. Boston: J.H. Eastburn's Press, 1864.

Roberston, James I. *The Civil War Letters of General Robert McAllister.* New Brunswick, NJ: Rutgers University Press, 1965.

Sears, Stephen W. *Chancellorsville.* Boston: Houghton Mifflin, 1996.

Stackpole, Edward J. *Chancellorsville: Lee's Greatest Battle.* Harrisburg, PA: The Stackpole Company, 1958.

Smith, Charles R., ed. *The Journals of Marine Second Lieutenant Henry Bulls Watson, 1845-1848*. Washington, D.C.: History and Museum Division Headquarters, U.S. Marine Corps, 1990.

Sagerman, Paula. *The Willows: Restoration Manual*. University of Pennsylvania Graduate School of Historic Preservation, 1991.

Walker, Francis Amasas. *History of the Army Second Corps in the Army of the Potomac*. New York: Charles Scribner's Sons, 1886.

War of the Rebellion: a Compilation of the Official Records of the Union and Confederate Armies. Seventy Volumes. Washington: Government Printing Office, 1881-1901.

INDEX

CPSIA information can be obtained at www.ICGtesting.com
Printed in the USA
BVOW010259200513

321149BV00006B/28/P